THE CAKE BOOK

TISH BOYLE

PHOTOGRAPHY BY JOHN UHER

WILEY

JOHN WILEY & SONS, INC.

Published by John Wiley & Sons, Inc., Hoboken, New Jersey
Published simultaneously in Canada

For general information about our other products and services, please contact our Customer Care Department within the United States at (800) 762-2974, outside the United States at (317) 572-3993 or fax (317) 572-4002.

Wiley also publishes its books in a variety of electronic formats. Some content that appears in print may not be available in electronic books. For more information about Wiley products, visit our web site at www.wiley.com.

Library of Congress Cataloging-in-Publication Data

Boyle, Tish.
  The cake book / by Tish Boyle ; photography by John Uher.
     p. cm.
  Includes index.
  ISBN-10: 0-471-46933-5 (cloth)
  ISBN-13: 978-0-471-46933-9 (cloth)
  1. Cake. I. Title.
  TX771.B69 2006
  641.8'653—dc22
                              2005021384
Printed in the United States of America

10 9 8 7 6 5 4 3 2 1

Designed by Elizabeth Van Itallie
Photography by John Uher
Food styling by Tish Boyle

To Dilys and Ambrose, who let me eat cake

Contents

ACKNOWLEDGMENTS vi

1. INTRODUCTION 1

2. INGREDIENTS FOR CAKES 4

3. CAKE-BAKING EQUIPMENT 20

4. CAKE-MAKING TECHNIQUES, TIPS,
   AND TROUBLESHOOTING 30

5. CAKE DECOR 40

6. ANGEL FOOD, CHIFFON,
   AND SPONGE CAKES 58

7. POUND CAKES AND COFFEE CAKES 88

8. BUTTER- AND OIL-BASED CAKES 116

9. FRUIT-BASED CAKES 172

10. FLOURLESS CAKES 196

11. CHEESECAKES 214

12. MOUSSE AND ICE CREAM CAKES 244

13. MERINGUE CAKES 284

14. FILLINGS AND FROSTINGS 298

15. BASIC RECIPES AND ACCOMPANIMENTS .. 330

16. SOURCES 366

INDEX 369

ACKNOWLEDGMENTS

Without the support and enthusiasm of a number of key people, this book would have been considerably more difficult to write.

Pam Chirls, my talented and good-natured editor, suggested this project and guided me through it seamlessly.

Mickey Choate, ace agent, led me through some puzzling legal minutiae with great dexterity and, more important, cooked up some incredible meals along the way.

John Uher, food photographer and gourmet, took beautiful photographs of my cakes and infused each photo shoot with adventure, laughter, and good wine (or tequila). Bob Piazza and Paul Williams ensured that each photo was perfect.

In the propping department, I am extremely grateful to Carolyn Humphrey, owner of A Brooklyn Table in Brooklyn Heights. She went out of her way to provide just the right plate, cake stand, or napkin. Thanks also to my stylish friend Ina Slote, who lent me advice as well as more than a few of her own props.

Lauren Salkeld and Kim Steckler researched and helped write some of the chapter intros; both are bound to go far as food writers. Deborah Schure diligently proofread my manuscript, while Jill Vogel and Cameron Levkoff helped out with prop and food styling at the shoots.

Baking professionals Carole Harlam, David DiFrancesco, Melanie Dubberley, and Lisa Yockelson generously contributed wonderful cake recipes to this book.

My dear friend Judith Sutton painstakingly copyedited my manuscript, and did a stellar job.

Many thanks to the membership and staff of the The Heights Casino, especially Gloria Donnelly and Norman Bridge, who enthusiastically ate all those cakes. Thanks also to my loyal tennis buddies, who gave me lots of encouragement (and helped me burn off some of those cake-induced calories).

My great friend Stephanie Banyas was always there for me with kind words, good advice, and an occasional reality check.

My wonderful family, especially my parents, Dilys and Ambrose, continues to inspire me and nurture my love of food.

Finally, thanks to my adorable husband, Dick, for making my life so sweet.

1

INTRODUCTION

Cakes evoke powerful memories. They are symbols of life's celebrations, from birthdays to weddings to anniversaries and every other important occasion in between. They convey messages, carry brightly lit candles, and generally put everyone in a good mood. Because of their star status in the world of desserts, cakes can turn even the simplest meal or gathering into a party.

While you can always head to the bakery to pick up a cake when you need one, there's something magical about the process of making one from scratch, a process that transforms a few simple ingredients—butter, sugar, flour, and eggs—into culinary artistry. For some, even otherwise accomplished cooks, the idea of concocting a cake from scratch can be intimidating. Perhaps it's something about the alchemy of baking, its required precision and unforgiving nature, that makes people think an advanced degree in chemistry is necessary to bake a successful cake. Cake mixes are as popular as ever in this era of convenience cooking. The truth is, though, that baking a cake from scratch is only marginally more difficult than baking one from a boxed mix—and the results are far superior. Yes, you'll need to pick up a few more ingredients at the market and do a bit more mixing and folding, but if it's worth making a cake at all, why not take these few extra steps and bake something you can really be proud of?

Use a cake mix, and you relinquish control. Your cake will be loaded with whatever additives the food scientists at some food conglomerate deemed necessary to turn out a perfect, focus group–tested product. That product will be predictable in appearance and texture, with a pleasing but faintly chemical endnote. Make a cake from scratch, and you're in control. You decide what ingredients will go into your cake. You can splurge and use premium butter and organic eggs, or tailor a recipe to suit your budget and flavor preferences.

The one essential requirement for making a good homemade cake is to start with a good recipe. This book will provide you with a collection of great cake recipes of varying levels of difficulty, resulting in an assortment of textures and flavors. Beyond that, it will also explain all the techniques required to make and decorate these cakes.

The recipes range from simple (e.g., pound cakes) to advanced (layer cakes with multiple components). Each one is given a difficulty rating, ranging from "one cake slice" (◥ simple—if you can make a cake from a mix, you can make this) to "four cake slices" (◥ ◥ ◥ ◥ very advanced—you're not in a rush and you enjoy a good baking challenge). "Two cake slices" (◥ ◥) means the recipe is at the intermediate level (such as a simple frosted layer cake or cheesecake with a crust), while "three cake slices" (◥ ◥ ◥) denotes an advanced-level recipe (e.g., a cake that has multiple components, such as layers of meringue, buttercream, and sponge cake). Overall, though, the difference between a "one cake slice" recipe and a "four cake slice" recipe is mostly the total time it takes to finish the cake rather than the inherent trickiness of any required technique.

Before you begin to bake, make sure you read the recipe through from beginning to end so that you have a general idea of the process and so there won't be any surprises along the way. Gather your equipment and ingredients together and make sure items such as eggs and butter are at the proper temperature. Take a close look at each ingredient and see if you need to do anything to it before adding it the batter. For example, if the recipe calls for "1 cup walnuts, chopped," better to chop the nuts now than when you're in the middle of mixing the batter. When all that is done, it's time to follow the recipe, from preheating the oven to garnishing the finished cake. Some steps take time, like allowing a cake to cool completely or refrigerating a filling before using. Be patient; rushing the process can mean disastrous results. Above all, enjoy yourself—baking a cake is not merely a means to an end. If it were, we might as well all hang up our aprons and head to the bakery.

2

INGREDIENTS
FOR
CAKES

For many, following a cake recipe is an adventure of sorts. No matter how specific an author is, there are always little decisions or interpretations to be made along the way, and the outcome is always uncertain. Frequently those decisions involve ingredients. Someone who regularly substitutes margarine for butter, for example, may do so in a cake recipe without hesitation, not realizing how much the flavor and texture of the finished product will be affected. Another baker might use reduced-fat sour cream in a cake as a matter of course. The cake, however, will lack the richness and texture of one made with full-fat sour cream. If you put great things into your cakes, with a little effort and some luck, great things will come out of your oven.

FLOURS

Flour is the foundation of a cake: it provides structure and binds the ingredients together. Using the right flour is a key factor in a cake's success, and the type of flour is reflected, sometimes subtly, sometime overtly, in its texture and crumb. Flours vary in many ways, but the crucial difference is in protein content. Flours with a high protein content, such as unbleached all-purpose flour, develop more gluten, which gives elasticity and strength to a batter. Cake flour, which is lower in protein, is designed to produce a tender cake crumb. Each recipe in this book specifies a particular flour, and it is important to use the right one. When all-purpose flour is called for, you can use either bleached or unbleached, as you prefer.

ALL-PURPOSE FLOUR. This is made from a blend of hard (high-gluten) and soft (low-gluten) wheat, to produce a flour of medium strength and protein content of 10.5 to 13 percent. There are two kinds: Bleached all-purpose flour has been chemically treated with bleaching agents that whiten the flour and make it easier to blend with ingredients with higher percentages of fat and sugar. Bleached flour produces a slightly more tender cake. Unbleached all-purpose flour is creamier in color and slightly heavier, and it will yield a firmer crumb.

CAKE FLOUR. Cake flour is made from soft winter wheat and contains less gluten than all-purpose flour, about 6.5 to 10 percent. It is more refined than all-purpose flour. Cakes made with it will have a delicate grain and texture.

SELF-RISING CAKE FLOUR. This contains added monocalcium phosphate or calcium acid phosphate, bicarbonate of soda, and salt. It should not be used in place of regular cake flour.

WHOLE WHEAT FLOUR. Milled from whole wheat kernels, wheat flour is sometimes used in place of or in combination with other flours. It gives a nutty flavor and a coarse texture to cakes. Store whole wheat flour in an airtight container in the refrigerator.

BREAD FLOUR. This is an unbleached hard-wheat flour that gives more structure than all-purpose or cake flour to baked goods. It has a gluten content of 12 to 15 percent.

Storing flour: Flour should be stored in an airtight container in a cool, dry place. All-purpose and cake flour should be used within fifteen months of purchase; whole wheat flour should be used within six to eight months. All flours can be frozen for up to two years. Double-seal the flour in resealable freezer bags before freezing.

Measuring flour: Measure flour by spooning it into a measuring cup until overflowing and then leveling the top with a knife; do not compress it. If you use too much flour, your cake will be dry and tough. Too little flour, and your cake will lack structure.

FATS

Fats make cakes rich and tender and provide aeration to help leaven the batter. They also add flavor, act as emulsifiers, and lubricate the gluten in the flour. There are several different types of fat used in baking cakes, each with its own properties that result in particular flavors and textures.

BUTTER. Its creaming abilities and flavor make butter the best fat for cake baking. It is available in salted and unsalted forms. Always use unsalted butter in baking, as that permits you to control the salt content in a recipe.

Each recipe in this book specifies the temperature the butter should be before using. Pay close attention and plan ahead if necessary, because butter temperature is crucial to the success or failure of a cake.

For cakes (and baking in general), I strongly recommend butter over butter-margarine blends or margarine. Do not use reduced-calorie or low-fat butter (or margarine). Nothing can replace the rich, flowery flavor of good fresh butter, and some recipes will not work with butter substitutes. By law, American butter must contain at least 80 percent butterfat. Recently, butters with a higher butterfat content (up to 86 percent) have shown up in gourmet food shops and many supermarkets. Use these butters for cake recipes in which butter is the star (e.g., pound cakes), where that extra buttery flavor and texture make all the difference.

Butter can be stored, wrapped in plastic, in the freezer for up to six months.

SOLID VEGETABLE SHORTENING. Shortening is 100 percent fat; it contains no water or minerals. It is soft and has the ability to surround air bubbles well, providing good aeration in batters. Since it is flavorless, though, shortening should be used in combination with butter. Avoid artificial butter-flavored shortening.

VEGETABLE OIL. Vegetable oil is used in some cakes, notably chiffon cakes, and makes for a very tender cake. Always use a neutral-flavored oil, such as safflower (my preference), peanut, corn, or sunflower.

SUGARS AND OTHER SWEETENERS

Sugar, in all its forms, is a carbohydrate that adds sweetness to cakes and baked goods. Granulated sugar crystals assist in aerating cake batters during the creaming process and add texture to finished cakes. Because of its ability to attract moisture, sugar also keeps cakes fresh longer.

BROWN SUGAR. Brown sugar is granulated sugar with added molasses. There are two basic types: light and dark. Light brown sugar has a more delicate flavor and lighter color than its darker counterpart, which contains more molasses (dark brown sugar has about 6.5 percent molasses, light brown sugar contains about 3.5 percent). Because it has a tendency to dry out and become rock hard, brown sugar should be stored tightly sealed in a plastic bag inside an airtight container.

CONFECTIONERS' SUGAR. Also called powdered sugar, this is granulated sugar that has been commercially processed to a fine powder. Although a small amount of cornstarch is added to prevent clumping, it should be sifted before use. Because it has a finer texture than granulated sugar, it should not be considered a substitute for granulated sugar.

CORN SYRUP. This thick, sweet syrup is made from cornstarch processed with enzymes or acids. There are two types: light and dark; in general, they can be used interchangeably. The dark has a richer flavor reminiscent of brown sugar.

CRYSTALLIZED SUGAR. Also known as coarse or crystal sugar, this decorating sugar has granules that are much larger than those of ordinary granulated sugar. It is available at cake-decorating supply stores.

GRANULATED SUGAR. Derived from sugarcane or sugar beets, this is the most common sweetener in cake and other baking recipes.

BOILED SUGAR SYRUP STAGES

Sugar syrups, boiled solutions of sugar and water, are the basis of many recipes, from soaking syrups to meringues and buttercreams. Because the temperature ranges for each stage are relatively narrow, it's important to determine the correct stage. A syrup that is not at the correct temperature can cause a recipe to fail. To make the task less daunting, always start with a perfectly clean, grease-free heavy-bottomed pot. Have a good candy thermometer on hand (see page 27), and be patient.

Below are the basic stages of cooked sugar you will need for the recipes in this book (precise temperatures vary in different sources).

215° TO 230°F — THREAD STAGE.
When you dip a metal spoon into the syrup, a thin thread drips from its edge.

234° TO 240°F — SOFT BALL STAGE.
When you drip a small amount of the syrup into a bowl of ice water, you will be able to form a very soft, malleable ball, which may not hold its shape. This syrup is used for French-style buttercreams.

244° TO 248°F — FIRM BALL STAGE.
When you drip a small amount of the syrup into a bowl of ice water, you will be able to form a firm, flexible ball that holds its shape.

250° TO 265° — HARD BALL STAGE.
When you drip a small amount of the syrup into a bowl of ice water, you will be able to form a hard ball that is slightly malleable.

270° TO 290°F — SOFT CRACK STAGE.
When you drip a small amount of syrup into a bowl of ice water, a string of syrup will form; it will crack when broken but will still be pliable.

300° TO 310°F — HARD CRACK STAGE.
The color is light gold and when you drip a small amount of syrup into a bowl of ice water, a brittle string of syrup will form; it will crack when broken.

320° TO 338°F — LIGHT CARAMEL STAGE.
The syrup is light amber brown.

338° TO 356°F — MEDIUM CARAMEL STAGE.
The syrup is medium amber brown.

356° TO 374°F — DARK CARAMEL STAGE.
The syrup is dark amber brown. Caramel can burn very quickly at this stage, so watch it carefully.

MUSCOVADO SUGAR. This is a dark cane sugar with a fine, moist texture and a lingering, musky molasses flavor. In the past few years it has become available in many supermarkets, and it is worth seeking out to use as a substitute for light or dark brown sugar.

SANDING SUGAR. A fine granulated sugar that is available in a variety of textures and colors. Great for decorating cakes, it is available at cake-decorating supply stores.

SUPERFINE SUGAR. Also known as bar or castor sugar, superfine sugar is very fine grained and dissolves more easily than regular granulated sugar. It can be substituted for granulated sugar in equal amounts in recipes.

TURBINADO SUGAR. Sold under the brand name Sugar in the Raw, this is a coarse, pale blond raw sugar with a delicate molasses flavor.

VANILLA SUGAR. This subtly flavored sugar can be substituted for plain granulated sugar in some recipes. To make vanilla sugar, split a vanilla bean lengthwise in half, place in a jar, and fill the jar with enough sugar to cover the bean. Cover and let stand for at least twenty-four hours to allow the sugar to absorb the vanilla flavor. The bean will be potent for up to a year; replenish the sugar as you use it. If the seeds begin to mix with the sugar, strain the sugar through a fine-mesh sieve before using, then return the seeds to the jar. Vanilla sugar can also be made with confectioners' sugar.

HONEY. Honey is a golden syrup with a distinct flavor and a slightly higher sweetening power than sugar. Its flavor varies depending on the flowers the bees fed on. In most recipes, honey can be used in place of sugar in equal amounts, but you must reduce the amount of liquid in the recipe by ¼ cup for each cup of honey used.

LYLE'S GOLDEN SYRUP. Also known as refiner's syrup, this thick, delicious golden syrup is a by-product of the sugar-refining process. Available at gourmet food shops and many supermarkets, it can be used interchangeably with light corn syrup.

MOLASSES. Another by-product of the sugar-refining process, molasses is a thick brownish-black syrup with a distinctive hearty flavor. It comes in three forms: unsulphured, sulphured, and blackstrap. Unsulphured molasses has a relatively mild flavor, sulphured has a more pronounced flavor. Blackstrap molasses has the strongest flavor of the three and would overwhelm the flavor of any cake. Measure molasses with a liquid measuring cup.

STABILIZERS

CORNSTARCH. Derived from corn, this powdery starch is generally used as a thickening agent. It can also be used to make your own cake flour when you only have all-purpose flour. Substitute 2 tablespoons cornstarch for 2 tablespoons flour in each cup.

CREAM OF TARTAR. Also known as potassium acid tartrate, cream of tartar is used to stabilize egg whites in beating and to inhibit crystallization of sugar syrups.

LEAVENERS

Leaveners help make batters rise and give cakes a light, airy texture. It's important to store them properly to maintain their effectiveness.

BAKING POWDER. This is composed of baking soda, cream of tartar, and cornstarch. When combined with a liquid, it releases carbon dioxide. Use double-acting baking powder, the most common type, which releases some carbon dioxide when it is combined with a liquid and then more when exposed to the oven heat. Baking powder has a shelf life of about a year, after which it loses its strength. To test it, sprinkle some over hot water. If it fizzes, it is still active.

BAKING SODA. Baking soda produces carbon dioxide bubbles when combined with an acid such as buttermilk or yogurt. It has an almost indefinite shelf life if stored in a dry place.

YEAST. A living organism, yeast leavens doughs and batters through the process of fermentation. The recipes in this book call for active dry yeast; do not substitute instant or rapid-rise (quick-rising) dry yeast. Store yeast in the refrigerator.

EGGS

Eggs bring richness and moisture to cakes, as well as give them structure. Egg yolks, rich in fat, are generally used in baking as a thickener and binder; they also make cakes tender. Egg whites, high in protein, are often whipped to add volume and air to cakes.

Eggs are graded for quality and freshness as AA, A, or B. Most eggs sold in supermarkets are Grade AA or A. Grade AA is best for baking; it has a thick white and strong yolk. Eggs should be stored in the coldest part of the refrigerator in their original carton, with the more pointed end down. Because of the potential threat of salmonella poisoning, keep eggs refrigerated until shortly before using them. Since eggs should be at room temperature for use in cake batters, bring them quickly to room temperature by setting them in a bowl of very warm water for 10 to 15 minutes (then dry the shells before cracking the eggs). Do not use eggs with cracked shells.

If you can, buy organic eggs from free-range hens. Organic eggs are produced by hens whose feed is composed of ingredients grown with minimal use of pesticides, fungicides, herbicides, and commercial fertilizers. Free-range hens have daily access to the outdoors. Because the production cost of such eggs is higher, and the hens produce fewer eggs, they're more expensive, but organic, free-range eggs generally have better flavor and brighter yolks. They are worth the extra price, especially in cakes where the egg flavor is particularly noticeable (e.g., Plainly Perfect Pound Cake, page 90).

CHOCOLATE

For cake baking, use the best chocolate you can afford; it will make all the difference in the finished cake. There are many excellent chocolates available in supermarkets today.

To store chocolate, wrap it first in plastic wrap, then in heavy-duty aluminum foil, and place it in an airtight container. Ideally, it should be stored in a cool, dry place with a consistent temperature of around 65°F. White chocolate must be stored away from light because of the milk solids it contains. (Light will accelerate its oxidation, so the chocolate may turn rancid overnight.) Properly stored, unsweetened and dark chocolates may keep for as long as two years; milk chocolate will keep for one year and white chocolate for seven to eight months. (See page 36 for instructions on melting chocolate and page 364 for instructions on tempering chocolate.)

UNSWEETENED CHOCOLATE. Also known as baking chocolate, this consists of pure chocolate liquor (ground cacao nibs) and lecithin (a stabilizer). It does not contain sugar, and it cannot be used as a substitute for semisweet or bittersweet chocolate.

BITTERSWEET AND SEMISWEET CHOCOLATES. These are the chocolates used most often in baking. Sugar, lecithin, vanilla, and cocoa butter are added to unsweetened chocolate to create these chocolates, which are virtually interchangeable (the FDA does not distinguish between the two categories). Both types must contain at least 35 percent chocolate liquor. Semisweet chocolate is generally sweeter than bittersweet chocolate, but this varies according to brand—one company's semisweet chocolate may be comparable in sweetness to another's bittersweet chocolate. Use your own taste as a guide in choosing between the two.

MILK CHOCOLATE. Milk chocolate contains much less chocolate liquor than bittersweet (10 percent as compared to about 35 percent). It also contains a minimum of 3.7 percent milk fat and 12 percent milk solids. Because of the milk components, it is sensitive to heat and is therefore more difficult to melt and bake with.

WHITE CHOCOLATE. White chocolate contains no chocolate solids at all, just chocolate's natural fat, cocoa butter. Different brands contain various proportions of cocoa butter, butterfat, sugar, milk solids, lecithin, and flavorings. Avoid so-called "coating" products, which are made with vegetable fat instead of cocoa butter.

CHOCOLATE MORSELS. Chocolate morsels, or chips, are especially formulated to retain their shape when used in baking, with vegetable fat substituted for some of the chocolate's natural fat, cocoa butter. Because of this, chocolate morsels should not be substituted for semisweet or bittersweet chocolate.

COCOA POWDER. Cocoa powder is the result of a hydraulic press operation that separates virtually all of the cocoa butter from the pure chocolate liquor. The "cake" that results is ground into a powder. There are two types of unsweetened cocoa powder: alkalized, or Dutch-processed, and nonalkalized, or natural. Dutch-processed cocoa powder has been treated with an alkali to neutralize its acidity, a process that results in a darker cocoa with less harshness. Nonalkalized cocoa powder tends to have a more chocolate flavor. Instant cocoa mixes, which contain sugar, cannot be substituted for cocoa powder in recipes.

NUTS AND DRIED FRUITS

Nuts, ground or chopped, are frequently added to cake batters to contribute both flavor and texture. Shelled nuts are available unblanched (raw, with skins intact, also referred to as natural) or blanched (skins removed). Always buy whole nuts and chop or grind them as necessary. Look for the freshest nuts in specialty food markets and health food stores.

ALMONDS. Almonds are grown in Australia, the Mediterranean, South Africa, and California. Their flavor is mellow and sweet. Almonds in their shells do not spoil as quickly as shelled nuts do. Once the package has been opened, store any leftover almonds in a tightly sealed container in a cool, dark place for up to three months; or freeze for up to a year.

CASHEWS. Buttery and slightly sweet, cashews are grown throughout the world, especially in India. Because they have a high fat content (48 percent), they can turn rancid quickly and should be stored in an airtight container in the refrigerator.

HAZELNUTS. Also known as filberts, hazelnuts are grown in Spain, France, and Turkey, and production is now thriving in Washington and Oregon as well. They are sweet and rich and pair beautifully with chocolate.

MACADAMIAS. Rich and buttery, these are grown primarily in Hawaii. Macadamias are expensive because they are labor-intensive to cultivate and process, and because they are relatively scarce—a 100-pound harvest yields a mere 15 pounds of edible nuts.

PEANUTS. Peanuts are grown throughout the American South. There are several varieties, but the most common ones are the Virginia and the Spanish peanut. Store shelled peanuts in an airtight container in the refrigerator for up to three months, or in the freezer for up to six months.

PECANS. These sweet, rich nuts are a member of the hickory family. The best pecans are from Georgia and Texas; their peak season is fall. Pecans can turn rancid quickly. Refrigerate them for up to three months or freeze for up to six months.

PISTACHIOS. These sweet nuts originated in Turkey and are now grown in Central Asia, the Near East, the Mediterranean, and California (a latecomer, as the first decent crop was not harvested there until 1978). Buy shelled pistachios if you can. If you can't find them shelled, look for nuts in the shell that have not been dyed bright red, and buy twice as much, by weight, as you need for the recipe. Shelled, they will keep for three months in the refrigerator, or up to six months frozen. Unshelled, they can be refrigerated for six months or frozen for a year.

WALNUTS. These nuts are grown in temperate areas throughout the world. American black walnuts have the richest flavor, faintly buttery and woodsy. The English, or Persian, variety is the most common, and it comes in three sizes: large, medium, and baby. Walnuts in the shell should not have any cracks or holes; out of the shell, they should look healthy, not shriveled. Shelled walnuts can be stored in a cool, dry place for several months; in the refrigerator, tightly covered, for six months; or in the freezer, well wrapped, for up to a year.

Information on chopping, toasting, and blanching nuts can be found in Chapter 4 (see pages 36–37).

NUT PASTES. Nut pastes are now available in many supermarkets, as well as in specialty and health food stores. The most commonly available nut paste, almond paste, is a close cousin to marzipan—which is a mixture of ground almonds, confectioners' sugar and corn syrup—but it has a higher proportion of nuts and, unlike marzipan, is not cooked. Once you open a container of nut paste, it can be stored in the refrigerator for up to six months. Commercially prepared praline paste and hazelnut paste are also available. If you have trouble finding them, see Sources (page 366). Recipes for making your own praline and pistachio pastes are on pages 333 and 335.

DRIED FRUITS. Myriad fruits are available dried: apples, pears, apricots, cherries, cranberries, figs, and dates, to name a few. They are found in specialty food shops, health food stores, and the produce or baking sections of supermarkets. Stored in airtight containers in a cool, dry place, they will keep for six to twelve months. Some of these products contain sulfites, so check the labels if you're allergic. They also contain preservatives to keep them from hardening or discoloring and to inhibit mold and fungi. Dried fruit should be moist when you use it. If it is dried out, you may be able to bring it back by placing it in a steamer for a minute or two. See also raisins, below.

RAISINS. These are grapes of a certain type, usually Thompson, that have been dried either in the sun or by a special dehydrating process. Sunmaid has recently been marketing a "baking raisin" that is exceptionally moist and plump and is wonderful in cakes. Golden raisins have been treated with sulfites to keep them from darkening.

FLAVOR ACCENTS

Because they are used in small quantities, ingredients like salt and vanilla extract might seem almost optional in recipes. But flavor accents are critical to the success of cakes, frostings, and their accompaniments.

SALT. Salt, which acts as a flavor enhancer, is an extremely important ingredient in cake batters and frostings. Unless otherwise specified, use table salt for the recipes in this book. The larger crystals of kosher or coarse salt will make your measurements inaccurate.

VANILLA. The sweet, mellow flavor and aroma of vanilla is irreplaceable. It finds its way into many cake recipes, whether as the forward flavor or as a backnote. Vanilla is a pod fruit found on a vine that is in the orchid family. Two high-quality varieties of vanilla beans are Tahitian and Madagascar (or Bourbon).

Most of the recipes in this book call for vanilla extract. When the vanilla flavor must be especially fresh and full, the recipe calls for vanilla beans. To use a vanilla bean, split it lengthwise with a paring knife and scrape out the seeds, then either add just the seeds or the seeds and the pod, depending on the recipe. Wrapped tightly in plastic, vanilla beans can be stored for up to three months in a cool, dry place or in the refrigerator. Never freeze vanilla beans, as this affects their subtle flavor.

Nielsen-Massey has recently come out with a vanilla paste, which is full of tiny vanilla bean seeds and has an excellent flavor. You can use vanilla paste interchangeably with vanilla extract. It is especially nice in whipped cream and white frostings, when you can see the vanilla seeds.

3

CAKE-BAKING
EQUIPMENT

ake baking demands an attention to detail, a precision, that borders on the scientific. Like any good scientist, the successful baker must have the right equipment at hand to transform raw ingredients into the perfect cake. Buy top-quality equipment—it will last a lifetime. Here are the basic tools you will need.

BENCH SCRAPER. A rectangular metal device with a wooden handle on one edge, a bench scraper is an excellent tool for cutting and portioning yeast doughs, transferring chopped nuts and other ingredients, and cleaning off countertops and cutting boards. It is also called a dough scraper.

CAKE-DECORATING COMB. Also known as a confectioners' comb, this is a triangular or square tool made of plastic or metal with jagged teeth of varying sizes on each side. It is used to create decorative patterns on the tops and sides of frosted cakes.

CAKE DIVIDER. This device, which resembles a comb with a handle and long metal prongs, is used for cutting ultra-delicate cakes such as angel food without compacting or squashing them.

CAKE LEVELER. This device consists of a long serrated blade mounted on a frame that can be adjusted to specific thicknesses to cut cakes into thinner layers or to even tops. It is particularly helpful when making wedding cakes.

CAKE PANS. The best cake pans are made of medium-weight aluminum with a dull surface or tin-plated steel. They should be sturdy and have straight sides. Avoid dark metal pans, which absorb more heat and can overbrown cakes. To make all of the recipes in this book you will need:

- two 8 x 2-inch round pans
- two 9 x 2-inch round pans
- one 9 x 3-inch round pan
- one 10 x 3-inch round pan
- one 8 x 2-inch square pan
- one 9 x 2-inch square pan
- one 15 x 10-inch jelly-roll pan
- one 17½ x 11½-inch jelly-roll pan (also known as a half sheet pan)
- one 9-inch tube or Bundt pan (9-cup capacity)
- one 10-inch tube pan with a removable bottom (12-cup capacity)
- one 10-inch Bundt pan (12-cup capacity)
- one 8 x 3-inch springform pan
- one 9 x 3-inch springform pan
- one 8½ x 4½ x 2½-inch loaf pan (6-cup capacity)
- one 9 x 5 x 3-inch loaf pan (8-cup capacity)
- one standard 12-cup muffin pan (3½-ounce capacity cups)
- two 6-cup Texas muffin pans (7-ounce capacity cups)
- two 6-cup Bundtlette pans (6-ounce capacity cups)

CAKE TESTER. A thin metal wire with a looped handle, a cake tester is inserted into the center of a cake as a test for doneness. Wooden toothpicks and bamboo skewers also work well.

CAKE TURNTABLE. A heavy revolving cake turntable is a useful piece of equipment for frosting and decorating cakes. When you set the cake on top, it allows you to turn the stand with one hand and frost or decorate the cake with the other. Select one that is made of heavy-duty aluminum and has a 12-inch-diameter platform.

CARDBOARD CAKE ROUNDS. These disks of corrugated cardboard are used for supporting and transporting cake layers. Sold in a variety of sizes, they come in plain brown or white cardboard or covered in silver or gold foil, with plain or fluted edges. They are available in small quantities at cake-decorating supply shops or in bulk through restaurant supply stores via the Internet (see Sources, page 366).

DREDGER. A small metal container with perforated holes in its top, this is used to dust the top of a cake or a work surface with ingredients such as confectioners' sugar, flour, cocoa powder, or cinnamon.

DOUBLE BOILER. A double boiler consists of two pans that nest together. The top pan, which holds the ingredient to be melted, warmed, or cooked, sits in the larger bottom pan, which is filled with an inch or two of water heated to a simmer. A double boiler is used for ingredients like chocolate that require gentle indirect heat. Be sure that the bottom of the top pan does not touch the simmering water—only the steam should warm it. A stainless steel bowl set over a pot of simmering water works well as an improvised double boiler.

ELECTRIC MIXERS. If you bake cakes more than once a year, a *heavy-duty electric mixer,* which makes the task of mixing batters and doughs a breeze, is a worthwhile purchase. Choose a machine with a 4½- to 5-quart stainless steel bowl, a 325- to 350-watt motor, and at least three attachments: a whisk, a dough hook, and a paddle. A plastic splatter shield that prevents wet or dry ingredients and batter from flying out of the bowl is a handy attachment. A *handheld electric mixer* is handy for making fillings, whipping egg whites, and mixing many batters and doughs.

FLOWER NAIL. A flower nail looks like a long thin nail with an oversized head. Covered with a small square of waxed paper, it is used as a base for piping flowers that are then transferred to a cake.

FOOD PROCESSOR. A food processor can be used to mix doughs and batters, blend glazes and icings, and chop nuts and other ingredients. One with a large capacity and a powerful motor is best, especially if you will be mixing yeast doughs.

KNIVES. For baking, three knives are essential: A chef's knife with a tapered blade ranging in length from 10 to 12 inches is used for most cutting tasks, including slicing fruit, chopping nuts, and slicing cakes. A long offset serrated knife with a 12- to 14-inch blade is excellent for chopping chocolate and cutting delicate cakes like angel food. A paring knife with a 2- to 3-inch blade is easy to manipulate and can be used to peel fruit, split vanilla beans, create garnishes, and perform other tasks. Buy knives with blades that are made of carbon-stainless steel alloys, which sharpen well and resist rusting and pitting from acidic ingredients.

MEASURING EQUIPMENT. For accurate measurements, which are essential in baking, you should have:

> ➤ Heavy-duty 1-cup and 1-quart glass measuring cups made of heat-resistant glass (such as Pyrex) for measuring liquids.
>
> ➤ A set of nested metal measuring cups for dry ingredients in the following sizes: 1 cup, ½ cup, ⅓ cup, and ¼ cup.
>
> ➤ A set of graduated metal measuring spoons to measure small amounts of both dry and liquid ingredients: standard sets include 1-tablespoon, 1-teaspoon, ½-teaspoon, and ¼-teaspoon sizes.

Information on how to measure ingredients accurately follows in Chapter 4 (see page 34).

MIXING BOWLS. The best mixing bowls are made of Pyrex or stainless steel. Choose deep bowls with high sides and buy a nested set with a variety of sizes.

NONREACTIVE SAUCEPAN. Nonreactive pans are made from a material such as stainless steel or enameled ceramic rather than a material such as aluminum or unlined copper. Copper, a reactive metal, can have a negative effect on food (particularly acidic food) by changing its flavor or color.

OVEN. Accurate oven temperature is one of the most important factors contributing to the success of a cake. Test your oven's temperature frequently with a high-quality oven thermometer. If you are using a convection oven, reduce the temperature indicated in the recipe by 25 degrees.

PARCHMENT PAPER. Also known as baking parchment, this is used for lining baking pans to give them a nonstick surface, making it easy to unmold cakes. It's available in full professional-size sheets, which can be cut in half to fit an 11½ x 17½-inch baking sheet, or in rolls. Parchment paper is also used to make disposable cones for cake decorating.

PASTRY BAG. More durable and larger than parchment cones, pastry bags are used for piping frostings and some batters and decorations through a pastry tip. They are available in polyester, which is easy to clean; nylon; and disposable plastic. I prefer the disposable plastic kind, which can be tossed after using (don't forget to detach your tip first, though). Have at least a 10-, 12-, and 14-inch bag.

PASTRY BRUSH. A small flat brush from ½ to 2 inches wide, this is used to grease cake pans or imbibe cake layers with syrup. I prefer a 1½-inch-wide brush for these tasks.

PASTRY TIPS. A set of nickel-plated cake-decorating tips is a worthwhile investment and allows you to do any type of piped cake décor from rosettes to roses.

SIFTER. A sifter is used to aerate and remove lumps from flour and other dry ingredients. Turning the handle passes the ingredient through a fine-mesh screen, giving it a uniform consistency and/or blending several ingredients evenly.

SIEVE. A fine-mesh sieve is indispensable for straining sauces and fillings. It can also be used to sift dry ingredients.

SILICONE BAKING MATS. Sold under the brand names Silpat and Exopat, baking mats have recently become available to nonprofessionals at good kitchen supply stores. They are flexible sheets of a nonstick silicone that is strong enough to withstand very high heat. They are reusable—some up to 2000 times.

SPATULAS. An *offset* or *angled-metal spatula* is an ideal tool for smoothing cake batter into pans and spreading frosting or glaze onto a baked cake. A *narrow metal spatula* is useful for leveling off dry ingredients when you measure them and for releasing the sides of a cake from a pan. A *wide inflexible metal spatula,* also known as a pancake turner, is ideal for lifting and moving iced cake layers. A *rubber spatula* is useful for folding ingredients into a batter, scraping batter into a baking pan, and a multitude of other cake-making tasks.

THERMOMETERS. An accurate *oven thermometer* is essential to ensure that your cakes bake properly. As oven thermostats can often be inaccurate, use an oven thermometer every time you bake. A *candy thermometer,* which registers temperatures up to 500°F, is essential for tasks such as making sugar syrups and French-style butter-creams. An *instant-read thermometer* is handy for checking the temperature of sauces such as crème anglaise.

TIMER. A reliable timer is crucial for cake baking. The timer built into your oven or your microwave should be fine if you stay in the kitchen, but I like to hang a digital timer on a string around my neck when I bake so I know that my cake is done no matter where I am.

TIP SAVER. This inexpensive tool is used to reshape bent pastry tips.

TRIANGULAR SCRAPER. Used to make chocolate ruffles and cigarettes, this tool consists of a triangular-shaped metal blade set into a handle. Also used for spackling, they are sold in hardware stores as well as cake-decorating supply stores.

WHISKS. Whisks are made in different sizes and shapes, suited to different functions. Large balloon-type whisks are for whipping ingredients when a lot of air must be incorporated (such as egg whites or cream) and for folding other ingredients into these delicate "foams." Medium to small whisks are good for making egg- or starch-based mixtures and combining ingredients when you don't want to incorporate a lot of air but want to prevent lumps. Look for a balloon whisk in the 12- to 14-inch size and two or three smaller sauce whisks in graduated sizes up to 10 inches.

WOODEN SPOONS. Used to mix batters, liquids, sugars, and fats, wooden spoons are available with flat (great for stirring sauces) or concave bowls. Since they don't conduct heat, they are useful for stirring hot sauces. Since wood is porous and will absorb odors, though, I suggest you keep separate sets for baking and savory cooking.

WIRE RACKS. Wire racks are used to support cake layers so that they cool properly after baking; the stubby legs and wire surface allow air to circulate around the layers so they cool evenly. These racks can also be used for glazing cakes—the excess glaze drips off the cake, creating a clean bottom edge and allowing you to collect the excess on a baking sheet underneath for reuse. Have at least two good wire racks on hand.

ZESTER. This handy tool consists of a handle and a blade with sharp-edged holes in it; it is used to remove the zest from citrus fruits. I highly recommend the Microplane Zester, a device that looks like a carpenter's rasp and finely grates the colored peel of citrus fruit quickly and efficiently.

A GUIDE TO CAKE PAN SIZES

The volumes listed below indicate the full capacity of each pan. To allow for rise, use about half that amount of batter. For example, with a 6 x 2-inch round pan, which has a volume of 4 cups, use about 2 cups of batter.

SURFACE AREA	VOLUME (APPROXIMATE)

ROUND PANS

6 x 2 inches / 28 square inches	4 cups
8 x 2 inches / 50 square inches	7 cups
8 x 3 inches / 50 square inches	10 cups
9 x 2 inches / 63 square inches	9 cups
9 x 3 inches / 63 square inches	13 cups
10 x 2 inches / 79 square inches	11 cups
10 x 3 inches / 79 square inches	16 cups
12 x 2 inches / 113 square inches	16 cups
14 x 2 inches / 154 square inches	22 cups

SQUARE AND RECTANGULAR PANS

8 x 8 x 2 inches / 64 square inches	8 cups
9 x 9 x 2 inches / 81 square inches	11 cups
13 x 9 x 2 inches / 117 square inches	15 cups
15½ x 10½ x 1 inches (jelly roll) / 163 square inches	10 cups
17½ x 11½ x 1 inches (jelly roll) / 201 square inches	12 cups

LOAF PANS

5½ x 3⅛ x 2¼ inches	2½ cups
7½ x 3¾ x 2¼ inches	4 cups
8½ x 4½ x 2½ inches	6 cups
9 x 5 x 3 inches	8 cups

TUBE AND BUNDT PANS

6¼ x 3¼-inch fluted tube or Bundt	5 cups
8¼ x 3¼-inch fluted tube or Bundt	6 cups
8 x 4-inch fluted tube or Bundt	9 cups
10 x 3¾-inch fluted tube or Bundt	13 cups
9½ x 4¼-inch tube	17 cups
9¾ x 4¼-inch tube	19 cups

4

CAKE-MAKING TECHNIQUES, TIPS, AND TROUBLE-SHOOTING

ake baking is science, not magic, and begins with solid formulas. But to achieve success, even the best recipe demands good technique, with proper attention paid to details such as the temperature of various ingredients and beating and baking times. It is good technique that makes the difference between a tall and tender angel food cake with a light-textured crumb and one that could double as a doorstop. So, be organized, follow the recipe down to the smallest detail, and work with care and patience—a memorable cake will be your reward.

PREPARING PANS

Preparing the pan or pans is the first step, and a very important one, in making a cake. If a cake sticks stubbornly to a pan, removed only in big chunks with the aid of spoon or spatula, it can be devastating. So take the time to prepare your pans properly.

Angel food and chiffon cakes are usually baked in ungreased pans to give the batter some traction so it can climb up the sides of the pan during baking. Most other cakes are baked in greased or greased and floured pans. I prefer to use solid vegetable shortening for this job, which, unlike butter, is 100 percent fat and allows for flawless release. Spread a thin layer of shortening over the bottom and sides of the pan, then dust with flour if specified in the recipe. For some cakes, include the extra step of lining the pan with parchment paper cut to fit. The bottom of the pan is usually greased first to prevent the paper from slipping, and the paper is sometimes greased as well, depending on the stickiness factor of the batter.

INGREDIENTS

MEASURING INGREDIENTS

Accurate measuring of ingredients is critical to the success of any cake, so take your time with this task. Too much flour can make a cake dry and heavy, while too little can cause its sides to cave in.

To measure flour: Spoon the flour lightly into the measuring cup until it is mounded over the rim, then sweep a straight-edged knife or spatula across the cup to level it; do not tap the cup or pack the flour into it. Sift the flour before measuring only if the recipe specifies so (e.g., "1 cup sifted cake flour"). If you think your flour has been compacted in storage, stir it with a spoon to aerate it before measuring. If sifted flour is called for, pay attention to how it is described: "½ cup cake flour, sifted" means that you should measure the flour first, then sift it; "½ cup sifted cake flour" means that you should sift slightly more flour than you need (about ¾ cup), then measure out ½ cup sifted flour.

To measure other dry ingredients: Always use dry measuring cups in the amount you need (don't try to eyeball ¼ cup of an ingredient in a ⅓-cup measure), and sweep a knife across the top of the cup to level the ingredient. Do the same when measuring tablespoon or teaspoon amounts of a dry ingredient; don't use rounded or heaping measures unless specified in the recipe.

To measure liquid ingredients: Pour the ingredient into a liquid measuring cup, set it on a flat surface, and check to be sure the liquid is at the mark you desire.

SOFTENING BUTTER

The temperature and consistency of the butter you use will affect the outcome of your cake. Generally butter should be softened before use in baking. That means that it is cool and malleable, not runny or squishy. To soften butter, let it stand at room temperature or unwrap it and place it on a microwave-safe plate. Microwave on the defrost setting (30 percent power) for 30 to 45 seconds, until it yields to your finger when gently pressed.

SEPARATING EGGS

To separate one egg, set out two bowls. Tap the egg against a flat surface to crack it and, holding the egg over one bowl, break the shell apart with your fingers, keeping the jagged edges somewhat close together, and allow the egg white to drip into the bowl. Then pour the contents of one half shell into the other, and repeat the process until all of the white has dripped into the bowl. Pour the yolk into the other bowl. If separating more than one egg, use three bowls: one to crack the egg over, one to pour the whites into as they are separated, and one for the yolks. This will save you from contaminating all the whites if a yolk breaks when you crack the egg over the first bowl.

CREAMING BUTTER AND SUGAR

Butter and sugar are creamed together to incorporate air bubbles into the batter and create volume, making this a vital step in the cake-making process (baking powder will only enlarge air bubbles already present in the batter). So make sure your butter is properly softened (it should be about 65°F to 70°F) and don't skimp on the amount of time specified for beating the butter and sugar.

BEATING EGGS

Eggs are beaten to incorporate air, making cakes light and airy. They may be beaten whole, or the whites and yolks beaten separately. Before beating egg whites, make sure the bowl is absolutely clean. Cream of tartar, an acid, is often added to egg whites before beating to help stabilize them. Pay close attention to the cues given in the recipes. Often, beaten egg whites are ready when they are shiny and have reached the soft peak stage—if you dip a spoon into the whites and lift it up, soft, curved peaks form. For stiffly beaten whites, the peaks should stand straight up. Egg whites that are lumpy, dull, and dry looking have been overbeaten.

FOLDING

Folding is a delicate mixing motion designed to combine two mixtures of different densities, used often in cake recipes. The goal is to preserve as many of the air bubbles in the lighter mixture (such as a meringue or whipped cream) as possible. Folding is usually done with a long-handled rubber spatula. To fold one ingredient into another, hold the bowl in one hand and spoon about one-quarter of the lighter mixture onto the heavier one. Using a rubber spatula, cut down through both mixtures, sweeping the spatula along the bottom of the bowl and up the side of the bowl to lift the heavier mixture up and over the lighter one. Give the bowl a quarter turn and repeat the motion, working gently and without deflating the lighter mixture. Continue until the mixtures are almost blended. Add the remainder of the lighter mixture and repeat until the two mixtures are mostly blended. If a few streaks remain, that's alright—it's better than overworking the batter.

MELTING CHOCOLATE

To melt chocolate in a double boiler: The easiest way to melt chocolate is in a double boiler. Place the coarsely chopped chocolate in the top of the double boiler over barely simmering water and heat, stirring frequently, until melted. Because it contains milk solids, white chocolate can be particularly difficult to melt. Always use high-quality, recently purchased white chocolate (white chocolate has a shelf life, when stored properly, of only eight months) and be sure to heat it only very gently when melting.

To melt chocolate in a microwave oven: Place the coarsely chopped chocolate in a microwave-safe bowl and microwave it at medium (50 percent) power for $1\frac{1}{2}$ to 4 minutes, until the chocolate turns shiny. Check often, because the chocolate will retain its shape and look solid even though it has actually liquefied. Stir milk and white chocolates after about $1\frac{1}{2}$ minutes. On average, 6 ounces chopped semisweet chocolate will require 3 minutes to melt at medium power. (Oddly, chocolate actually melts faster at medium or low microwave heat than it does at high.)

To melt chocolate with a liquid: Melting chocolate will seize (clump up) if it comes in contact with only a small amount of liquid. In general, 2 ounces of chocolate can be safely melted with 1 tablespoon of liquid, such as milk, cream, liquor, coffee, or water. Chocolate can be melted with a liquid, or butter, in a saucepan directly over low heat, or in a double boiler.

BLANCHING AND TOASTING NUTS

To blanch whole almonds: Place the nuts in a pot of simmering water for about 1 minute. Drain in a strainer, then place them in a bowl of cold water. Pinch each nut; the skin will slide off. Dry the nuts thoroughly before toasting, chopping, or grinding.

To toast nuts: Position a rack in the center of the oven and preheat the oven to the temperature called for below, depending on the type of nut. Place the nuts in a single layer on a baking sheet and toast for the time specified, shaking the pan two or three times. After toasting, transfer the nuts to a room-temperature baking sheet to cool completely.

> ➤ HAZELNUTS: Toast at 350°F for 8 to 12 minutes, until fragrant. After toasting, wrap the nuts in a clean towel and cool completely. Transfer the nuts to a large sieve and rub them back and forth against the mesh to remove the loose skins.
>
> ➤ WHOLE ALMONDS: Toast at 350°F for 10 to 15 minutes. Blanched almonds will be golden when done; unblanched almonds are done when they are a light brown all the way through (cut one in half to check).
>
> ➤ SLICED OR SLIVERED ALMONDS: Toast at 325°F for 5 to 10 minutes, until golden and fragrant.
>
> ➤ WALNUTS AND PECANS: Toast at 350°F for 5 to 10 minutes, until fragrant.

STORING CAKES

Most cakes can be stored in an airtight container (such as a Tupperware cake keeper) at room temperature for two days. Cheesecakes and cakes that are made with mousses, custards, whipped cream, or meringue should be loosely covered with plastic wrap and refrigerated. Follow the storage instructions given in each recipe.

FREEZING CAKES

In general, cakes should be frozen unfilled and unfrosted. Cool each layer completely before freezing. Wrap each layer individually in plastic wrap, then slip it into a sealable freezer bag. Seal the bag (eliminating as much air as possible from the bag) and then store the cake on a flat surface in the freezer. Most cakes can be frozen for up to three months. Cheesecakes freeze particularly well. Chill the cake for several hours first, then wrap in plastic wrap, place in an airtight container, and freeze. To thaw cakes, place them, still wrapped, in the refrigerator overnight.

HIGH-ALTITUDE BAKING

Approaches to high-altitude baking vary greatly. Some bakers argue for making recipe adjustments at 3,000 feet above sea level, while others insist that no adjustments be made until 3,500 feet. There really are no hard-and-fast rules. When it comes right down to it, each and every recipe should be tested and adapted individually.

The main obstacle to baking at high altitudes involves overcoming low air pressure. At higher altitudes, the air is thinner and, consequently, exerts less pressure. As a result, cakes rise before they can absorb all the liquid ingredients or set, which means they cannot hold their expanded state, and thus collapse. A secondary but related problem is that water boils at a lower temperature as altitude increases. The resulting lack of moisture tends to make for a crumbly and dry cake and alters the sugar-to-liquid ratio. Too much sugar proportionately weakens the cake structure, further exacerbating the fallen cake problem. Another problem, albeit one without a scientific explanation, is that cakes tend to stick to the pan more at higher altitudes. Heavily greasing and lightly flouring your pans can easily overcome this. Lining flat-bottomed pans with parchment paper also helps.

To surmount the more challenging problems of high-altitude baking, here are some general guidelines or tips. One of the easiest solutions, before attempting to adjust a recipe, is to raise the oven temperature by 25 degrees when baking at 3,500 feet or more. This sets the structure of the cake more quickly, helping to prevent its collapse. Other techniques include using cold eggs—they won't trap as much air, and so expand less when baking—and underbeating eggs (beat to soft peaks when stiff peaks are required; beat eggs and sugar together only until a weak ribbon or trail has formed), which also inhibits the rise. And don't fill the pans more than half-full, so that if the cake does rise too much, at least it won't overflow.

A different approach to high-altitude baking is to adjust the recipe, changing the proportions of ingredients. This can be a bit risky, as it may affect the cake's taste and texture, but with some experimentation, such adjustments can be successful. Since quick and excessive rise is one of the main problems, decreasing the leavener (baking soda and/or baking powder) and thereby limiting the rise is often helpful. Another solution is to improve the set or structure of the cake. Increasing the amount of flour can help to set and dry the batter. Increasing the liquid so that there is more to gelatinize the starch and so set the cake can also be helpful. Lastly, try using less sugar, as sugar weakens cake structure.

CAKE TROUBLESHOOTING GUIDE

➤ CAKE DOESN'T RISE WELL. *Cause:* Not enough baking powder; baking powder was stale; butter and/or eggs were cold; batter was not properly aerated	*Solution:* Make 2 more layers to stack with the other layers; or, as a last resort, call the cake a "European torte," which is supposed to be low
➤ CAKE IS DRY AND TOUGH. *Cause:* Too much egg or flour or too little liquid or fat; not enough sugar or baking powder; batter was overbeaten after flour was added; cake was overbaked	*Solution:* Brush cake layers generously with sugar syrup to moisten them and frost cake with a generous amount of fluffy frosting
➤ CAKE SINKS IN CENTER. *Cause:* Too much fat or leavening; leavening was stale; batter was overbeaten	*Solution:* Compensate for depression by topping with extra frosting or fresh fruit
➤ CAKE DOMES IN CENTER. *Cause:* Too much or wrong type of flour; too little fat and/or sugar; oven was too hot	*Solution:* Slice off domed top so that cake is level and frost as usual
➤ CRUST IS HARD. *Cause:* Oven temperature was too high or cake was overbaked; cake was baked too high in oven; cake pan was too large	*Solution:* Trim hard crust off using serrated knife
➤ SIDES CAVED IN. *Cause:* Too much liquid	*Solution:* Turn cake into trifle by cutting into chunks and layering it with custard, berries, and whipped cream

5

CAKE

DECOR

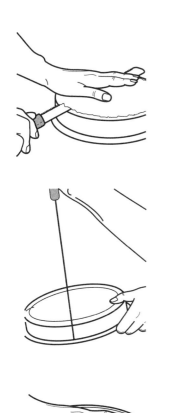

A professional-looking decorated cake is bound to impress even the most jaded food enthusiast. But that does not automatically imply elaborate. Sometimes a simple touch, such as a light dusting of confectioners' sugar or a coating of sleek chocolate glaze, is all a cake needs. When a more ornate look is in order, choose one of the garnishing methods below, or let your imagination be your guide.

TRIMMING AND DIVIDING CAKE LAYERS

For a professional look, domed or uneven cake layers should be trimmed before filling and frosting. Place each cake layer on a cardboard cake round and, using a long serrated knife, trim the top crust as necessary so that the cake is level. Before dividing a cake layer, cut a vertical notch down one side of the cake so you'll know where to line up the divided layers when assembling them. With the layer on a cake round, place one hand on top of it, hold the blade of a serrated knife against the side of the cake at the level where you want to cut it, and cut into the cake with a gentle sawing motion, rotating it away from the blade as you cut. Continue to cut into the center of the cake while rotating it until it is cut completely through.

FILLING AND FROSTING THE CAKE

When you're ready to fill cake layers, dab a little frosting on the center of a cardboard cake round to anchor the bottom layer and

make the assembled cake more stable, and place one layer, cut side up, on top. To fill the cake, use the amount of filling specified in the recipe, spreading it to within ¼ inch of the edges of the cake, then top with another layer.

To frost the cake: Brush off any loose crumbs from the surface of the cake. Using a small offset metal spatula, spread a generous amount of frosting around the sides of the cake, then over the top. To smooth the sides, run the spatula under hot water and wipe it dry. Place the warm blade of the spatula upright against the side of the cake and rotate the cake (a turntable comes in handy here), keeping the spatula in a fixed position. If you want the top of your cake to be completely smooth, use a longer spatula. Run it under hot water and wipe it dry, then sweep it over the top of the cake in a smooth motion, making the layer of frosting as even as possible.

STACKED CAKES

If you are making a stacked cake, with each tier appearing to rest on the one below, some advance planning is in order, as you will need to insert supports for each tier. Begin by placing the bottom cake tier, on a cardboard cake round, onto a decorative plywood or Masonite presentation board. Insert several ¼-inch dowels, cut to the height of the tier, into the cake, inside the perimeter of what will be the next tier. Place the next cake tier on a cardboard cake round that is the same size or slightly smaller than it is, and center the cake on the base tier. Repeat with any remaining tiers. The cake is now ready to be frosted.

DECORATIVE TOUCHES

To add texture to the top and sides of a cake, you can use a triangular confectioners' comb, a flat plastic or metal tool with small teeth on its edges. To decorate the sides, dip the comb in hot water and wipe it dry. Hold one edge of the comb against the side of the cake at a 45-degree angle and, keeping the comb in a fixed position, rotate the cake on its turntable slowly to create a grooved pattern. Or, if you are not using a turntable, simply sweep the comb around the sides, keeping it as straight and steady as possible. The comb can also be used to create a wavy textured pattern on the top of the cake. Beginning at one side, sweep the comb over the top in an even wavy motion.

Another interesting design for the top of a cake is a simple spiral pattern. To do this, you must use a cake-decorating turntable. Run a small metal spatula under hot water and wipe it dry. Lightly place the blade of the spatula, flat side down, in the center of the frosted cake. Slowly rotate the turntable, letting the spatula slide in a spiral pattern out to the edges of the cake.

An easy decorative touch is to coat the sides of a frosted cake with chopped or ground toasted nuts or cake or meringue crumbs. Have the garnish in a bowl and make sure your cake is secured with a dab of frosting to a cardboard cake round. Supporting the cake with one hand under the cake round, hold it over the bowl. With your other hand, scoop up some of the nuts or crumbs and pat them onto the side of the cake. Let the excess fall back into the bowl. Rotate the cake and repeat until the sides are completely covered.

PIPED DECORATIONS

USING A PASTRY BAG

Buttercream, ganache, frosting, and stabilized whipped cream can be piped through a pastry bag to decorate a cake. Always use a bag that's a little larger than you think you might need, and never fill it more than halfway. To fill the bag, first fold back a generous cuff at the top. Use a rubber spatula to scoop the frosting into the bag, filling it half full. Unfold the cuff, squeeze the frosting toward the tip, and twist the bag closed at the top. Squeeze out a small amount of the frosting at the tip to eliminate any trapped air. To pipe, hold the bag at the top between the thumb and fingers of one hand; this hand both holds the bag closed and squeezes the frosting toward the tip. Use the other hand to support and guide the tip. For most decorations, you should hold the bag at either a 90-degree angle (e.g., for stars or simple rosettes) or a 45-degree angle (e.g., rope or shell borders).

ADDING A TOUCH OF COLOR

Buttercream, royal icing, and light-colored frosting can be shaded in various colors with paste food coloring. I prefer paste to liquid food coloring because it doesn't alter the consistency of the frosting as much. Add tiny amounts of the coloring using the tip of a toothpick; you can always add more, but once you've added too much, you can't remove it. Keep the colors pale and subtle. Garishly colored decorations belong on cakes that are sold in supermarkets.

BASIC PIPED DECORATIONS

Even the simplest piped decoration can make a cake look elegant and professional. Here are the techniques for the basic piped decorations.

DOT

PASTRY TIP: Any round tip

BAG POSITION: 90-degree angle

MOTION: Squeeze the pastry bag with a steady motion, letting the force of the icing lift the tip off the surface. Leaving the tip partially buried in the icing, stop squeezing the bag. Smooth the surface of the dot as you pull away in a slightly circular motion, so that a point doesn't form.

STAR

PASTRY TIP: Any star tip

BAG POSITION: 90-degree angle

MOTION: Squeeze the pastry bag until the star is the size you want it. Stop squeezing and pull the tip straight up.

ROSETTE

PASTRY TIP: Any star tip

BAG POSITION: 90-degree angle

MOTION: Squeeze the pastry bag, forming a tight circle. Release the pressure and drag the tip to the side and up, continuing the circular motion.

SHELL

PASTRY TIP: Any star tip

BAG POSITION: 45-degree angle

MOTION: Squeeze frosting onto the cake, letting it bulge out as you lift the tip slightly. Then release the pressure as you pull away the tip on the surface of the cake, forming a pointed tail. Start the next shell at the tip of the first one; the wide part of the second shell will cover the tail of the first one.

REVERSE SHELL

PASTRY TIP: Any star tip

BAG POSITION: 45-degree angle

MOTION: Squeeze the frosting onto the cake as you would to form a shell. Move the tip slightly to the left and in a clockwise direction to form a question mark as the frosting is squeezed out, then gradually release the pressure. Start the next shell at the tip of the first one, repeating the motion in the reverse direction. Continue to alternate directions.

FLEUR-DE-LIS

PASTRY TIP: Any star tip

BAG POSITION: 45-degree angle

MOTION: A fleur-de-lis design is composed of three shells: one shell and two reverse shells. First pipe a centered shell with a long tail. Move the tip slightly to the left and pipe a reverse shell, making its tip line up on top of the first shell's tip. Pipe another reverse shell in the opposite direction on the other side of the plain shell, making its tail line up with the other reverse shell's tail.

ROPE

PASTRY TIP: Any star tip

BAG POSITION: 45-degree angle

MOTION: Starting just above the surface of the cake and using steady pressure on the pastry bag, pipe out an elongated sideways S shape. Release the pressure on the bag and lift up the tip. Tuck the tip into the top curve of the S and repeat the procedure.

C Scroll

Pastry tip: Any star tip

Bag position: 45-degree angle

Motion: This is a series of sideways Cs, with the openings facing up. It is frequently used to decorate the sides of a cake. Begin to pipe a tight counterclockwise circle, but instead of closing it, loop it around to form a large C shape, then end with another tight circle at the other end of the C. Pipe the next C scroll so that it just touches the first one.

S Scroll

Pastry tip: Any star tip

Bag position: 45-degree angle

Motion: This is a series of sideways Ss, frequently used to decorate the sides of a cake. Begin to pipe a tight counterclockwise circle, but instead of closing it, loop it around to form an elongated S shape, then end with another tight circle at the other end of the S. Pipe the next S scroll so that it just touches the first one.

Basket Weave

Pastry tips: Small round tip (such as Ateco #3 or #4), ribbon tip (such as Ateco #46, #47, or #48)

Bag position: 90-degree angle

Motion: You will need two bags of icing, one fitted with a small round tip and another fitted with a ribbon tip. Pipe the vertical lines with the round tip and the horizontal lines with the ribbon tip. Start with the round tip and pipe a straight vertical line from the top to the bottom of the area you are decorating. Switch to the bag fitted with the ribbon tip and pipe a straight horizontal band over the top of the vertical line, centering it over the line. Pipe another horizontal band below the first one, spacing it one bandwidth below. Repeat piping bands to the bottom of the vertical line.

Switch to the bag fitted with the round tip and pipe another vertical line down the side of the cake so that it covers the right ends of the horizontal bands. Starting just to the right of the vertical line, pipe another row of horizontal bands, as above. Continue piping in the same pattern until the area you want to decorate is filled.

PIPED FLOWER DECORATIONS

DROP FLOWER

PASTRY TIP: Any drop flower tube (such as Ateco #129, #136, #190, or #193)

BAG POSITION: 90-degree angle

MOTION: For a plain drop flower: Holding the bag just above the surface of the cake, squeeze it until the flower is as wide as you want it. Release the pressure and swiftly lift the tip straight up and away.

For a swirled drop flower: Start with the hand holding the bag positioned as far to the left as possible. As you pipe out the flower, turn your hand to the right in a fluid motion to create a swirled effect.

SWEET PEA

PASTRY TIP: Rose tip (such as Ateco #101s to #104), small round tip (such as Ateco #2)

BAG POSITION: 45-degree angle

MOTION: Fit one bag with a rose tip and fill with petal shade; fit another bag with a small round tip and fill with pale green. For this flower, you make a center petal first, then two petals on either side. Hold the pastry bag against the surface so that the wide end of the rose tip is facing down. Gently squeeze the bag and, as the icing flows out, raise the tip about ⅛ inch above the surface. Hold that position briefly, then lower the tip to the position in which you started, release the pressure, and pull the bag away. Move the bag so that the tip is just to the left of the point at which you started the first petal, angle the tip slightly to the left, and repeat the procedure to make a second petal. Position the bag just to the right of the point at which you started the first petal, angle the tip slightly to the right, and repeat the procedure to make a third petal. Use a small round tip to pipe a calyx in a pale green shade where the petals meet at the bottom.

ROSEBUD

PASTRY TIP: Any rose tip (such as Ateco #101s to #104)

BAG POSITION: 45-degree angle

MOTION: The first piping motion will form a cupped petal with a standing edge: Position the pastry bag so that the wide end of the tip is closest to the surface. Squeeze the bag, lifting the tip about ¼ inch off the surface and moving your hand slightly to the right. Then continue to squeeze the bag, coming down on the surface about ⅛ inch to the right of where you started piping the petal. Release the pressure when you touch the surface and pull the bag away. For the second petal, position the tip where you ended the first petal and angle it so that it is facing the inside of the cupped petal. Squeezing the bag lightly, lift the tip about ¼ inch off the surface and form a mirror image of the first petal, catching the standing edge and pulling it inward. Relax the pressure as the petal lays itself down on the surface, and pull the bag away.

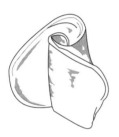

HALF ROSE

PASTRY TIP: Any rose tip (such as Ateco #101s to #104)

BAG POSITION: 45-degree angle

MOTION: This is a rosebud with two petals added to it. Pipe a rosebud as directed above. Then center the wide end of the tip at the base of the rosebud. Pivot the tip slightly to the left and squeeze the bag, lifting the tip slightly as you move it toward the center of the bud to form a left petal. Pivot the tip slightly to the right and repeat the procedure to form a right petal.

ROSE

PASTRY TIPS: Round tip (such as Ateco #12) and any rose tip (such as Ateco #101s to #104) for petals

BAG POSITION: 90-degree angle for base cone, 45-degree angle for petals

MOTION: The classic rose should be piped onto a small square of waxed paper set on a flower nail and then, when set, carefully transferred to the cake. Pipe a small dab of icing onto the nail to secure the waxed paper. Half-fill two bags with firm icing: Fit one bag with a round #12 tip and the other with a rose tip. Using the round tip and holding the bag at a 90-degree angle, pipe a large cone (about ¾ inch high) onto the waxed paper (until you are proficient at piping a rose, let the cone firm up before piping the petals—if using royal icing, let it harden at room temperature before proceeding; if using buttercream, refrigerate it until firm before proceeding). For the first layer of petals, gently place the rose tip wide end down against the base of the cone, with the narrow end straight. Pipe a petal around the cone, moving the tip up, around, and then down while turning the nail counterclockwise about one-third of a turn. Pipe a second petal next to the first, starting at the base of the first petal and overlapping it slightly, then moving the tip up and then down on the cone's surface as you rotate the nail. Pipe a third petal in the same way to complete the row. For the second row of petals, begin with the rose tip wide end down, just touching the center of one of the petals, and the narrow end angled outward at about a 45-degree angle to the cone. Squeeze the bag while rotating the nail one-quarter of a turn and moving the tip up, around, and down to form a petal. Start the next petal at the base of the previous one, and pipe three more petals to complete the row. For the third row of petals, begin with the rose tip wide end down, just touching the center of one of the petals, and the narrow end angled so that it is almost perpendicular to the cone. Pipe the first petal as before, giving the nail one-quarter of a turn. Pipe four more petals to complete the rose.

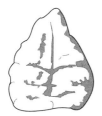

Leaves

Pastry tip: Any leaf tip (such as Ateco #65s to #70)

Bag position: 45-degree angle

Motion: Lightly touch the surface and then squeeze the bag until the icing fans out to the desired width. Release the pressure gradually as you pull the tip away, ending in a point.

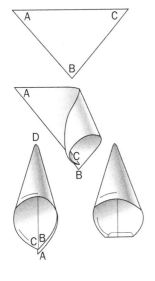

FINE PIPING AND WRITING

To write a message on a cake or decorate it with fine piped decorations or drizzled lines, use a fluid mixture such as royal icing or melted chocolate (blended with a little vegetable oil if necessary) and pipe it out through a parchment cone. To form a parchment cone:

- Cut a square of parchment paper diagonally in half, forming two triangles. Place one triangle before you as shown.
- Take the right-hand Point C (longest side/furthest point) of the triangle and fold it up and toward Point B.
- Take the opposite Point A and fold it up and around until it meets Points B and C at the top to form the closed tip of the cone, Point D.
- Fold Points A and C (at point B) down (in the direction of D) in order to prevent the cone from unraveling.

To use, fill the cone half full and fold over the open end to seal and tighten. Snip off the tip of the cone to the desired size (practice piping on a plate to determine if the opening is the right size). Pipe using one hand to squeeze the cone and the other hand, near the tip, to guide it.

An easy, if less professional, alternative to a parchment cone is a small sealable plastic bag. Scrape the icing into the bag and seal it. Snip a tiny hole in one of the bottom corners of the bag, and squeeze the bag gently to drizzle the icing over the cake. Since you have less control with a bag, I suggest that you use a parchment cone for the exacting task of writing on a cake.

CORNELLI LACE DECORATION: This free-form lacy piping makes an unusual and pretty pattern for the top of a cake. Use an icing or chocolate that contrasts with the color of the frosted or glazed cake. For example, if you decorated the cake with a dark chocolate glaze, use white chocolate or milk chocolate to pipe the lace. Pipe the design through a parchment cone.

STENCILING

A simple way to decorate an unfrosted or frosted cake is to dust the top with confectioners' sugar or cocoa powder through a parchment paper stencil or doily. If you are decorating a frosted cake, refrigerate it for about an hour to firm up the frosting before stenciling.

Cut out a circle of parchment paper that is slightly larger than the cake. Fold the circle into sixteenths (fold it in half, then in half again three more times). Using scissors, cut out small shapes along the fold lines to create a pattern. Unfold the circle and place it under a heavy pan or phone book to flatten it out. Or simply use a paper doily. Right before serving the cake, center the stencil (or doily) on the cake and sift an even coating of confectioners' sugar or cocoa powder over it. Very carefully lift the stencil straight up and off the cake.

CHOCOLATE DECOR

CHOCOLATE BANDS

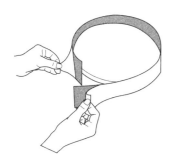

Wrapping a chocolate band, plain or decorated, around the sides of a cake creates a dazzling visual effect. Food-grade acetate, available in cake-decorating supply shops, gives the chocolate band an ultra-shiny finish and a professional look. To make a band: Cut a strip of acetate (or two strips, if necessary) or an acetate transfer sheet to fit around the frosted or glazed cake (the cake should be cool, but not cold, when you apply the band). Place the acetate on a piece of parchment paper (if you are using a transfer sheet, make sure that the cocoa butter–coated side is facing up). Temper the chocolate (see instructions on page 364). Pour a line of chocolate down the length of the strip and, using a small offset metal spatula, spread it into a thin even layer over the acetate, covering it completely (you shouldn't be able to see through the chocolate in any spots). Let the chocolate set for about 5 minutes, until tacky.

Very carefully lift up the chocolate-covered strip by the ends and press it onto the sides of the cake just so that it adheres. Repeat with a second strip if needed, lining up the seams so that they meet. Refrigerate the cake until the chocolate is completely set, about 40 minutes.

Gently peel off the acetate.

CHOCOLATE RUFFLES

Although working with chocolate is challenging by nature, forming perfect chocolate ruffles for the top of a cake is not as difficult as it looks; it just requires a little patience. First temper the chocolate (see instructions on page 362). Meanwhile, warm up a large baking sheet (11½ x 17½ inches) by running it under hot water for several seconds. Wipe the sheet completely dry and place it upside down on a work surface. Pour about ¾ cup tempered chocolate onto the sheet and, using an offset metal spatula, spread it evenly over the entire sheet. Place the coated sheet in the refrigerator for 5 minutes, or until the top looks slightly dull. Then let the chocolate set at room temperature for about 20 minutes.

Use a triangular metal scraper to form the ruffles. Put on a pair of plastic or latex gloves (available at cake decorating supply stores) to prevent leaving fingerprints on the ruffles. Hold the scraper at a shallow angle, about 25 degrees. Starting at a short end of the baking sheet and working away from yourself, push the chocolate with the scraper, angling it slightly to the left and using your other hand to pleat the chocolate on the right side. If the chocolate is too warm and does not form pleats, let it set a bit longer at room temperature. Set the chocolate ruffles on a piece of parchment paper as you form them, and let set at room temperature until firm.

When ready to decorate, use a pancake turner to carefully transfer each ruffle to the top of the cake. Place the smallest ruffles in the center of the cake and the largest ones on the outside. Lightly dust the cake with confectioners' sugar before serving.

CHOCOLATE LEAVES

Though time-consuming to make, chocolate leaves are a striking decoration for the top of a cake, particularly one glazed with dark chocolate. To make chocolate leaves, gather organic leaves of different sizes (rose leaves are most often used, but you can also use citrus tree leaves). Wash and dry the leaves thoroughly. Line a baking sheet with parchment paper.

Temper the chocolate (see instructions on page 364) and put on a pair of plastic or latex gloves to avoid leaving fingerprints on the leaves. Using a new small soft artist's brush, brush the underside of

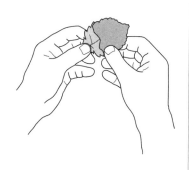

each leaf with a thin layer of chocolate, covering it completely, then place chocolate side up, on the baking sheet. Refrigerate the chocolate leaves for 5 minutes, or until dull and dry to the touch. Holding each leaf by the stem with one hand, gently peel the chocolate leaf off with the other hand. You should be able to reuse the green leaves three or four times before the chocolate begins to stick. Store the leaves in an airtight container in the refrigerator until ready to use.

CHOCOLATE CURLS

The best way to form chocolate curls is from a chunk (about 3 or 4 inches) cut from a thick block of chocolate, preferably couverture. The key to forming perfect curls is the temperature of the chocolate: too warm, and the chocolate will not curl; too cold, and it will splinter. Place the chocolate chunk in a microwave oven for 20-second intervals at medium power until it just starts to soften. This can take several tries, depending on the wattage of the microwave oven. Alternatively, use the gentle heat of a hair dryer to soften the chocolate. Line a baking sheet with waxed or parchment paper. Holding the chocolate chunk at one end with a piece of parchment paper, scrape a vegetable peeler over the other end of the chunk, pulling it toward you and letting the curls drop onto the parchment sheet. The lighter the pressure you apply, the tighter the curl will be. Use a toothpick or bamboo skewer to transfer the curls carefully to the top or sides of a cake.

GRATED CHOCOLATE

To grate chocolate, start with a small chunk of chocolate at cool room temperature. Grate the chocolate on the medium holes of a box or handheld grater onto a piece of parchment paper. To decorate the top of a cake, use a spoon to sprinkle spoonfuls of the grated chocolate onto it. To decorate the sides of a frosted cake, first make sure your hands are cold by running them under cold water and wiping them dry. Pick up handfuls of the grated chocolate and pat onto the sides of the cake.

GOLD LEAF

Decorating cakes with edible gold leaf results in a dramatic and elegant look, particularly if set against a rich dark chocolate glaze. When purchasing gold leaf, choose 22-karat grade, also known as patent gold, which is sold in booklets of 3½-inch square sheets separated by tissue paper. The sheets can be purchased from cake-decorating and art supply stores. Always work with gold leaf in a draft-free environment, as even a small breeze will cause the sheets to fly up or become jumbled. To apply a small piece of gold leaf to a cake, use a new small artist's brush. Gently touch the brush to the gold leaf and then bring the gold leaf as close as possible to the surface of the cake, until it sticks. Don't let the brush touch the surface of the cake, or it may leave a mark.

MARZIPAN

Marzipan can be used as a smooth elegant covering for a cake or formed into small decorations, such as fruit or flowers. To cover a cake with marzipan, place the cake on a cardboard cake round. To prevent the marzipan coating from cracking, you need to bevel the top edge of the cake. To do this, use a serrated knife, positioned at a 45-degree angle, to shave off a ¼-inch-wide strip from the top edge of the cake. Spread the top and sides of the cake with a smooth layer of buttercream, ganache, or other tacky frosting for the marzipan to cling to. To cover a 9- or 10-inch cake, you will need about 1 pound of marzipan. Dust a work surface liberally with confectioners' sugar. Shape the marzipan into a disk and roll it out, rotating it frequently to prevent sticking and dusting lightly with confectioners' sugar as needed, until it is about 16 inches in diameter. Move the cake as close as possible to the marzipan. Lightly roll the marzipan round halfway up on the rolling pin. Position the draped end of the marzipan so that it slightly overlaps the bottom of the far side of the cake, and gently drape the marzipan over the top of the cake, gradually unrolling it as you go. Smooth the marzipan onto the top of the cake as you unroll it, then smooth the sides so that there are no wrinkles, folds, or trapped air bubbles. Using a paring knife or pizza cutter,

trim away the excess marzipan at the base of the cake.

To form realistic marzipan fruit decorations, it is helpful to have a few professional tools on hand, such as a veined leaf cutter, a candy-maker's knife, an arrow-tipped gum paste tool, and a burnisher. You will also need a box grater, several small artist's paintbrushes, and paste food coloring and petal dust in various colors. Have real fruits on hand to inspire you and remind you of the details. Color portions of marzipan with paste food coloring appropriate to the fruit you are making (i.e., use yellow paste coloring for lemons and bananas, orange paste coloring for oranges). Pinch off pieces of the colored marzipan and form it by hand into fruit shapes such as apples, cherries, oranges, pears, peaches, raspberries, and/or bananas. Roll oranges and raspberries over the small holes of the box grater to give definition to their surface. Use the candy-maker's knife to form a crease down one side of cherries and the arrow-tipped tool to make a hole in the top of stemmed fruit. For leaves, roll out a thin layer of marzipan and use the veined leaf cutter to cut out leaves. Dab some corn syrup onto the fruit to attach the leaves to the fruit, and press the leaves in place with the burnisher. Lightly brush each piece of fruit with petal dust in the appropriate shade.

6

Angel Food,
Chiffon,
and Sponge
Cakes

HEAVENLY ANGEL FOOD CAKE • MICHAEL'S DOUBLE CHOCOLATE ANGEL FOOD CAKE • CLASSIC CHIFFON CAKE • SPICED CHIFFON CAKE *(variation)* • LIME CHIFFON CAKE *(variation)* • BANANA WALNUT CHIFFON CAKE *(variation)* • VANILLA-FLECKED CHIFFON CAKE • ORANGE CHIFFON CAKE • HOT MILK SPONGE CAKE • CLASSIC GÉNOISE • ALMOND GÉNOISE • BOSTON CREAM PIE • THE ULTIMATE LEMON ROLL • OPERA CAKE • CHOCOLATE HAZELNUT BÛCHE DE NOËL

Angel food, chiffon, and sponge cakes all belong to a category known as foam cakes, which contain a high ratio of eggs in relation to other ingredients. Angel food cakes are tall, airy, and delicate, made with only egg whites and, consequently, fat-free. The whites are beaten with cream of tartar (which stabilizes them) and sugar to the meringue stage, then flavoring (such as vanilla extract or lemon zest) and a mixture of sifted flour, confectioners' sugar, and salt is very gently folded in. Because the batter contains no chemical leavening, such as baking powder, the volume of an angel food cake depends solely on incorporated air (from the beaten whites) and steam, and therefore it is especially important not to deflate the batter during the folding process. Angel food cakes are usually baked in ungreased tube pans, which allows the batter to climb the sides of the pan and achieve high volume.

Most sponge cakes rely on beaten eggs, either whole or separated, for their volume. Baking powder, which adds extra volume and yields a finer crumb, occasionally shows up in recipes for American-style sponge cakes. Generally, the only fat in sponge cakes comes from the egg yolks, but the French génoise is sometimes enriched with butter. As with angel food cakes, the success of sponge cakes depends mostly on the volume of the beaten eggs and the ability of the baker to preserve this volume when folding in the dry ingredients. European-style sponge cakes tend to be slightly drier and less tender than their American counterparts. They are meant to be "imbibed" with a liqueur-flavored sugar syrup and are usually only one element of a cake that is layered with multiple components.

Chiffon cakes, invented by insurance salesman Harry Baker in 1927, are foam cakes enriched with oil. Because they have a high proportion of eggs, they are exceptionally light. The oil makes these cakes moist and tender—and allows them to stay that way even after refrigeration. The egg yolks contribute richness, while the beaten whites and baking powder give chiffon cakes volume. Always use a neutral-tasting vegetable oil, such as safflower (my preference), corn, or peanut oil. Like angel food cakes, chiffon cakes can be served unadorned or can be glazed, frosted, or lightly dusted with confectioners' sugar.

HEAVENLY ANGEL FOOD CAKE

Occasionally when I'm in the middle of making an angel food cake, I think, "This is a lot of trouble to go to for a cake that doesn't even haven't any butter in it." Then I taste it, and realize that, despite its absence of fat, the cake really is a little slice of heaven. Guilt-free heaven at that. Since the lightness of this cake relies on the air cells in the beaten egg whites, it is essential that the whites be at room temperature for maximum volume.

➤ MAKES ONE 10-INCH CAKE, SERVING 10 TO 12
➤ SPECIAL EQUIPMENT: LONG-NECKED BOTTLE (IF THE CAKE PAN DOESN'T HAVE "FEET")

1 cup (3.5 oz/100 g) sifted cake flour

¾ cup (3 oz/86 g) sifted confectioners' sugar

¼ teaspoon salt

12 large egg whites, at room temperature

1 teaspoon cream of tartar

1 cup (7 oz/200 g) superfine sugar

2 teaspoons vanilla extract

¼ teaspoon almond extract (optional)

1. Position a rack in the center of the oven and preheat the oven to 325°F.

2. Sift together the cake flour, confectioners' sugar, and salt into a medium bowl. Whisk together until well blended, and set aside.

3. In the clean dry bowl of an electric mixer, using the whisk attachment, beat the egg whites at low speed until frothy. Add the cream of tartar and mix just until blended. Increase the speed to medium and beat until the whites are fluffy and begin to form soft peaks. Gradually add the superfine sugar, about 1 tablespoon at a time. Increase the speed to high and whip until the whites are glossy and smooth and form almost stiff peaks; they should not be dry. Using a balloon whisk, gently whisk in the vanilla and almond extract, if using (just a few strokes of the whisk—don't overwork the whites).

4. Sift a few tablespoons of the flour mixture over the whites and, using a large rubber spatula or a balloon whisk, very gently fold it in. Repeat until all the flour mixture is added, using a light touch to deflate the batter as little as possible. Scrape the batter into an ungreased 10-inch tube pan with a removable bottom. Smooth the top with a spatula.

5. Bake the cake for 40 to 45 minutes, until it is golden brown and springs back when lightly touched with a finger and a cake tester inserted into the center comes out clean. Invert the pan and place

the center tube on a long-necked bottle. (If the pan has "feet," it can be inverted directly onto a work surface.) Let stand upside down until completely cooled, about 1½ hours.

6. To unmold the cake, slide a thin-bladed knife around the side of the cake, making sure to press the knife against the side of the pan to avoid marring the surface of the cake. Repeat with the center tube. Lift the tube up to remove the cake from the pan, and slide the knife under the cake to detach it from the pan bottom. Invert the cake onto a serving plate. Dust the top lightly with confectioners' sugar.

7. Slice the cake using an angel food cake divider or a serrated knife (use a sawing motion) to avoid compressing its airy texture.

STORE *in an airtight container at room temperature for up to 3 days, or refrigerate for up to a week.*

MICHAEL'S DOUBLE CHOCOLATE ANGEL FOOD CAKE

My brother-in-law, Michael Bellas, is an authority on beverage marketing. Owing to a mild obsession with his health, he is also an authority on the fat content of most foods. But he loves chocolate, and chocolate angel food cake is one of the few chocolate desserts in which he will occasionally indulge. Though Michael might not approve, a slice of this chocolaty cake is lovely topped with a dollop of softly whipped cream and perhaps even a little chocolate (dare we say *fudge*?) sauce. Note that you will need to whip the whites in a 5-quart or larger bowl.

➤ MAKES ONE 10-INCH CAKE, SERVING 10 TO 12
➤ SPECIAL EQUIPMENT: LONG-NECKED BOTTLE (IF THE CAKE PAN DOESN'T HAVE "FEET")

1 cup (3.5 oz/100 g) sifted cake flour

¾ cup (3 oz/86 g) sifted confectioners' sugar

¼ cup (0.8 oz/23 g) Dutch-processed cocoa powder

¼ teaspoon salt

2 ounces (57 g) bittersweet chocolate, finely grated

14 large egg whites, at room temperature

1½ teaspoons cream of tartar

1 cup (7 oz/200 g) superfine sugar

1½ teaspoons vanilla extract

1. Position a rack in the center of the oven and preheat the oven to 325°F.

2. Sift together the cake flour, confectioners' sugar, cocoa powder, and salt in a medium bowl. Whisk in the grated chocolate until blended, and set aside.

3. In the clean dry bowl of an electric mixer, using the whisk attachment, whip the egg whites at low speed until frothy. Add the cream of tartar and mix just until blended. Increase the speed to medium and gradually add the superfine sugar, about 1 tablespoon at a time. Increase the speed to high and whip until the whites are glossy and smooth and form stiff peaks; they should not be dry. Using a balloon whisk, gently whisk in the vanilla extract (just a few strokes of the whisk—don't overwork the whites). If you have a larger bowl, transfer the whipped whites to it now.

4. Sprinkle a few tablespoons of the flour mixture over the whites and, using a large rubber spatula or a balloon whisk, very gently fold it in. Repeat until all the flour mixture is added, using a light touch to deflate the batter as little as possible. Scrape the batter into an ungreased 10-inch tube pan with a removable bottom. Smooth the top with a spatula.

5. Bake the cake for 42 to 48 minutes, until it springs back when lightly touched with a finger and a cake tester inserted into the center comes out clean. Invert the pan and place the center tube on a long-necked bottle. (If the pan has "feet," it can be inverted directly onto a work surface.) Let stand upside down until completely cooled, about 1½ hours.

6. To unmold the cake, slide a thin-bladed knife around the side of the cake, making sure to press the knife against side of the pan to avoid marring the surface of the cake. Repeat with the center tube. Lift the tube up to remove the cake from the pan, and slide the knife under the cake to detach it from the pan bottom. Invert the cake onto a serving plate. Dust the top lightly with confectioners' sugar.

7. Slice the cake using an angel food cake divider or a serrated knife (use a sawing motion) to avoid compressing its airy texture.

STORE *at room temperature, under a cake keeper or covered with foil, for up to 5 days.*

CLASSIC CHIFFON CAKE

The original recipe for chiffon cake was developed by Hollywood insurance salesman Harry Baker in 1927. Baker had a side business of making and selling cakes for parties, and one day he discovered that adding vegetable oil to sponge cake batter made an exceptionally moist and tender cake. He eventually sold his coveted recipe to General Mills (for an undisclosed sum) twenty years later. Because it remains soft and moist even when refrigerated or frozen, chiffon cake is ideal as a base for mousse and ice cream cakes.

➤ MAKES ONE 9-INCH CAKE, SERVING 8

1¼ cups (4.4 oz/125 g) sifted cake flour

¾ cup (5.3 oz/150 g) granulated sugar, divided

1½ teaspoons baking powder

¼ teaspoon salt

3 large eggs, separated, at room temperature

⅓ cup (80 ml) water

¼ cup (60 ml) safflower or other neutral vegetable oil

1 teaspoon vanilla extract

1 large egg white

¼ teaspoon cream of tartar

1. Position a rack in the center of the oven and preheat the oven to 325°F. Grease the bottom (not the sides) of a 9-inch springform pan. Line the bottom of the pan with a round of parchment paper and grease the paper.

2. Sift together the flour, ½ cup of the granulated sugar, the baking powder, and salt in a medium bowl. Whisk until well blended, and set aside.

3. In a large bowl, whisk together the egg yolks, water, oil, and vanilla extract. Whisk in the flour mixture one-third at a time, mixing just until blended.

4. In the bowl of an electric mixer, using the whisk attachment, beat the 4 egg whites and the cream of tartar at medium speed until soft peaks form. Gradually beat in the remaining ¼ cup sugar, then increase the speed to high and beat until the whites are stiff but not dry. Using a large rubber spatula, briskly fold about one-third of the whites into the cake batter. Gently fold in the remaining whites. Scrape the batter into the prepared pan and smooth the top.

5. Bake the cake for 28 to 32 minutes, until a cake tester inserted into the center comes out clean. Place the pan on a wire rack and run a paring knife around the edge of the pan to loosen the cake. Cool the cake in the pan for 20 minutes.

6. Invert the cake onto the wire rack and peel off the parchment paper. Cool the cake completely.

STORE *in an airtight container at room temperature for up to 5 days.*

SPICED CHIFFON CAKE: In Step 2, add ½ teaspoon ground cinnamon, ¼ teaspoon ground ginger, ¼ teaspoon ground cloves, and ¼ teaspoon freshly grated nutmeg to the flour mixture.

LIME CHIFFON CAKE: In Step 3, add 2 teaspoons finely grated lime zest to the yolk mixture. Reduce the water to 1 tablespoon (15 ml) and add ¼ cup (60 ml) strained freshly squeezed lime juice.

BANANA WALNUT CHIFFON CAKE: In Step 2, add ½ teaspoon ground cinnamon, ¼ teaspoon ground ginger, and ¼ teaspoon freshly grated nutmeg to the flour mixture. In Step 3, replace the water with ¾ cup (180 ml) mashed very ripe banana (about 1½ large or 2 medium bananas). In Step 4, fold in ½ cup (2.1 oz/60 g) finely chopped walnuts with the second batch of beaten egg whites. Bake the cake for 35 to 40 minutes.

VANILLA-FLECKED CHIFFON CAKE

Here's an incomparable vanilla chiffon cake: tall, moist, and flecked with fragrant vanilla bean seeds. It's marvelous on its own or paired with Gingered Berry Compote (page 351), Red Berry Sauce (page 350), or Cacao Nib Whipped Cream (page 342). If you don't have a vanilla bean, substitute 1 tablespoon vanilla paste (available from The Baker's Catalogue; see Sources, page 367) or, as a last resort, 1 tablespoon pure vanilla extract.

➤ MAKES ONE 10-INCH CAKE, SERVING 12 TO 14
➤ SPECIAL EQUIPMENT: LONG-NECKED BOTTLE (IF THE CAKE PAN DOESN'T HAVE "FEET")

2½ cups (8.8 oz/250 g) sifted cake flour

1¾ cups (12.3 oz/350 g) granulated sugar, divided

1 tablespoon baking powder

¾ teaspoon salt

1 plump Tahitian vanilla bean, split lengthwise in half

6 large eggs, separated, at room temperature

⅔ cup (160 ml) water

½ cup (120 ml) safflower or other neutral vegetable oil

1 teaspoon finely grated lemon zest

3 large egg whites

½ teaspoon cream of tartar

Confectioners' sugar for dusting

1. Position a rack in the center of the oven and preheat the oven to 325°F.

2. Sift together the cake flour, 1¼ cups of the sugar, the baking powder, and salt in a large bowl. Whisk until well blended, and set aside.

3. Using a spoon, scrape the small seeds out of the vanilla bean into the bowl of an electric mixer fitted with the paddle attachment (discard bean). Add the egg yolks, water, vegetable oil, and lemon zest and beat at medium speed until blended, about 1 minute. Reduce the speed to low and add the flour mixture one-quarter at a time, mixing just until blended.

4. In a clean mixer bowl, using the whisk attachment, beat the 9 egg whites and the cream of tartar at medium speed until soft peaks form. Gradually beat in the remaining ½ cup sugar. Increase the speed to high and beat until the whites are stiff but not dry. Using a large rubber spatula, briskly fold about one-quarter of the whites into the cake batter. Gently fold in the remaining whites. Scrape the batter into an ungreased 10-inch tube pan with a removable bottom and smooth the top.

5. Bake for 55 to 65 minutes, until a cake tester inserted into the center comes out clean. Invert the pan and place the center tube on

a bottle. (If the pan has "feet," it can be inverted directly onto a work surface.) Let stand upside down until completely cooled, about 1½ hours.

6. To unmold the cake, slide a thin-bladed knife around the side of the cake, making sure to press the knife against the side of the pan to avoid marring the surface of the cake. Repeat with the center tube. Lift the tube up to remove the cake from the pan, and slide the knife under the cake to detach it from the pan bottom. Invert the cake onto a serving plate. Dust the top lightly with confectioners' sugar.

7. Slice the cake using an angel food cake divider or a serrated knife (use a sawing motion) to avoid compressing its airy texture.

STORE *at room temperature, under a cake keeper or covered with foil, for up to 5 days. Or freeze, well wrapped, for up to 2 weeks.*

ORANGE CHIFFON CAKE

Tall, moist, and exceptionally light, this simple cake has a bright fresh-squeezed-orange flavor. Serve it with fresh berries and, if you're feeling indulgent, sweetened whipped cream.

➤ MAKES ONE 10-INCH CAKE, SERVING 12 TO 14
➤ SPECIAL EQUIPMENT: LONG-NECKED BOTTLE (IF THE PAN DOESN'T HAVE "FEET")

2½ cups (8.8 oz/250 g) sifted cake flour

1¾ cups (12.3 oz/350 g) granulated sugar, divided

¾ teaspoon baking soda

¾ teaspoon salt

6 large eggs, separated, at room temperature

⅔ cup (160 ml) freshly squeezed orange juice

½ cup (120 ml) safflower or other neutral vegetable oil

1 tablespoon finely grated orange zest

1 teaspoon finely grated lemon zest

½ teaspoon Fiori di Sicilia (see Sources, page 366) or 1 teaspoon orange oil or vanilla extract

3 large egg whites

½ teaspoon cream of tartar

Confectioners' sugar for dusting

1. Position a rack in the center of the oven and preheat the oven to 325°F.

2. Sift together the cake flour, 1¼ cups of the sugar, the baking soda, and salt in a large bowl. Whisk until well blended, and set aside.

3. In the bowl of an electric mixer, using the paddle attachment, beat the egg yolks, orange juice, vegetable oil, citrus zest, and Fiori di Sicilia or orange oil or vanilla extract at medium speed until blended, about 1 minute. Reduce the speed to low and add the flour mixture one-quarter at a time, mixing just until blended.

4. In a clean mixer bowl, using whisk attachment, beat the 9 egg whites and the cream of tartar at medium speed until soft peaks form. Gradually beat in the remaining ½ cup sugar. Increase the speed to high and beat until the whites are stiff but not dry. Using a rubber spatula, briskly fold about one-quarter of the whites into the cake batter. Gently fold in the remaining whites. Scrape the batter into an ungreased 10-inch tube pan with a removable bottom and smooth the top.

5. Bake the cake for 55 to 65 minutes, until a cake tester inserted into the center comes out clean. Invert the pan and place the center tube on a bottle (if the pan has "feet," it can be inverted directly onto a work surface). Let stand upside down until completely cooled, about 1½ hours.

6. To unmold the cake, slide a thin-bladed knife around the side of the cake, making sure to press the knife against the side of the pan to avoid marring the surface of the cake. Repeat with the center tube. Lift the tube up to remove the cake from the pan, and slide the knife under the cake to detach it from the pan bottom. Invert the cake onto a serving plate. Dust the top lightly with confectioners' sugar.

7. Slice the cake using an angel food cake divider or a serrated knife (use a sawing motion) to avoid compressing its airy texture.

STORE *at room temperature, under a cake keeper or covered with foil, for up to 5 days. Or freeze, well wrapped, for up to 2 weeks.*

HOT MILK SPONGE CAKE

A gloriously moist and tender all-purpose sponge cake with a fine crumb and lovely golden color.

➤ MAKES ONE 9-INCH CAKE, SERVING 8

1⅓ cups (4.7 oz/133 g) sifted cake flour

1¼ teaspoons baking powder

¼ teaspoon salt

½ cup (120 ml) whole milk

4 tablespoons (2 oz/57 g) unsalted butter, cut into tablespoons

3 large eggs, at room temperature

¾ cup (5.3 oz/150 g) granu-lated sugar

1 teaspoon vanilla extract

1. Position a rack in the center of the oven and preheat the oven to 350°F. Grease the bottom and sides of a 9-inch cake pan. Dust the pan with flour.

2. Sift together the cake flour, baking powder, and salt two times. Set aside.

3. In a small saucepan, combine the milk and butter and heat over medium heat just until the butter is melted. Remove the pan from the heat and set aside.

4. In the bowl of an electric mixer, using the whisk attachment, beat the eggs at high speed until blended, about 1 minute. Gradually add the sugar and vanilla extract and beat until pale and tripled in volume, about 6 minutes.

5. Sift one-third of the flour mixture over the egg mixture and gently fold it in with a rubber spatula. Repeat with the remaining flour mixture in two more additions.

6. Reheat the milk mixture to just under a boil. Add it all at once to the egg mixture and gently fold it in. Scrape the batter into the prepared pan.

7. Bake the cake for 20 to 25 minutes, until it springs back when lightly touched and a cake tester inserted into the center comes out clean. Cool the cake in the pan on a wire rack for 10 minutes.

8. Run a paring knife around the edge of the pan and invert the cake onto the wire rack. Reinvert the cake, so that it is right side up, and cool completely.

STORE *in an airtight container at room temperature for up to 3 days, or refrigerate for up to a week.*

CLASSIC GÉNOISE

This classic European cake is not as moist or rich as an American layer cake, but it is wonderful when brushed with a flavored sugar syrup and frosted with a rich ganache or buttercream.

➤ MAKES ONE 9-INCH CAKE OR TWO 9-INCH CAKE LAYERS

1 cup (3.5 oz/100 g) sifted cake flour

½ teaspoon salt

6 large eggs

¾ cup (5.3 oz/150 g) granulated sugar

½ teaspoon finely grated lemon zest

1½ teaspoons vanilla extract

6 tablespoons (3 oz/85 g) unsalted butter, melted and cooled

1. Position a rack in the center of the oven and preheat the oven to 350°F. Grease the bottom and sides of one 9 x 3-inch springform pan or two 9-inch round cake pans. Dust the pan(s) with flour.

2. Sift together the flour and salt into a medium bowl. Whisk to combine, and set aside.

3. In the bowl of an electric mixer, whisk together the eggs and sugar by hand. Set the bowl over a saucepan of simmering water, making sure that the bottom of the bowl does not touch the water, and heat the mixture, whisking constantly, until the eggs are warm. Transfer the bowl to the electric mixer stand and, using the whisk attachment, beat on high speed until the mixture has tripled in volume, about 8 minutes. Reduce the speed to low and beat in the lemon zest and vanilla extract.

4. Sift one-third of the flour mixture over the batter and gently fold it in with a rubber spatula. Sift in the remaining flour mixture in two more additions, again folding in gently.

5. Transfer the melted butter to a small bowl if necessary, and scoop about ¾ cup of the batter into the bowl. Stir until blended. Fold this mixture into the remaining batter. Scrape the batter into the prepared pan(s).

6. If using two 9-inch pans, bake the cakes for 12 to 15 minutes, until the tops spring back when lightly touched and a cake tester inserted into the center comes out clean. If using a 9-inch spring-

form pan, bake for 25 to 30 minutes. Cool the cake(s) in the pan(s) on a wire rack for 15 minutes.

7. Invert the cake(s) onto the wire rack (if using a springform pan, remove the side first) and cool completely.

STORE *at room temperature, wrapped in plastic wrap, for up to 3 days, or refrigerate for up to a week.*

Almond Génoise

What's unusual about this flavorful almond génoise is that it doesn't call for whole eggs—instead, the eggs are separated and the yolks and whites are beaten independently, as in a French biscuit cake. The result is a wonderfully light all-purpose sponge cake that can simply be brushed with syrup and glazed or layered with mousse and meringue rounds for a more elaborate production.

➤ **MAKES TWO 9-INCH CAKE LAYERS**

1 cup (4 oz/114 g) cake flour

¼ teaspoon salt

1½ cups (6.3 oz/180 g) slivered almonds, lightly toasted

8 large eggs, separated, at room temperature

1½ cups (10.5 oz/300 g) granulated sugar, divided

¼ teaspoon cream of tartar

5 tablespoons (2.5 oz/71 g) unsalted butter, melted and still warm

½ teaspoon almond extract

1. Position a rack in the center of the oven and preheat the oven to 350°F. Grease the bottom and sides of two 9-inch round cake pans. Dust the pans with flour.

2. Sift together the flour and salt into a medium bowl. Transfer the mixture to the bowl of a food processor and add the almonds. Process until the almonds are finely ground. Set aside.

3. In the bowl of an electric mixer, using the whisk attachment, beat the egg yolks and 1 cup of the sugar at high speed until light and thick, about 3 minutes. Transfer the mixture to a large bowl.

4. In a clean dry mixer bowl, using the clean whisk attachment, beat the egg whites at medium speed until frothy. Add the cream of tartar and beat at medium-high speed until soft peaks just begin to form. Gradually add the remaining ½ cup sugar and beat at high speed until the whites form stiff peaks.

5. Using a rubber spatula, gently fold about one-third of the whites into the yolk mixture. Sprinkle about one-third of the flour mixture over the egg yolk mixture and gently fold it in. Continue adding the egg whites and flour mixture alternately, folding very gently.

6. In a small bowl, stir together the butter and almond extract. Scoop about 1 cup of the cake batter into the bowl and stir until blended. Gently fold this mixture into the remaining batter. Scrape the batter into the prepared pans.

7. Bake the cakes for 18 to 22 minutes, until the tops spring back when lightly touched and a cake tester inserted into the center comes out clean. Cool the cakes in the pans on a wire rack for 15 minutes.

8. Invert the cakes onto the rack and cool completely.

STORE *at room temperature, wrapped in plastic wrap, for up to 3 days, or refrigerate for up to a week.*

BOSTON CREAM PIE

In 1855, a German-born pastry chef at Boston's Parker House Hotel added a rich chocolate glaze to a custard-filled sponge cake known as Boston Pie, and a new American classic was born. One mouthful, and you'll realize that although Bostonians might not know their pie from their cake, they know a good thing when they taste it.

➤ MAKES ONE 9-INCH CAKE, SERVING 10

VANILLA CUSTARD FILLING

3 large egg yolks

¼ cup (1.7 oz/50 g) granulated sugar

2 tablespoons (0.5 oz/15 g) cornstarch

1 cup (240 ml) whole milk

1 tablespoon unsalted butter

1 teaspoon vanilla extract or paste

¼ cup (60 ml) heavy cream

Hot Milk Sponge Cake (page 72)

⅔ cup Bittersweet Chocolate Glaze (page 306)

MAKE THE FILLING

1. In a medium bowl, whisk together the yolks, sugar, and cornstarch; set aside.

2. In a medium saucepan, bring the milk to a gentle boil. Remove the pan from the heat and whisk about ⅓ cup of the hot milk into the yolk mixture. Return the entire mixture to the saucepan, place over medium-high heat, and bring to a boil, whisking constantly. Continue to boil, whisking constantly, for 1 minute. Remove the pan from the heat, scrape the bottom of the pan with a spatula, and whisk until smooth. Whisk in the butter until melted.

3. Immediately strain the custard through a fine-mesh sieve into a medium bowl. Whisk in the vanilla extract or paste. Cover the surface of the custard with plastic wrap, and let cool to room temperature, then refrigerate for 2 hours, or until well chilled.

ASSEMBLE THE CAKE

4. Using a long serrated knife, cut the cake horizontally in half to make 2 layers.

5. Transfer the custard filling to the bowl of an electric mixer. Add the ¼ cup heavy cream and, using the whisk attachment, beat the mixture at high speed until it is light and forms soft peaks, about 1 minute.

6. Save the smooth bottom layer for the top of the cake, and place the remaining cake layer cut side up on a serving plate. Scrape the

filling onto the layer and, using a small offset metal spatula, spread it into an even layer. Top with the other cake layer, cut side down.

GLAZE THE CAKE

7. Pour the warm glaze over the top of the cake, allowing some of it to drizzle down the sides. Serve the cake immediately, or refrigerate.

STORE *in the refrigerator in a covered container for up to a day; bring to room temperature before serving.*

THE ULTIMATE LEMON ROLL

Composed of a tangy, silk-textured filling enveloped in a moist lemon chiffon roll, this cake is a ray of sunshine for lemon lovers. Though best eaten the day it's assembled, the cake can be made in stages—the filling can be made up to two days in advance, the chiffon cake (store it rolled up) up to three days ahead.

➤ MAKES ONE 11-INCH ROLL, SERVING 10

LEMON SILK FILLING

7 large egg yolks

1⅓ cups (9.3 oz/266 g) granulated sugar

1 tablespoon finely grated lemon zest

⅔ cup (160 ml) freshly squeezed lemon juice

Pinch of salt

½ cup (1 stick/4 oz/112 g) cold unsalted butter, cut into tablespoons

½ cup (120 ml) heavy cream

LEMON CHIFFON SHEET CAKE

Confectioners' sugar for sprinkling

1¼ cups (4.4 oz/125 g) sifted cake flour

¾ cup (5.3 oz/150 g) granulated sugar, divided

1½ teaspoons baking powder

¼ teaspoon salt

3 large eggs, separated

1 tablespoon finely grated lemon zest

MAKE THE FILLING

1. Set a fine-mesh sieve over a medium bowl and set aside. In a medium heavy nonreactive saucepan, whisk together the egg yolks and sugar until blended. Stir in the lemon zest and juice, salt, and butter and cook over medium heat, whisking constantly, until the mixture thickens, 7 to 10 minutes (do not let the mixture boil, or it will curdle). The custard should leave a path on the back of a wooden spoon when you draw your finger across it. Immediately strain the mixture through the sieve, pressing it through with a rubber spatula.

2. Set the bowl containing the lemon mixture in a larger bowl filled about one-third full with ice water (be careful that the water doesn't splash into the lemon mixture). Stir the lemon mixture frequently until it is slightly chilled, about 15 minutes.

3. In the bowl of an electric mixer, using the whisk attachment, beat the heavy cream at high speed until soft peaks form. Fold a large spoonful of the whipped cream into the lemon mixture to lighten it. Gently fold in the remaining cream. Cover the bowl and refrigerate the cream until ready to use; it will firm up as it chills. (The filling can be made up to 2 days in advance.)

MAKE THE SHEET CAKE

4. Position a rack in the center of the oven and preheat the oven to 325°F. Grease the bottom and sides of an 11½ x 17½-inch jelly-roll pan. Line the bottom of the pan with parchment paper. Place a sheet of parchment paper about the same size as the pan on a work surface and sprinkle it lightly with confectioners' sugar.

¼ cup (60 ml) freshly squeezed
lemon juice

¼ cup (60 ml) vegetable oil

1 tablespoon (15 ml) water

1 teaspoon vanilla extract

1 large egg white

½ teaspoon cream of tartar

GARNISH

Confectioners' sugar for dusting

5. Sift together the cake flour, ½ cup of the sugar, the baking powder, and salt into a medium bowl. Whisk until well blended, and set aside.

6. In the bowl of an electric mixer, using the paddle attachment, beat the egg yolks, lemon zest, lemon juice, vegetable oil, water, and vanilla extract at medium speed until blended, about 1 minute. Reduce the speed to low and add the flour mixture, one-quarter at a time, mixing just until blended.

7. In a clean mixer bowl, using the whisk attachment, beat the 4 egg whites and the cream of tartar at medium speed until soft peaks form. Gradually beat in the remaining ¼ cup sugar. Increase the speed to high and beat until the whites are stiff but not dry. Using a rubber spatula, briskly fold about one-quarter of the whites into the cake batter. Gently fold in the remaining whites. Scrape the batter into the prepared pan and smooth the top.

8. Bake the cake for 14 to 18 minutes, until it is just starting to brown lightly and springs back when lightly touched. Run a paring knife around the sides of the pan to loosen the cake. Invert the hot cake onto the prepared sheet of parchment paper and carefully remove the pan. Peel the parchment paper from the cake. Starting with a short end, gently roll the cake up, rolling the bottom sheet of parchment paper along with it. Let cool completely.

FILL THE ROLL

9. Gently unroll the cake. Spread the chilled filling over the surface of the cake, spreading it to within 1 inch of the edges. Reroll the cake, using the parchment paper to help push it along. Using a serrated knife, trim off the crusty ends of the roll, cutting about a ¼-inch slice from each end. Place the roll on a serving plate and refrigerate for at least 1 hour before serving.

10. Just before serving, sift confectioners' sugar generously over the top of the cake.

STORE *in the refrigerator, well wrapped, for up to a day; this cake is best served the day it is made.*

Opera Cake

Its origins are obscure, but the opera cake remains one of the most popular desserts in French pâtisseries. It is a very low cake made of thin layers of coffee-soaked almond biscuit and chocolate and espresso buttercream, topped with a chocolate glaze. Pastry chefs traditionally write its name in glaze across the top, but if your handwriting is shaky, garnish it with edible gold leaf instead (available from Easy Leaf Products; see Sources, page 367).

➤ MAKES ONE 5½ X 11-INCH CAKE, SERVING 8
➤ SPECIAL EQUIPMENT: CANDY THERMOMETER

ALMOND BISCUIT

1 cup (3 oz/85 g) unblanched sliced almonds

½ cup (2 oz/58 g) confectioners' sugar

3 large eggs, at room temperature

⅓ cup (1.3 oz/38 g) cake flour

3 large egg whites, at room temperature

⅛ teaspoon salt

⅛ teaspoon cream of tartar

3 tablespoons (1.3 oz/37 g) granulated sugar

3 tablespoons (1.5 oz/43 g) unsalted butter, melted

ESPRESSO SYRUP

⅓ cup (80 ml) hot espresso or coffee

¼ cup (1.7 oz/50 g) granulated sugar

3 tablespoons (44 ml) Kahlúa or other coffee liqueur

MAKE THE BISCUIT

1. Position a rack in the center of the oven and preheat the oven to 400°F. Grease the bottom and sides of an 11½ x 17½-inch jelly-roll pan. Line the bottom of the pan with parchment paper and grease the paper. Dust the paper and sides of the pan with flour.

2. In the bowl of a food processor, pulse together the almonds and confectioners' sugar just until the almonds are finely ground (don't overprocess, or the nuts will form a paste); set aside.

3. In the bowl of an electric mixer, using the whisk attachment, beat the eggs at high speed until light, thick, and tripled in volume, about 3 minutes. Reduce the speed to low, add the almond mixture, and mix just until blended. Remove the bowl from the mixer stand. Sift half of the cake flour over the batter and gently fold it in. Sift over the remaining flour and fold it in.

4. In a clean mixer bowl, using the clean dry whisk attachment, beat the egg whites at medium speed until frothy. Add the salt and cream of tartar and beat at medium-high speed until soft peaks just begin to form. Gradually add the granulated sugar and beat at high speed until the whites form stiff, shiny peaks. Using a rubber spatula, gently fold one-third of the whites into the batter. Gently fold in the remaining whites, then the melted butter. Gently scrape the batter into the prepared pan, trying not to deflate it too much, and smooth it into an even layer.

¾ cup (5.3 oz/150 g) granulated sugar

⅓ cup (80 ml) water

2 large eggs, at room temperature

14 tablespoons (7 oz/200 g) unsalted butter, slightly softened

½ teaspoon vanilla extract

2½ ounces (71 g) bittersweet chocolate, melted and cooled

1 teaspoon instant espresso powder, dissolved in 1 teaspoon hot water

⅔ cup Bittersweet Chocolate Glaze (page 306)

5. Bake the cake for 8 to 10 minutes, until golden brown. Cool the cake in the pan on a wire rack for 10 minutes.

6. Run a paring knife around the edges of the pan to loosen the cake, then transfer it, still on the paper, to a cutting board. Using a serrated knife, trim off about ⅛ inch from each side of the cake. Cut the cake crosswise into 3 even strips, each about 5½ x 11 inches. Carefully peel each strip off the paper.

MAKE THE SYRUP

7. In a small saucepan, combine the espresso and sugar and heat over medium heat, stirring frequently, until the sugar dissolves. Stop stirring, increase the heat to high, and bring the syrup to a boil. Remove the pan from the heat and let the syrup cool for 10 minutes, then stir in the Kahlúa.

MAKE THE BUTTERCREAMS

8. In a small heavy saucepan, combine the sugar and water and bring to a boil over medium heat, stirring to dissolve the sugar. Stop stirring and increase the heat to high.

9. In the bowl of an electric mixer, using the whisk attachment, beat the eggs at medium speed until the sugar syrup is ready.

10. Cook the sugar syrup until it reaches 238°F on a candy thermometer (watch the syrup very carefully—it's easy to overcook it). Remove the pan from the heat and, with the mixer off, immediately pour about ¼ cup of the hot syrup over the beaten eggs. Beat at high speed until blended, about 10 seconds. Turn the mixer off and add another ¼ cup syrup. Beat at high speed for another 10 seconds. Repeat this process until all of the syrup is used. Using a rubber spatula, scrape down the sides of the bowl. Then continue to beat at medium-high speed until the egg mixture is completely cool, about 5 minutes.

11. At medium speed, beat the softened butter 1 tablespoon at a time into the egg mixture. Add the vanilla extract, increase the speed to medium-high, and beat until the buttercream is smooth and shiny, about 2 minutes.

12. Transfer half of the buttercream (about 1 cup) to a medium bowl. Stir in the melted chocolate until blended. Stir the espresso mixture into the other half of the buttercream.

ASSEMBLE THE CAKE

13. Place one of the cake strips on a rectangular platter or piece of cardboard covered with foil. Brush a generous amount of the espresso syrup over the strip, saturating it. Scrape all but ½ cup of the chocolate buttercream onto the cake strip, spreading it evenly all the way to the edges. Top with another cake strip and brush it generously with syrup. Scrape all but ½ cup of the espresso buttercream over the cake, spreading it evenly as before. Top with the remaining cake strip. Brush the cake with syrup.

14. In a small bowl, stir together the reserved chocolate and espresso buttercreams. Spread this over the top of the cake strip as evenly as possible. Refrigerate the cake for at least 30 minutes (or up to 24 hours).

GLAZE THE CAKE

15. Remove the cake from the refrigerator. Carefully pour all but 2 tablespoons of the glaze over the top of the cake, then, using a small offset metal spatula, spread the glaze just over the top of the cake to the edges. Refrigerate the cake for 10 minutes, to set the glaze. Scrape the remaining glaze into a parchment paper cone or small sealable plastic bag. (If using a bag, seal it and snip a tiny hole in one of the bottom corners.) Pipe the word "OPERA" on top of the cake. Chill the cake for at least 30 minutes to set the glaze.

16. To serve, bring the cake to room temperature (this is imperative!). Use a long serrated knife to cut rectangular slices of cake.

STORE *in the refrigerator for up to 1 day or place the cake in the freezer until firm, then wrap in plastic wrap and freeze for up to a month (defrost the cake, still wrapped, in the refrigerator overnight).*

CHOCOLATE HAZELNUT BÛCHE DE NOËL

ABûche de Noël, or Yule Log Cake, is as much a holiday showpiece as it is a delectable dessert. Complete with charming little meringue mushrooms and chocolate leaves, this festive show-stopper takes some time and effort, but its appearance alone is bound to generate a chorus of oohs and aahs. It'll also get rave reviews on the taste front—this version is a moist chocolate chiffon cake soaked with a Frangelico-fueled syrup, filled with a hazelnut buttercream, and then frosted with chocolate buttercream. To maximize the flavor and silky texture of the buttercream, it is essential that you bring this cake to room temperature before serving.

➤ MAKES ONE 14-INCH ROLL, SERVING 10 TO 12

CHOCOLATE CHIFFON SHEET CAKE

⅔ cup (2.3 oz/66 g) sifted cake flour

⅔ cup (4.6 oz/132 g) granulated sugar, divided

⅓ cup (1 oz/30 g) Dutch-processed cocoa powder, sifted

1¼ teaspoons baking powder

¼ teaspoon salt

2 large eggs, at room temperature

6 tablespoons (89 ml) safflower or other neutral vegetable oil

1 teaspoon vanilla extract

3 large egg whites

¼ teaspoon cream of tartar

Confectioners' sugar for dusting

MAKE THE SHEET CAKE

1. Position a rack in the center of the oven and preheat the oven to 350°F. Grease the bottom and sides of an 11½ x 17½-inch jelly-roll pan. Line the bottom of the pan with a sheet of parchment paper and grease the paper. Dust the paper and sides of the pan with flour.

2. In a small bowl, whisk together the cake flour, ⅓ cup of the sugar, the cocoa powder, baking powder, and salt; set aside.

3. In a large bowl, whisk together the eggs, oil, and vanilla until well blended. Stir in the flour mixture just until blended (the mixture will be thick).

4. In the bowl of an electric mixer, using the whisk attachment, beat the egg whites and cream of tartar at medium-high speed until soft peaks form. Gradually beat in the remaining ⅓ cup sugar. Increase the speed to high and beat until the whites are stiff but not dry. Using a rubber spatula, briskly fold about one-third of the whites into the chocolate batter. Gently fold in the remaining whites just until blended. Scrape the batter into the prepared pan and smooth it into an even layer.

⅓ cup (80 ml) water

2 tablespoons (0.8 oz/25 g) granulated sugar

1 tablespoon Frangelico (hazelnut liqueur; brandy or dark rum can be substituted)

HAZELNUT AND CHOCOLATE BUTTERCREAMS

¾ cup (5.3 oz/150 g) granulated sugar

4 large egg whites

3 tablespoons (44 ml) water

1½ cups plus 2 tablespoons (13.5 oz/385 g) unsalted butter, softened but still cool

1 teaspoon vanilla extract

4 ounces (113 g) bittersweet chocolate, melted with 2 tablespoons water and cooled

2 tablespoons (1.3 oz/38 g) praline paste, homemade (page 333), or store-bought (see Sources, page 366)

GARNISH

Meringue Mushrooms (page 362)

Chocolate Leaves (page 54)

Confectioners' sugar for sprinkling

5. Bake the cake for 12 to 15 minutes, until it springs back when lightly touched in the center. Place a sheet of parchment paper about the same size as the pan on a work surface and generously dust it with confectioners' sugar. Run a paring knife around the edges of the cake pan and carefully invert the cake onto the parchment paper. Remove the pan and carefully peel off the parchment paper on top. Starting at a long side, roll the cake up with the parchment paper jelly roll–style, forming a tight cylinder with the seam hidden at the bottom of the roll. Cool the rolled cake completely on a wire rack.

MAKE THE SYRUP

6. In a small saucepan, combine the water and sugar, and cook over medium heat, stirring constantly with a wooden spoon, just until the sugar dissolves. Stop stirring, increase the heat to high, and bring the syrup to a boil. Remove the pan from the heat and let the syrup cool for 10 minutes, then stir in the liqueur.

MAKE THE BUTTERCREAMS

7. Pour ½ inch of water into a large skillet. Bring the water to a simmer, then reduce the heat to medium-low to maintain a simmer.

8. In the bowl of an electric mixer, combine the sugar, egg whites, and water. Place the bowl in the skillet of water and whisk gently until the mixture registers 160°F on an instant-read thermometer. Transfer the bowl to the mixer stand and, using the whisk attachment, beat at medium-high speed until the meringue is cool and forms stiff, shiny peaks, about 5 minutes.

9. Reduce the speed to medium and beat in the butter 1 tablespoon at a time. Beat in the vanilla. Beat at high speed until the buttercream is smooth, about 1 minute.

10. Transfer 2½ cups of the buttercream to a medium bowl and stir in the melted chocolate until completely blended. Set the chocolate buttercream aside.

11. Add the praline paste to the buttercream remaining in the mixer bowl and, using the whisk attachment, beat on high speed until well blended.

ASSEMBLE THE CAKE

12. Carefully unroll the cooled cake. Using a long serrated knife, trim off about ⅛ inch from the short ends of the cake. Brush the cake with the hazelnut syrup. Spread with an even layer of the hazelnut buttercream. Cut a 3 x 11-inch strip from one of the short ends of the cake, and cut the strip crosswise into two 3 x 5½-inch strips. From a short end, roll each strip into a tight cylinder, wrap in aluminum foil, and freeze for about 30 minutes, until firm. Reroll the large cake roll, without the parchment paper, and transfer it, seam side down, to a long serving platter. Refrigerate until the small rolls are frozen.

13. Unwrap the small cake rolls. Trim one end of one roll on the diagonal so that the roll can be attached to the log to form one of the branch knobs. Attach it to the cake log with a dab of the chocolate buttercream. Trim the remaining small roll in the same manner and attach it to the cake log near the other knob but facing in the opposite direction.

14. Using a small metal spatula, cover the stump ends of the cake and the branch knobs with a smooth layer of chocolate buttercream. Scrape the remaining buttercream into a large pastry bag fitted with a medium closed star tip (such as Ateco #4). Pipe slightly wavy lines, simulating tree bark, lengthwise over the cake log, covering it completely. Refrigerate the cake until ready to decorate and serve it.

15. About 45 minutes before serving, remove the cake from the refrigerator. Decorate it with the meringue mushrooms and chocolate leaves. Right before serving, lightly sprinkle the cake with confectioners' sugar to represent snow.

STORE *in the refrigerator, loosely covered, for up to 24 hours.*

7

POUND CAKES

AND

COFFEE CAKES

PLAINLY PERFECT POUND CAKE • LIME POPPY SEED POUND CAKE *(variation)* • LEMON POPPY SEED POUND CAKE *(variation)* • TOASTED ALMOND POUND CAKE • LUXE POUND CAKE • LEMON-SOAKED GINGER POUND CAKE • CHERRY-ALMOND CREAM CHEESE POUND CAKE • CINNAMON SWIRL BUTTERMILK POUND CAKE • RICH MARBLE POUND CAKE WITH CHOCOLATE GLAZE • DEEP CHOCOLATE SOUR CREAM POUND CAKE • SOUR CREAM–BLUEBERRY CRUMB CAKE • BUTTERMILK PEACH COFFEE CAKE • FILLED COFFEE CAKE • BRIOCHE CAKE WITH CARAMEL CUSTARD CREAM

The richest of all butter cakes, the pound cake was named for the fact that original versions contained a pound each of flour, sugar, eggs, and butter. The leavening for these cakes traditionally came only from the air bubbles created by creaming the butter and sugar; baking powder was not used, and the cakes were dense and heavy. Modern pound cakes usually contain a small amount of chemical leavening and are moister and more tender than their predecessors, with a more open crumb and delicate texture.

The formula for pound cakes is simple: butter and sugar are creamed together to incorporate air, eggs are added, and then flour and other dry ingredients are blended in at low speed. The classic pound cake is baked in a loaf pan, but more decorative pans, such as a fluted Bundt pan, can be used. Since the classic pound cake has a mild, buttery taste, it is an ideal cake to convey a host of flavors, from ginger to lemon to chocolate. Whatever the flavor, the beauty of the pound cake is its simplicity; it is one of the easiest cakes to make and, though not as flashy as a frosted layer cake, one of the most satisfying to eat.

Like pound cakes, coffee cakes are relatively simple butter cakes that can carry a panoply of flavors beautifully. Most are leavened with baking powder and/or baking soda, but some are leavened with yeast. Though they are typically served at breakfast or brunch, coffee cakes can be enjoyed any time of day (or night). In fact, the Brioche Cake with Caramel Custard Cream (page 112) is an ideal dessert to end a grand meal.

PLAINLY PERFECT POUND CAKE

A good pound cake is simple, buttery, and rich. Think of it as the vanilla ice cream of the cake world. It is essential that you cream the butter and sugar for a full four minutes to achieve the fine crumb and tender texture of this classic cake. Serve a slice of this cake on its own or with ice cream or berries and softly whipped cream.

➤ MAKES ONE 9 X 5-INCH LOAF CAKE, SERVING 10

2 cups (7 oz/200 g) sifted cake flour

¼ teaspoon baking powder

¼ teaspoon salt

1 cup (2 sticks/8 oz/227 g) unsalted butter, softened

1¼ cups (8.8 oz/250 g) granulated sugar

4 large eggs

1 teaspoon finely grated lemon zest

1 teaspoon finely grated orange zest

1 teaspoon vanilla extract

⅓ cup (80 ml) heavy cream

1. Position a rack in the center of the oven and preheat the oven to 325°F. Grease the bottom and sides of a 9 x 5-inch loaf pan. Dust the pan with flour.

2. Sift together the flour, baking powder, and salt into a medium bowl. Whisk to combine well, and set aside.

3. In the bowl of an electric mixer, using the paddle attachment, beat the butter at medium speed until very creamy, about 2 minutes. Gradually add the sugar and beat the mixture at medium-high speed until very light, about 4 minutes. Reduce the speed to low and add the eggs one at a time, beating well after each addition and scraping down the sides of the bowl occasionally (the mixture will look curdled at this point). Beat in the citrus zest and vanilla extract. Add the flour mixture at low speed in three additions, alternating it with the heavy cream in two additions and mixing just until the flour is incorporated. Scrape the batter into the prepared pan and smooth the top.

4. Bake the cake for 60 to 70 minutes, until a cake tester inserted into the center comes out clean. Place the cake pan on a wire rack and let cool for 20 minutes.

5. Unmold the cake and cool completely, right side up, before slicing.

STORE *in an airtight container at room temperature for up to a week, or refrigerate for up to 2 weeks.*

LIME POPPY SEED POUND CAKE: Stir 3 tablespoons poppy seeds into the sifted flour mixture in Step 2. Omit the orange zest and add 2 teaspoons finely grated lime zest along with the lemon zest in Step 3. While the cake is baking, combine $\frac{1}{3}$ cup granulated sugar and $\frac{1}{4}$ cup water in a small saucepan. Cook over medium heat, stirring constantly, until the sugar is dissolved. Remove the pan from the heat and stir in 3 tablespoons freshly squeezed lime juice and 2 tablespoons freshly squeezed lemon juice.

When the cake is done, let it cool in the pan on a wire rack for 10 minutes, then poke the top of the cake all over at 1-inch intervals with a bamboo skewer and brush it with half the lime syrup. Let the cake stand for 5 minutes. Invert the cake onto the wire rack and poke the bottom all over with the skewer. Brush the bottom and sides with the remaining syrup. Turn the cake upright on the rack and let cool completely.

LEMON POPPY SEED POUND CAKE: Stir 3 tablespoons poppy seeds into the sifted flour mixture in Step 2. Omit the orange zest and increase the lemon zest to 1 tablespoon in Step 3. While the cake is baking, combine $\frac{1}{3}$ cup granulated sugar and $\frac{1}{4}$ cup water in a small saucepan. Cook over medium heat, stirring constantly, until the sugar is dissolved. Remove the pan from the heat and stir in $\frac{1}{3}$ cup freshly squeezed lemon juice.

When the cake is done, let it cool in the pan on a wire rack for 10 minutes, then poke the cake all over at 1-inch intervals with a bamboo skewer and brush it with half the lemon syrup. Let the cake stand for 5 minutes. Invert the cake onto the wire rack and poke the bottom all over with the skewer. Brush the bottom and sides with the remaining syrup. Turn the cake upright on the rack and let cool completely.

TOASTED ALMOND POUND CAKE

The rustic appearance of this homey loaf cake belies its sophisticated almond flavor. The crust is a deep brown, but the interior is a buttery golden yellow. As it bakes, the heady fragrance of almonds will fill your kitchen, and you may not be able to wait for the cake to cool before you try a slice. Use canned almond paste for this cake; it has a much better flavor than the brand sold in a tube.

➤ MAKES ONE 9 X 5-INCH LOAF CAKE, SERVING 10

1¾ cups (6.2 oz/175 g) sifted cake flour

1 teaspoon baking powder

½ teaspoon salt

½ cup (2.1 oz/60 g) blanched slivered almonds, toasted (see page 36)

1 cup (7 oz/200 g) granulated sugar, divided

1 cup (2 sticks/8 oz/227 g) unsalted butter, softened

½ cup (5 oz/142 g) canned almond paste

4 large eggs

1 teaspoon vanilla extract

¼ teaspoon almond extract

½ cup (120 ml) heavy cream or whole milk

Confectioners' sugar for dusting

1. Position a rack in the center of the oven and preheat the oven to 325°F. Grease the bottom and sides of a 9 x 5-inch loaf pan. Dust the pan with flour. Stack two baking sheets on top of one another and set aside. (This will be used to insulate the cake while it is baking—you can use an insulated baking sheet instead if you have one.)

2. Sift together the flour, baking powder, and salt into a medium bowl. Whisk to combine, and set aside.

3. Combine the almonds and ¼ cup of the sugar in the bowl of a food processor and process until the almonds are just finely ground (don't overprocess, or the nuts will become oily). Stir the ground almonds into the flour mixture and set aside.

4. In the bowl of an electric mixer, using the paddle attachment, beat the butter and almond paste at medium speed until very creamy, about 2 minutes. Gradually add the remaining ¾ cup sugar and beat the mixture at high speed until very light, about 4 minutes. Reduce the speed to medium and add the eggs one at a time, beating well after each addition and scraping down the sides of the bowl occasionally. Beat in the vanilla and almond extract. Add the flour mixture at low speed in three additions, alternating it with the heavy cream in two additions and mixing just until the flour is incorporated. Scrape the batter into the prepared pan and smooth the top.

5. Place the cake in the oven on top of the stacked baking sheets. Bake for 70 to 85 minutes, until a cake tester inserted in the center of the cake comes out clean. Place the cake pan on a wire rack and let cool for 20 minutes.

6. Unmold the cake and cool completely, right side up.

7. Dust the top of the cake with confectioners' sugar before serving.

STORE *in an airtight container at room temperature for up to a week, or refrigerate for up to 2 weeks.*

LUXE POUND CAKE

Baking expert Lisa Yockelson created this rich and aromatic pound cake. The mingling of the two extracts—vanilla and almond—adds a rounded scent to the creamy batter. The superfine sugar keeps the crumb of the baked cake tender and delicate, the eggs contribute to its volume and defined texture, and the heavy cream develops its richness. Cut it into thick slices; it is wonderful as a cushion for sliced, sweetened peaches or fresh berries and dollops of whipped cream.

➤ MAKES ONE 10-INCH CAKE, SERVING 16

3 cups (12 oz/342 g) cake flour

¼ teaspoon baking powder

1 teaspoon salt

1 cup (2 sticks/8 oz/227 g) unsalted butter, softened

3 cups (21.2 oz/600 g) superfine sugar

7 large eggs

1 tablespoon (15 ml) vanilla extract

1½ teaspoons almond extract

1 cup (240 ml) heavy cream

Confectioners' sugar for sifting

1. Position a rack in the center of the oven and preheat the oven to 325°F. Grease the inside of a 10-inch Bundt pan.

2. Sift together the flour, baking powder, and salt into a medium bowl. Whisk to combine, and set aside.

3. In the bowl of an electric mixer, using the paddle attachment, beat the butter at medium speed until very creamy, about 5 minutes. Add the sugar in four additions, beating for 1 minute after each one, or until light. Beat in the eggs one at a time, beating for 30 seconds after each addition and scraping down the sides of the bowl with a rubber spatula as necessary. Beat in the vanilla and almond extract.

4. At low speed, beat in the flour mixture in three additions, alternating it with the cream in two additions; scrape down the sides of the bowl thoroughly after each addition. Beat for 30 to 45 seconds longer. Scrape the batter evenly into the prepared pan.

5. Bake the cake for 65 to 75 minutes, or until it is golden on top and a toothpick inserted in the center comes out clean; the cake should pull away slightly from the sides of the pan. Cool the cake in the pan on a rack for 10 to 12 minutes.

6. Carefully invert the cake onto another rack and let cool completely.

7. Sift confectioners' sugar over the top of the cake just before serving.

STORE *in an airtight container at room temperature for up to a week, or refrigerate for up to 2 weeks.*

Lemon-Soaked Ginger Pound Cake

This ginger pound cake is wonderful as is, unadorned. But when it's brushed with a punchy lemon syrup, it enters a new realm of moistness and flavor. The intense warm ginger flavor of the cake comes from a combination of ground ginger, grated fresh ginger, and finely chopped crystallized ginger (available at many supermarkets and gourmet markets).

➤ Makes one 10-inch Bundt cake, serving 12 to 14

GINGER POUND CAKE

2½ cups (10.7 oz/302 g) all-purpose flour

½ cup (2 oz/57 g) cake flour

2½ teaspoons ground ginger

½ teaspoon baking powder

½ teaspoon baking soda

½ teaspoon salt

1 cup (2 sticks/8 oz/227 g) unsalted butter, softened

1¾ cups (12.3 oz/350 g) granulated sugar

4 large eggs, at room temperature

2 tablespoons (1 oz/30 g) grated peeled fresh ginger

½ cup (2.8 oz/80 g) finely chopped crystallized ginger

2 teaspoons finely grated lemon zest

1 teaspoon vanilla extract

1 cup (8.5 oz/242 g) sour cream

MAKE THE CAKE

1. Position a rack in the center of the oven and preheat the oven to 350°F. Grease the inside of a 10-inch Bundt pan. Dust the pan with flour.

2. Sift together the flours, ground ginger, baking powder, baking soda, and salt into a large bowl. Set aside.

3. In the bowl of an electric mixer, using the paddle attachment, beat the butter at medium speed until creamy, about 2 minutes. Gradually add the sugar and beat at medium-high speed until the mixture is light in texture and color, about 3 minutes. Beat in the eggs one at a time, beating for 30 to 40 seconds after each one. Scrape down the sides of the bowl as necessary. Beat in the grated ginger, crystallized ginger, lemon zest, and vanilla extract. At low speed, add the sifted mixture in three additions, alternating it with the sour cream in two additions. Scrape the batter into the prepared pan and smooth the top with a spatula.

4. Bake the cake for 50 to 55 minutes, or until a toothpick inserted in the center comes out clean. Cool the cake in the pan on a cooling rack for 10 minutes, then invert it onto another rack. Place the cake, on the rack, over a baking sheet.

MEANWHILE, MAKE THE SYRUP

5. Combine the lemon juice and sugar in a small nonreactive saucepan and cook over medium heat, stirring, until the sugar dis-

⅓ cup (80 ml) freshly squeezed
lemon juice

⅔ cup (4.7 oz/133 g) granulated
sugar

Confectioners' sugar for dusting

solves, 3 to 4 minutes. Remove the pan from the heat. Using a pastry brush, dab the syrup generously all over the surface of the warm cake, allowing it to soak into the cake before reapplying. Dab any syrup that has dripped onto the baking sheet onto the cake. Let the cake cool completely.

6. Dust the top of the cake with confectioners' sugar just before serving.

STORE *in an airtight container at room temperature for up to 4 days, or refrigerate for up to a week.*

CHERRY-ALMOND CREAM CHEESE POUND CAKE

A velvet-textured plain cake with the subtle tang of cream cheese and a fragrant almond under-note, and little bursts of tart cherry throughout. This is a pound cake that is bound to garner some attention, and rightly so.

➤ MAKES ONE 10-INCH BUNDT CAKE, SERVING 16

¼ cup (about 4 oz/113 g) dried cherries, coarsely chopped

2 tablespoons (30 ml) kirsch or hot water

3 cups (12 oz/342 g) cake flour

¾ teaspoon baking powder

¼ teaspoon baking soda

¾ teaspoon salt

1 cup (2 sticks/8 oz/227 g) unsalted butter, softened

8 ounces (227 g) cream cheese, softened

2 cups (14 oz/400 g) granu-lated sugar

5 large eggs

1½ teaspoons vanilla extract

1 teaspoon almond extract

Confectioners' sugar for dusting

1. Place the cherries and kirsch in a small bowl and let stand for 20 minutes.

2. Position a rack in the center of the oven and preheat the oven to 325°F. Grease the inside of a 10-inch Bundt pan. Dust the pan with flour.

3. Sift together the flour, baking powder, baking soda, and salt into a medium bowl. Whisk to blend, and set aside.

4. In the bowl of an electric mixer, using the paddle attachment, beat the butter and cream cheese at medium speed until creamy, about 1 minute. Gradually add the sugar and beat at medium-high speed until well blended and light, about 2 minutes. Add the eggs one at a time, beating well after each addition and scraping down the sides of the bowl as necessary. Beat in the vanilla and almond extract. Add the flour mixture at low speed, mixing just until blended. Add the cherries, along with any remaining liquid, and mix until blended. Scrape the batter into the prepared pan.

5. Bake the cake for 55 to 65 minutes, until a toothpick inserted in the center comes out clean. Cool the cake in the pan on a wire rack for 15 minutes.

6. Unmold the cake onto the rack and let cool completely.

7. Dust the cake lightly with confectioners' sugar right before serving.

STORE *at room temperature, under a cake keeper or covered with foil, for up to 5 days.*

Cinnamon Swirl Buttermilk Pound Cake

A sure-fire bake sale hit, this fine-crumbed buttermilk Bundt cake has a mellow sweet orange backnote and a crumbly, cinnamon-scented brown sugar streusel swirled throughout. Like many pound cakes, its appearance is unassuming, but its flavor and texture are unparalleled.

➤ Makes one 10-inch Bundt cake, serving 12

CINNAMON STREUSEL SWIRL

½ cup (2.1 oz/60 g) all-purpose flour

⅓ cup (2.5 oz/72 g) firmly packed light brown sugar

¼ teaspoon ground cinnamon

Pinch of salt

3 tablespoons (1.5 oz/42 g) unsalted butter, melted

BUTTERMILK POUND CAKE

2 cups (8.5 oz/242 g) all-purpose flour

½ cup (2 oz/57 g) cake flour

1 teaspoon baking powder

¼ teaspoon baking soda

½ teaspoon salt

⅛ teaspoon ground cardamom

1 cup (2 sticks/8 oz/227 g) unsalted butter, softened

2 cups (14 oz/400 g) granulated sugar

1. Position a rack in the center of the oven and preheat the oven to 325°F. Grease the inside of a 10-inch Bundt pan. Dust the pan with flour.

MAKE THE CINNAMON SWIRL

2. In a small bowl, whisk together the flour, brown sugar, cinnamon, and salt, breaking up any large lumps of brown sugar. Add the melted butter and stir until blended and crumbly.

MAKE THE POUND CAKE

3. Sift together the flours, baking powder, baking soda, salt, and cardamom into a medium bowl. Whisk to combine, and set aside.

4. In the bowl of an electric mixer, using the paddle attachment, beat the butter at medium speed until very creamy, about 2 minutes. Gradually add the sugar and beat at medium-high speed until well blended and light, about 4 minutes. At medium speed, add the eggs one at a time, beating well after each addition and scraping down the sides of the bowl as necessary. Beat in the vanilla extract and orange zest. At low speed, add the dry ingredients in three additions, alternating with the buttermilk in two additions and mixing just until combined.

5. Scrape half of the batter into the prepared pan and smooth it into an even layer. Sprinkle the streusel mixture evenly over the batter. Scrape the remaining batter on top and smooth it into an even layer.

3 large eggs

2 teaspoons vanilla extract

1 teaspoon finely grated orange zest

1 cup (240 ml) buttermilk

GARNISH

Confectioners' sugar for dusting

6. Bake the cake for 65 to 75 minutes, until a cake tester inserted into the center comes out clean. Cool the cake in the pan on a wire rack for 15 minutes.

7. Invert the cake onto the rack and cool completely.

8. Dust the cake lightly with confectioners' sugar right before serving.

STORE *in an airtight container at room temperature for up to a week, or refrigerate for up to 2 weeks.*

RICH MARBLE POUND CAKE WITH CHOCOLATE GLAZE

This very tender cake features a stunning striated pattern of alternating vanilla and deep chocolate batter. It is a big, over-the-top pound cake made all the more elegant with a coating of shiny dark chocolate glaze. If you prefer a more homespun version, skip the glaze and give it a light dusting of confectioners' sugar. Wonderful served with vanilla ice cream or ice-cold milk.

➤ MAKES ONE 10-INCH BUNDT CAKE, SERVING 12 TO 14

MARBLE POUND CAKE

3 cups (12 oz/342 g) cake flour

2 teaspoons baking powder

½ teaspoon salt

2½ cups (17.6 oz/500 g) granulated sugar, divided

½ cup (1.4 oz/41 g) natural (not Dutch-processed) cocoa powder

6 tablespoons (90 ml) water

1½ cups (3 sticks/12 oz/340 g) unsalted butter, softened

1½ teaspoons vanilla extract

5 large eggs

½ cup (120 ml) whole milk

⅔ cup Bittersweet Chocolate Glaze (page 306)

MAKE THE CAKE

1. Position a rack in the center of the oven and preheat the oven to 325°F. Grease the inside of a 10-inch Bundt pan. Dust the pan with flour.

2. Sift together the flour, baking powder, and salt into a medium bowl. Set aside.

3. In a medium bowl, whisk together ½ cup of the sugar, the cocoa powder, and water until smooth; set aside.

4. In the bowl of an electric mixer, using the paddle attachment, beat the butter at medium speed until very creamy, about 2 minutes. Gradually beat in the remaining 2 cups sugar. Increase the speed to medium-high and beat until the mixture is well blended and light, about 4 minutes. At medium speed, beat in the vanilla, then beat in the eggs one at a time, mixing well after each addition and scraping down the sides of the bowl as necessary. At low speed, add the dry ingredients in three additions, alternating with the milk in two additions and mixing just until blended.

5. Add 3 cups of the batter to the cocoa mixture and stir until blended. Spoon one-third of the remaining plain batter into the prepared pan and smooth it into an even layer. Spoon one-third of the chocolate batter over the plain batter and smooth it into an even layer. Spoon over another third of the plain batter, then another third of the chocolate batter, smoothing the layers. Repeat with the remaining batters, ending with the chocolate batter.

6. Bake the cake for 60 to 70 minutes, until a cake tester inserted into the center comes out clean. Cool the cake in the pan on a wire rack for 15 minutes.

7. Invert the cake onto the rack and cool completely.

GLAZE THE CAKE

8. Place the cake on the rack, on a wax paper– or foil-lined baking sheet. Slowly pour the glaze over the top of the cake, letting it drip down the sides of the cake. Let the glaze set for about 30 minutes before slicing the cake.

STORE *in an airtight container or well wrapped at room temperature for up to 4 days, or refrigerate for up to a week.*

DEEP CHOCOLATE SOUR CREAM POUND CAKE

A truly moist cake that gets its deep chocolate flavor from an abundance of Dutch-processed cocoa powder (which is less bitter than natural cocoa powder). Unglazed, it's a great cake for snacking, brunch, or afternoon tea. Coated with glaze and accented with a flavored whipped cream (try White Chocolate Whipped Cream, page 346, or Caramel Cream, page 347), it's fancy enough to serve at a dinner party.

➤ MAKES ONE 10-INCH BUNDT CAKE, SERVING 12 TO 14

CHOCOLATE SOUR CREAM POUND CAKE

1½ cups (6.4 oz/181 g) all-purpose flour

½ cup (2 oz/57 g) cake flour

1 cup (3.2 oz/92 g) Dutch-processed cocoa powder

2¼ teaspoons baking powder

½ teaspoon salt

1½ cups (3 sticks/12 oz/340 g) unsalted butter, softened

2½ cups (17.6 oz/500 g) granulated sugar

4 large eggs

2 teaspoons vanilla extract

1 cup (8.5 oz/242 g) sour cream

⅔ cup Bittersweet Chocolate Glaze (page 306)

MAKE THE CAKE

1. Position a rack in the center of the oven and preheat the oven to 325°F. Grease the inside of a 10-inch Bundt pan. Dust the pan with flour.

2. Sift together the flours, cocoa powder, baking powder, and salt into a medium bowl. Set aside.

3. In the bowl of an electric mixer, using the paddle attachment, beat the butter at medium speed until very creamy, about 2 minutes. Gradually beat in the sugar. Increase the speed to medium-high and beat until the mixture is well blended and light, about 4 minutes. At medium speed, beat in the eggs one at a time, mixing well after each addition and scraping down the sides of the bowl as necessary.

4. In a small bowl, stir the vanilla extract into the sour cream. If your mixer has a splatter shield attachment, attach it now. At low speed, add the dry ingredients to the butter mixture in three additions, alternating with the sour cream mixture in two additions and mixing just until blended. Scrape the batter into the prepared pan and smooth the top.

5. Bake the cake for 65 to 75 minutes, until a cake tester inserted into the center comes out clean. Cool the cake in the pan on a wire rack for 15 minutes.

6. Invert the cake onto the rack and let cool completely.

GLAZE THE CAKE

7. Place the cake on the wire rack, on a wax paper– or foil-lined baking sheet. Slowly pour the glaze over the top of the cake, letting it drip down the sides. Let the glaze set for about 30 minutes before slicing the cake.

STORE *in an airtight container at room temperature for up to 4 days, or refrigerate for up to a week.*

SOUR CREAM–BLUEBERRY CRUMB CAKE

Talented baker and frequent *Chocolatier* magazine contributor Carole Harlam gave me this recipe from her personal file, and it's become a favorite of mine, particularly when I'm having guests for brunch. Sour cream and lots of butter make the cake tender and moist and offset the bold, tangy flavor of gleaming fresh, juicy blueberries. A crunchy cinnamon-infused crumb topping cloaks the cake, adding a buttery caramel flavor.

➤ MAKES ONE 9-INCH SQUARE CAKE, SERVING 9

CRUMB TOPPING

1 cup (4.3 oz/121 g) all-purpose flour

¼ cup (1.8 oz/50 g) granulated sugar

⅓ cup (2.8 oz/80 g) firmly packed dark brown sugar

1 teaspoon ground cinnamon

⅛ teaspoon salt

7 tablespoons (3.5 oz/100 g) unsalted butter, melted

SOUR CREAM BLUEBERRY CAKE

1½ cups (6.4 oz/181 g) all-purpose flour

1¼ teaspoons baking powder

¼ teaspoon baking soda

¼ teaspoon salt

1 cup (5 oz/142 g) fresh or unthawed frozen blueberries

1 cup (8.5 oz/242 g) sour cream

1½ teaspoons vanilla extract

MAKE THE TOPPING

1. In a medium bowl, stir the flour, sugar, brown sugar, cinnamon, and salt until well blended. Add the melted butter and mix with a fork, stirring until the butter is absorbed and the dry ingredients are uniformly moistened. Set aside.

MAKE THE CAKE

2. Position a rack in the center of the oven and preheat the oven to 350°F. Butter and flour the bottom and sides of a 9-inch square baking pan.

3. In a medium bowl, whisk together the flour, baking powder, baking soda, and salt until well blended.

4. In a medium bowl, toss the blueberries with 1 tablespoon of the flour mixture until the berries are coated; set aside. In a small bowl, whisk together the sour cream and vanilla extract; set aside.

5. In the bowl of an electric mixer, using the paddle attachment, beat together the butter and granulated sugar at medium speed until light and fluffy, 4 to 5 minutes. Beat in the eggs one at a time, beating well after each addition and scraping down the sides of the bowl as necessary. At low speed, beat in the flour mixture in three additions, alternating it with the sour cream in two additions. Using a rubber spatula, fold in the blueberries. Scrape the batter into the prepared pan and smooth the top with a spatula.

10 tablespoons (1¼ sticks/
5 oz/142 g) unsalted butter,
softened

1 cup (7 oz/200 g) granulated
sugar

2 large eggs

Sprinkle the crumb topping evenly over the batter, breaking up any large lumps with your fingers.

6. Bake the cake until a toothpick inserted into the center comes out clean, about 45 minutes. Place the cake in the pan on a wire rack and let cool completely.

7. Cut the cake into squares and serve from the pan.

STORE *at room temperature, covered with foil, for up to 4 days, or refrigerate for up to a week.*

BUTTERMILK PEACH COFFEE CAKE

This is a tender-crumbed buttermilk cake with fragrant, juicy peach slices and a crumbly nut and sugar filling and topping. It is ideal in the summer with fresh peaches, and almost as good with flash-frozen peach slices at any time of the year.

➤ MAKES ONE 9-INCH CAKE, SERVING 10

CRUMB TOPPING AND FILLING

1 cup (4.3 oz/121 g) all-purpose flour

½ cup (3.8 oz/108 g) firmly packed light brown sugar

1 teaspoon ground cinnamon

⅛ teaspoon salt

⅔ cup (2 oz/57 g) unblanched sliced almonds

7 tablespoons (3.5 oz/100 g) unsalted butter, melted

BUTTERMILK PEACH CAKE

2 cups (8.5 oz/242 g) all-purpose flour

½ teaspoon baking powder

½ teaspoon baking soda

¼ teaspoon salt

¾ cup (1½ sticks/6 oz/170 g) unsalted butter, softened

1¼ cups (8.8 oz/250 g) granulated sugar

2 large eggs

1 large egg yolk

MAKE THE TOPPING AND FILLING

1. In a medium bowl, stir together the flour, sugar, cinnamon, salt, and almonds until well blended. Add the melted butter and mix with a fork, stirring until the butter is absorbed and the dry ingredients are uniformly moistened. Set aside.

2. Position a rack in the center of the oven and preheat the oven to 350°F. Grease the bottom and sides of a 9-inch springform pan. Dust the pan with flour.

MAKE THE CAKE

3. In a medium bowl, whisk together the flour, baking powder, baking soda, and salt until well blended; set aside.

4. In the bowl of an electric mixer, using the paddle attachment, beat together the butter and granulated sugar at medium speed until light and fluffy, 4 to 5 minutes. Beat in the eggs and egg yolk one at a time, beating well after each addition and scraping down the sides of the bowl as necessary. Beat in the vanilla and almond extract. At low speed, beat in the flour mixture in three additions, alternating it with the buttermilk in two additions.

5. Scrape half of the batter into the prepared pan and smooth the top with a small offset metal spatula. Sprinkle half of the crumb topping evenly over the batter, breaking up any large lumps with your fingers. Arrange a circle of peach slices, overlapping them slightly, around the outer edge of the pan. Arrange another circle of the remaining slices in the center. Spoon the remaining batter over

1 teaspoon vanilla extract

¼ teaspoon almond extract

¾ cup (180 ml) buttermilk

1 heaping cup ¼-inch-thick fresh or frozen peach slices*

White Drizzle Glaze (page 305)

*Note: It's fine to leave the skin on fresh peaches. If using frozen peach slices, slice them ¼ inch thick while still frozen or slightly thawed.

the filling and smooth it into an even layer, covering the filling. Sprinkle the remaining crumb mixture on top of the cake.

6. Bake the cake for 50 to 60 minutes, until a toothpick inserted into the center comes out clean. (Cover the cake with foil during the last 15 minutes of baking if it is getting too brown.) Cool the cake in the pan on a wire rack for 20 minutes.

7. Remove the side of the pan and cool the cake completely.

GLAZE THE CAKE

8. Scrape the glaze into a parchment cone (see page 52) or small sealable plastic bag (seal the bag and snip a tiny hole in one of the bottom corners). Drizzle the glaze onto the cake. Let the glaze set for at least 10 minutes before serving the cake.

STORE *at room temperature, covered with foil, for up to 2 days, or refrigerate for up to 5 days.*

FILLED COFFEE CAKE

🍰 🍰 🍰

Sundays always bring back memories of family trips to the bakery for jelly doughnuts and sugar-glazed coffee cakes similar to this one. This is a simple ring-shaped coffee cake made from a risen yeast dough and filled with a fruit or almond filling. A light coating of egg wash gives the cake a shiny golden finish, and a drizzle of white sugar glaze gives it a festive look.

➤ MAKES ONE 9-INCH CAKE, SERVING 10

YEAST DOUGH

⅔ cup (160 ml) whole milk, heated until warm (105° to 110°F)

One ¼-ounce packet active dry yeast (about 2¼ teaspoons)

⅓ cup plus 1 teaspoon (2.5 oz/71 g) granulated sugar, divided

3 cups (12.8 oz/363 g) all-purpose flour, divided

6 tablespoons (3 oz/85 g) unsalted butter, softened

1 teaspoon salt

1 teaspoon vanilla extract

1 large egg

Apple Filling (page 303), Fig Filling (page 304), or Almond Filling (page 301)

1 large egg, whisked with 1 tablespoon water for egg wash

White Drizzle Glaze (page 303)

MAKE THE DOUGH

1. Pour the warm milk into the bowl of an electric mixer and sprinkle over the yeast. Stir in 1 teaspoon of the sugar and let stand for 5 minutes, until the yeast has dissolved and is creamy.

2. Stir in 1 cup of the flour. Transfer the bowl to the mixer stand. Using the paddle attachment, start mixing the dough at low speed. Gradually add the remaining ⅓ cup sugar, then add the butter 1 tablespoon at a time. Add the salt and vanilla extract. Add another cup of flour and mix until a smooth, sticky dough forms. Add the egg and mix until blended. Add the remaining cup of flour and mix until blended.

3. Switch to the dough hook and knead the dough at medium-low speed for 5 minutes. Form the dough into a ball, put it in a buttered bowl, and turn dough to coat. Cover the bowl with plastic wrap.

4. Set the bowl in a warm place and let the dough rise for 1½ hours, until it is one and a half times its original volume. (While the dough is rising, prepare the filling; let cool, or chill.)

ASSEMBLE THE CAKE

5. Transfer the dough to a work surface. Using a rolling pin, roll it out into a 12 x 20-inch rectangle. Spread the filling evenly over the dough, leaving a ½-inch border uncovered on both long sides of the rectangle. Starting with a long edge, roll the dough up jelly-roll style into a long tube.

6. Butter the bottom and sides of a 9-inch springform pan. Cut the log into ten 2-inch-wide slices. Arrange the slices cut side up in the pan (7 slices around the edge, 3 in the center; don't worry if the slices aren't perfectly shaped). Cover the pan with plastic wrap and set it aside in a warm place for 1½ hours, until the dough has puffed and filled out the pan.

7. Position a rack in the center of the oven and preheat the oven to 350°F.

8. Remove the plastic wrap from the cake and brush any exposed dough with the egg wash. Bake the cake for 28 to 35 minutes, until golden brown. Cool the cake in the pan on a wire rack for 10 minutes, then remove the sides of the pan and cool completely.

GLAZE THE CAKE

9. Scrape the glaze into a parchment cone (see page 52) or small sealable plastic bag (seal the bag and snip a tiny hole in one of the bottom corners). Drizzle the top and sides of the cake with glaze. Let the glaze set for at least 10 minutes before slicing the cake.

STORE *in an airtight container at room temperature for up to 3 days, or refrigerate for up to a week.*

Brioche Cake with Caramel Custard Cream

Enriched with eggs and lots of butter, brioche is a beautiful golden dough that is relatively easy to make, thanks to the electric mixer; it just takes time because of the rising and chilling process. The baked cake is brushed with a rum syrup and filled with a luscious caramel cream for a triumphant end to any special meal. A sprinkling of confectioners' sugar to finish is de rigueur.

➤ Makes one 9-inch cake, serving 10

BRIOCHE DOUGH

¼ cup (60 ml) whole milk

1 tablespoon (0.7 oz/21 g) honey

1½ teaspoons active dry yeast

2 large eggs, lightly beaten

¾ cup (3.2 oz/91 g) all-purpose flour

2 tablespoons (0.8 oz/25 g) granulated sugar

½ teaspoon salt

1 cup (4.5 oz/130 g) bread flour, or as needed

½ cup (1 stick/4 oz/113 g) unsalted butter, at room temperature

1 large egg, whisked with 1 tablespoon (15 ml) water for egg wash

2 tablespoons (0.4 oz/11 g) unblanched sliced almonds

MAKE THE DOUGH

1. In a small saucepan (or a small cup if you want to use the microwave), combine the milk and honey and heat until it registers 110°F to 115°F on an instant-read thermometer. Pour the mixture into the bowl of an electric mixer and sprinkle over the yeast. Let stand for 10 minutes, until the yeast is creamy.

2. Transfer the bowl to the mixer stand and attach the paddle attachment. Mixing at low speed, gradually add the eggs, all-purpose flour, sugar, and salt and mix until blended. Gradually add the bread flour. Mix at medium speed until the dough is smooth and elastic, about 5 minutes. The dough should not stick to the sides of the bowl; if it does, add up to 2 tablespoons more bread flour, mixing until the dough cleans the sides of the bowl. Add the butter 1 tablespoon at a time, mixing until it is well blended. The dough will be very soft.

3. Transfer the dough to a work surface and knead by hand a few times to ensure that the butter is completely incorporated. Shape the dough into a ball and transfer it to a medium buttered bowl. Cover the bowl with plastic wrap and set aside in a warm place for 1½ to 2 hours, until the dough has doubled in volume.

4. Punch the dough down to deflate it, and knead it a few times. Return the dough to the bowl, cover, and refrigerate for at least 4 hours (or up to 12 hours). The dough should double in volume; if it doesn't, let it stand at room temperature until it has.

1 large egg

2 tablespoons (0.5 oz/15 g) cornstarch

1⅓ cups (320 ml) whole milk, divided

⅓ cup (2.3 oz/67 g) granulated sugar

2 tablespoons (30 ml) water

½ tablespoon (0.3 oz/7 g) unsalted butter

1 teaspoon vanilla extract

Pinch of salt

½ cup (120 ml) heavy cream

1 cup Basic Soaking Syrup (page 332), flavored with dark rum

Confectioners' sugar for dusting

5. Butter the bottom and sides of a 9 x 3-inch springform pan. Divide the dough into 6 even pieces. Shape each piece into a ball. Arrange 5 of the balls around the edge of the pan, and place the last ball in the center. Flatten each ball gently with your palm to form a disk. Cover the pan and let the dough rise until it is puffed and almost fills the pan, about 1 hour.

6. Position a rack in the center of the oven and preheat the oven to 350°F.

7. Brush the dough with the egg wash and sprinkle over the almonds. Bake the cake for 30 to 35 minutes, until it is a lovely golden brown and a toothpick inserted into the center comes out clean. Cool the cake in the pan on a wire rack for 15 minutes.

8. Remove the side of the pan and cool completely on the wire rack.

MAKE THE CARAMEL CREAM

9. In a small bowl, whisk together the egg and cornstarch. Whisk in ⅓ cup of the milk until smooth; set aside.

10. Place the remaining 1 cup milk in a small microwaveable cup and microwave at high until boiling, 1½ to 3 minutes.

11. Meanwhile, in a small heavy-bottomed saucepan, combine the sugar with the water and cook over medium heat, stirring, until the sugar dissolves. Increase the heat to high and cook, without stirring, occasionally brushing down the sides of the pan with a wet pastry brush, until the syrup caramelizes and turns a golden amber color. Remove the pan from the heat and carefully add the hot milk (the mixture will bubble up). Return the pan to low heat and cook, stirring constantly, until any hardened caramel has dissolved and the mixture is smooth.

12. Whisk about ¼ cup of the hot caramel mixture into the egg and cornstarch mixture. Return the mixture to the saucepan and cook over medium-high heat, whisking constantly, until the custard comes to a boil. Continue to boil, whisking constantly, for 1 minute. Remove the pan from the heat, scrape the bottom of the pan with a spatula, and whisk until smooth. Whisk in the butter until melted. Immediately strain the custard through a fine-mesh sieve into a medium bowl. Whisk in the vanilla extract and salt.

13. Set the bowl containing the caramel custard in a large bowl filled about one-third full with ice water (be careful that the water doesn't splash into the custard). Stir the custard frequently until it is slightly chilled, about 15 minutes.

ASSEMBLE THE CAKE

14. Using a long serrated knife, cut the cake horizontally in half to make 2 layers. Brush the cut side of each layer well with the rum syrup.

15. Remove the caramel custard from the refrigerator and beat vigorously with a rubber spatula until smooth. In the bowl of an electric mixer, using the whisk attachment, beat the ½ cup heavy cream at high speed until it forms medium-stiff peaks. Gently fold the whipped cream into the caramel custard.

16. Spread the caramel cream over the bottom layer of the cake (it will be a thick layer). Top with the other cake layer. Sprinkle the top of the cake very lightly with confectioners' sugar. Serve immediately, or refrigerate for up to 1 hour before serving.

STORE, *once filled, in the refrigerator; leftover cake can be refrigerated, loosely covered, for up to 3 days.*

8

BUTTER-
AND OIL-BASED
CAKES

BASIC WHITE CAKE LAYERS • COCONUT CAKE LAYERS *(variation)* • BASIC GOLDEN CAKE LAYERS • DEVILISHLY MOIST CHOCOLATE CAKE • DEEPLY DARK DEVIL'S FOOD CAKE • SOUR CREAM CHOCOLATE CAKE LAYERS • CHOCOLATE BANANA QUICK CAKE • FRESH GINGER SPICE CAKE • GINGERBREAD • LEMON CORNMEAL CAKE • CHOCOLATE GUINNESS CAKE • PUMPKIN WALNUT CAKE • SAUCY CHOCOLATE PUDDING CAKE • TRES LECHES CAKE • STICKY TOFFEE PUDDING CAKE • SOUR CREAM POPPY SEED CAKE WITH WHIPPED WHITE CHOCOLATE LEMON GANACHE • SOUR CREAM FUDGE CAKE WITH PEANUT BUTTER FROSTING • INDIVIDUAL GLAZED CHOCOLATE BUTTERMILK CAKES • CHOCOLATE COCONUT CUPCAKES • SOLID GOLD CARROT CAKE • "SEVEN LAYER" CAKE • SACHER TORTE • GERMAN CHOCOLATE CAKE • BANANA CAKE WITH CARAMEL ESPRESSO FROSTING • BROOKLYN BLACKOUT CAKE 2003 • CHOCOLATE WALNUT TORTE WITH COGNAC CREAM • LEMON LUST CAKE • ORANGE GROVE CAKE • CREAMY COCONUT CAKE

When you think of the classic American layer cake, devil's food, German chocolate, carrot, white and golden birthday cakes, and countless others come to mind. What you may not know is that beside their iconic status, these cakes also have in common the fact that they're butter- or oil-based. It's no mere coincidence that this foolproof method of cake making has produced so many time-tested standards: the results are not only delicious, but also keep rather well.

What distinguishes the butter cake is its high proportion of butter in relationship to the other ingredients. Key to its success is the use of room-temperature butter, which produces a moist, light texture. In fact, this holds true even after baking: Butter cakes must be stored (airtight) at room temperature. Then they will reward you with peak freshness and flavor for up to five days. Refrigeration, on the other hand, will result in a dense texture akin to that of a pound cake, with the taste of butter dominating all other flavors.

Possessing the advantages of both fat and foam cakes, oil-based cakes achieve both lightness and richness. As a rule, you should choose a neutral oil such as safflower or grapeseed, unless the cake contains a nut whose flavor you want to underscore; then feel free to use a corresponding nut oil instead. The exceptionally moist and springy result is perhaps the antithesis of the French sponge cake. And, unlike butter cakes, oil-based cakes have a soft, tender texture that responds well to refrigeration.

BASIC WHITE CAKE LAYERS

Enriched by a good amount of butter and lightened by beaten egg whites, these snowy white cake layers are moist and tender and the perfect foil for flavorful fillings and frostings.

➤ MAKES TWO 9-INCH CAKE LAYERS

3¼ cups (11.5 oz/325 g) sifted cake flour

1 tablespoon baking powder

¾ teaspoon salt

1 cup (2 sticks/8 oz/227 g) unsalted butter, softened

1½ cups (10.6 oz/300 g) granulated sugar

6 large egg whites

1 teaspoon finely grated lemon zest (optional)

2 teaspoons vanilla extract

1⅓ cups (320 ml) whole milk

1. Position a rack in the center of the oven and preheat the oven to 350°F. Grease the bottom and sides of two 9-inch round cake pans. Dust the pans with flour.

2. Sift together the cake flour, baking powder, and salt into a medium bowl. Whisk to combine, and set aside.

3. In the bowl of an electric mixer, using the paddle attachment, beat the butter at medium-high speed until creamy, about 30 seconds. Gradually add the sugar and beat at high speed until light, about 2 minutes. Reduce the speed to low and add the egg whites one at a time, beating well after each addition and scraping down the sides of the bowl occasionally. Beat in the lemon zest and vanilla extract. If you have a splatter shield for your mixer, attach it now (the milk tends to splash up as you add it). Add the flour mixture at low speed in three additions, alternating it with the milk in two additions and mixing just until the flour is incorporated. Scrape the batter into the prepared pans, dividing it evenly, and smooth the tops.

4. Bake the cake for 25 to 30 minutes, until lightly browned around the edges. Cool the cakes in the pans on wire racks for 15 minutes.

5. Invert the layers onto the racks and cool upside down completely.

STORE *at room temperature, covered in foil, for up to 5 days.*

COCONUT CAKE LAYERS: Replace ⅔ cup of the whole milk with coconut milk in Step 3. Fold 1 cup sweetened flaked coconut into the batter after adding the flour mixture.

BASIC GOLDEN CAKE LAYERS

A warm golden color with a tender crumb, this cake works well with a variety of frostings, from a rich buttercream to a whipped ganache and everything in between.

➤ MAKES TWO 9-INCH CAKE LAYERS

3¼ cups (11.5 oz/325 g) sifted cake flour

1 tablespoon baking powder

¾ teaspoon salt

1 cup (2 sticks/8 oz/227 g) unsalted butter, softened

1½ cups (10.6 oz/300 g) granulated sugar

3 large eggs

2 large egg yolks

2 teaspoons vanilla extract

1⅓ cups (320 ml) whole milk

1. Position a rack in the center of the oven and preheat the oven to 350°F. Grease the bottom and sides of two 9-inch round cake pans. Dust the pans with flour.

2. Sift together the cake flour, baking powder, and salt into a medium bowl. Whisk to combine, and set aside.

3. In the bowl of an electric mixer, using the paddle attachment, beat the butter at medium-high speed until creamy, about 30 seconds. Gradually add the sugar and beat at high speed until light, about 2 minutes. Reduce the speed to low and add the eggs and egg yolks one at a time, beating well after each addition and scraping down the sides of the bowl as necessary. Beat in the vanilla extract. If you have a splatter shield for your mixer, attach it now (the milk tends to splash up as you add it). Add the flour mixture at low speed in three additions, alternating it with the milk in two additions and mixing just until the flour is incorporated. Scrape the batter into the prepared pans, dividing it evenly, and smooth the tops.

4. Bake the cake for 25 to 30 minutes, until lightly browned around the edges. Cool the cakes in the pans on wire racks for 15 minutes.

5. Invert the layers onto the racks and cool completely.

STORE *at room temperature, covered in foil, for up to 5 days.*

WHEN I AM IN TROUBLE, EATING IS THE ONLY THING THAT CONSOLES ME.
—OSCAR WILDE, *THE IMPORTANCE OF BEING EARNEST*

preceding page: CHOCOLATE VALEN-
TINE CAKE (PAGES 211–213) *left:*
INDIVIDUAL MERINGUE CUPS WITH
LIME CREAM AND FRESH BERRIES
(PAGES 290–291) *below:* APPLE
CHEESECAKE BRÛLÉE (PAGES
230–232) *bottom:* CHERRY-ALMOND
CREAM CHEESE POUND CAKE (PAGES
100–101) *right:* BROWNIE LATTE
CHEESECAKE (PAGES 242–243)

left: PLAINLY PERFECT POUND CAKE
(PAGE 90) *below:* ORANGES AND
CREAM CAKE (PAGES 267–269)
bottom: CHOCOLATE ALMOND-
COCONUT CAKE (PAGES 206–207)
right: CREAMY COCONUT CAKE
(PAGES 170-171)

left: CHOCOLATE PEANUT BUTTER
MOUSSE CAKE (PAGES 262–263)
below: SOUR CREAM POPPY SEED
CAKE WITH WHIPPED WHITE
CHOCOLATE LEMON GANACHE
(PAGES 138–139) *bottom:* BRIOCHE
CAKE WITH CARAMEL CUSTARD
CREAM (PAGES 112–114) *right:*
CHERRY-TOPPED CHEESECAKE CUPS
(PAGES 222–223)

left: BROOKLYN BLACKOUT CAKE 2003 (PAGES 158–160) *below:* CHOCOLATE COCONUT CUPCAKES (PAGES 144–145) *bottom:* PEACH TATIN CAKE (PAGES 186–187)

DEVILISHLY MOIST CHOCOLATE CAKE

Extremely moist and very chocolaty, this versatile cake can be used as a component in myriad recipes. Since it's made with oil, it remains soft and moist even when refrigerated or frozen, so it works particularly well in mousse or ice cream cakes.

➤ MAKES ONE 9-INCH CAKE

1⅓ cups (5.7 oz/161 g) all-purpose flour

¾ cup (2.2 oz/61 g) natural (not Dutch-processed) cocoa powder

1¼ teaspoons baking powder

½ teaspoon baking soda

¼ teaspoon salt

1⅔ cups (11.7 oz/332 g) granulated sugar

⅓ cup (80 ml) safflower or other neutral vegetable oil

2 large eggs

⅓ cup (80 ml) whole milk

2 teaspoons vanilla extract

1 cup (240 ml) boiling water

1. Position a rack in the center of the oven and preheat the oven to 325°F. Grease the bottom and sides of a 9 x 3-inch springform pan or a 9 x 3-inch round cake pan (if you use a springform pan, make sure it has a tight-fitting bottom, to prevent the batter from leaking). Dust the pan with flour and set aside.

2. Sift together the flour, cocoa powder, baking powder, baking soda, and salt into the bowl of an electric mixer. Add the sugar and, using the paddle attachment, mix at low speed until blended. Add the safflower oil and mix a few seconds, until the dry ingredients are crumbly.

3. In a small bowl, whisk together the eggs until blended. Whisk in the milk and vanilla extract until blended. With the mixer at low speed, add the egg mixture to the flour mixture and mix until blended, scraping down the sides of the bowl as necessary. Gradually add the boiling water and mix just until blended and smooth, scraping down the sides of the bowl as necessary. Pour the batter into the prepared pan.

4. Bake the cake for 45 to 55 minutes, until a toothpick inserted into the center comes out clean. Cool the cake in the pan on a wire rack for 20 minutes.

5. Remove the side of the springform pan, if using one. Invert the cake onto the wire rack. Remove the bottom of the pan, if using a springform, and cool the cake completely.

STORE *at room temperature, wrapped in foil, for up to 5 days.*

DEEPLY DARK DEVIL'S FOOD CAKE

Tnis moist chocolate cake is very similar to the one used in the Brooklyn Blackout Cake 2003 (page 158), but here the butter is not melted. The full recipe makes a relatively tall one-layer cake that can be sliced horizontally into two or three layers, while the half recipe makes a cake which can be used whole or sliced into two layers.

➤ MAKES ONE 9-INCH CAKE

FULL RECIPE

1¾ cups (7.5 oz/212 g) all-purpose flour

2 teaspoons baking powder

¾ teaspoon baking soda

¾ teaspoon salt

11 tablespoons (5.5 oz/156 g) unsalted butter, softened

1½ cups (10.5 oz/300 g) granulated sugar

⅔ cup (2.1 oz/61 g) Dutch-processed cocoa powder

2 large eggs

1 teaspoon vanilla extract

1⅓ cups (320 ml) warm water

HALF RECIPE

¾ cup plus 2 tablespoons (3.7 oz/106 g) all-purpose flour

1 teaspoon baking powder

¼ teaspoon plus ⅛ teaspoon baking soda

1. Position a rack in the center of the oven and preheat the oven to 325°F. Grease the bottom and sides of a 9 x 3-inch springform pan (make sure the pan has a tight-fitting bottom, to prevent the batter from leaking). Dust the pan with flour.

2. Sift together the flour, baking powder, baking soda, and salt into a medium bowl. Whisk until well blended, and set aside.

3. In the bowl of an electric mixer, using the paddle attachment, beat the butter at medium speed until creamy, about 1 minute. Gradually add the sugar and beat at high speed until the mixture is pale and well blended, about 3 minutes. Add the cocoa powder and beat at medium speed for 1 minute, scraping down the sides of the bowl with a rubber spatula as necessary. Beat in the eggs one at a time, beating well after each addition. Beat in vanilla extract. At low speed, add the flour mixture in three additions, alternating it with the warm water in two additions. Scrape down the sides of the bowl and mix at low speed for 30 seconds. Pour the batter into the prepared pan and smooth the top.

4. Bake the cake for 45 to 55 minutes for the full recipe, 25 to 30 minutes for the half recipe, until a cake tester inserted into the center of the cake comes out clean. Cool the cake in the pan on a wire rack for 20 minutes.

¼ teaspoon plus ⅛ teaspoon salt

5½ tablespoons (2.75 oz/78 g) unsalted butter, softened

¾ cup (5.3 oz/150 g) granulated sugar

⅓ cup (1.1 oz/31 g) Dutch-processed cocoa powder

1 large egg

½ teaspoon vanilla extract

⅔ cup (160 ml) warm water

5. Remove the side of the pan and invert the cake onto the rack. Remove the bottom of the pan and let the cake cool completely.

STORE *at room temperature, wrapped in foil, for up to 5 days.*

SOUR CREAM CHOCOLATE CAKE LAYERS

These moist and very chocolaty cake layers have a tender crumb. They make an excellent base for an over-the-top all-American layer cake when split in half, then frosted.

➤ MAKES TWO 9-INCH CAKE LAYERS

2⅔ cups (11.3 oz/322 g) all-purpose flour

2½ cups (17.5 oz/500 g) granulated sugar

½ cup (1.4 oz/41 g) natural cocoa powder (not Dutch-processed)

1½ teaspoons baking soda

½ teaspoon salt

3 large eggs, at room temperature

⅔ cup (5.6 oz/160 g) sour cream, at room temperature

1 tablespoon (15 ml) vanilla extract

10 tablespoons (1¼ sticks/5 oz/142 g) unsalted butter, melted and cooled

⅔ cup (160 ml) safflower or corn oil

1¼ cups (300 ml) ice-cold water

1. Position a rack in the center of the oven and preheat the oven to 350°F. Grease the bottom and sides of two 9-inch round cake pans. Line the bottom of each pan with a round of parchment paper and grease the paper. Dust the paper and sides of the pans with flour.

2. Sift together the flour, sugar, cocoa powder, baking soda, and salt into a medium bowl. Whisk to combine, and set aside.

3. In another medium bowl, whisk together the eggs until blended. Whisk in the sour cream and vanilla extract until blended. Set aside.

4. In the bowl of an electric mixer, using the paddle attachment, mix the melted butter and oil together at low speed. Add the cold water and mix to blend. Add the dry ingredients all at once and mix at medium-low speed for 1 minute. Add the egg mixture and mix for another minute, until well blended, scraping down the sides of the bowl with a rubber spatula as necessary. Scrape the batter into the prepared pans, dividing it evenly.

5. Bake the cakes for 35 to 40 minutes, until a toothpick inserted into the center comes out clean. Cool the cakes in the pans on wire racks for 15 minutes.

6. Invert the cakes onto the racks, peel off the paper, and cool completely.

STORE *at room temperature, wrapped in foil, for up to 5 days.*

CHOCOLATE BANANA QUICK CAKE

This recipe falls into the category of "quick breads," but it is really much more of a cake than a bread. It is a deep-chocolate fine-crumbed cake, made moist by the addition of sour cream and mashed banana, and studded with slivers of bittersweet chocolate. A slice of this cake served with a billowy dollop of Coconut Whipped Cream (page 344) is pure heaven.

➤ MAKES ONE 9 X 5-INCH LOAF CAKE, SERVING 8

1¼ cups (5.3 oz/151 g) all-purpose flour

¼ cup (0.8 oz/23 g) Dutch-processed cocoa powder

1 teaspoon baking soda

¼ teaspoon salt

½ cup (1 stick/4 oz/113 g) unsalted butter, softened

1 cup (7 oz/200 g) granulated sugar

2 large eggs

1⅓ cups (320 ml) mashed ripe bananas (about 3 medium bananas)

1 teaspoon vanilla extract

½ cup (4.2 oz/121 g) sour cream

4 ounces (113 g) bittersweet chocolate, finely chopped

1. Position a rack in the center of the oven and preheat the oven to 350°F. Grease the bottom and sides of a 9 x 5-inch loaf pan.

2. Sift together the flour, cocoa powder, baking soda, and salt into a medium bowl. Whisk to combine, and set aside.

3. In the bowl of an electric mixer, using the paddle attachment, beat the butter at medium speed until creamy, about 1 minute. Gradually beat in the sugar and beat at high speed until well blended, about 2 minutes. At medium speed, beat in the eggs one at a time, beating well after each addition and scraping down the sides of the bowl as necessary. Add the mashed bananas and vanilla extract and mix at low speed until blended. Add the flour mixture at low speed in three additions, alternating it with the sour cream in two additions. Remove the bowl from the mixer stand and stir in the chopped chocolate. Scrape the batter into the prepared pan and smooth the top with a spatula.

4. Bake the cake for 55 to 65 minutes, until a cake tester inserted into the center comes out clean (except for any melted chocolate). Cool the cake in the pan on a wire rack for 15 minutes.

5. Unmold the cake onto the rack, turn right side up, and cool completely.

STORE *at room temperature, covered in foil, for up to 5 days.*

FRESH GINGER SPICE CAKE

Fresh ginger—lots of it—along with chopped crystallized ginger, provide just the right note of warmth and intensity in this simple cake. Dust it with confectioners' sugar and serve it with a fruit or berry compote, or frost it with Cream Cheese Spice Frosting (page 310)—either way, this cake is bound to get attention.

— error —

➤ MAKES ONE 9-INCH CAKE, SERVING 10   *To make it rise ???*

GINGER SPICE CAKE

2½ cups (10.7 oz/302 g) all-purpose flour

½ teaspoon ground ginger

½ teaspoon ground cinnamon

¼ teaspoon salt

⅓ cup (1.9 oz oz/53 g) finely chopped crystallized ginger

1 cup (240 ml) unsulphured (mild) molasses

¾ cup (5.7 oz/163 g) firmly packed light brown sugar

2 large eggs

⅓ cup (2.8 oz/79 g) peeled, finely chopped fresh ginger

1 cup (2 sticks/8 oz/227 g) unsalted butter, cut into table-spoons

1 cup (240 ml) water

GARNISH

Confectioners' sugar for dusting

MAKE THE CAKE

1. Position a rack in the center of the oven and preheat the oven to 350°F. Grease the bottom and sides of a 9 x 3-inch springform pan. Line the bottom of the pan with a round of parchment paper.

2. In a medium bowl, whisk together the flour, ground ginger, cinnamon, and salt. Place the crystallized ginger in a small bowl, add 2 tablespoons of the flour mixture, and stir to coat the ginger pieces. Set aside.

3. In a large bowl, whisk together the molasses and brown sugar, breaking up any large lumps of sugar. Whisk in the eggs until well blended. Whisk in the finely chopped ginger.

4. In a small saucepan, combine the butter and water and heat over medium heat, stirring occasionally, until the butter is melted. Remove from the heat and whisk about ½ cup of the mixture into the molasses mixture until blended. Whisk in the remaining butter mixture. Whisk in the flour mixture just until blended. Whisk in the crystallized ginger. Pour the batter into the prepared pan.

5. Bake the cake for 50 to 60 minutes, until a toothpick inserted into the center comes out clean. Cook the cake in the pan on a wire rack for 20 minutes.

6. Remove the side of the pan and invert the cake onto the wire rack. Peel off the parchment paper, reinvert the cake, and let it cool completely.

7. Dust the top of the cake with sifted confectioners' sugar before serving.

STORE *at room temperature, under a cake keeper or covered with foil, for up to 5 days.*

GINGERBREAD

Aside from eating it, the thing I love most about gingerbread is the incredible fragrance that envelops the house as it bakes. Grated fresh ginger adds some zip to the panoply of spices in this version, while butter and sour cream give it a rich character and moist crumb. Serve this au natural, or with a dollop of Mascarpone Whipped Cream (page 345).

➤ MAKES ONE 9-INCH SQUARE CAKE, SERVING 16

3 cups (12.8 oz/363 g) all-purpose flour

1½ teaspoons baking powder

1 teaspoon baking soda

2 teaspoons ground ginger

1½ teaspoons ground cinnamon

½ teaspoon freshly grated nutmeg

⅛ teaspoon ground cloves

½ teaspoon salt

10 tablespoons (1¼ sticks/ 5 oz/142 g) unsalted butter, softened

1 cup (7 oz/200 g) granulated sugar

1 large egg

1 large egg yolk

½ cup (4.2 oz/121 g) sour cream

1 tablespoon (15 ml) vanilla extract

1 tablespoon (0.5 oz/15 g) finely grated fresh ginger root

¾ cup (180 ml) unsulphured (mild) molasses

1¼ cups (300 ml) very hot water

1. Position a rack in the center of the oven and preheat the oven to 325°F. Grease the bottom and sides of a 9-inch square baking pan. Dust the pan with flour.

2. Sift the flour, baking powder, baking soda, ground ginger, cinnamon, nutmeg, cloves, and salt into a medium bowl. Whisk to combine well, and set aside.

3. In the bowl of an electric mixer, using the paddle attachment, beat the butter at medium speed until creamy, about 1 minute. Gradually add the sugar and beat at medium-high speed until light, about 2 minutes, scraping down the sides of the bowl as necessary. Beat in the egg and egg yolk one at a time, beating well after each addition and scraping down the bowl as necessary. Beat in the sour cream, vanilla extract and grated ginger. Add the molasses and beat for another minute. If your mixer has a splatter shield attachment, attach it now. Add the dry ingredients at low speed, mixing just until blended. Carefully add the hot water (it may splash up as you add it) and beat until smooth, scraping down the sides and bottom of the bowl as necessary (the batter will be thin). Pour the batter into the prepared pan.

4. Bake the cake for 50 to 60 minutes, or until a toothpick inserted into the center comes out clean. Place the pan on a wire rack to cool. The cake can be served warm or at room temperature.

5. Cut the cake into squares and serve directly from the pan.

STORE *at room temperature, covered in foil, for up to 5 days.*

LEMON CORNMEAL CAKE

This homey cake combines the subtle nutty flavor of cornmeal with the brightness of lemon. Stone-ground cornmeal gives it a slightly crunchy texture that is very appealing. Serve it alone or, on more festive occasions, with Gingered Berry Compote (page 351) and sweetened whipped cream.

➤ MAKES ONE 9-INCH CAKE, SERVING 10

LEMON CORNMEAL CAKE

1⅓ cups (5.7 oz/161 g) all-purpose flour

1 cup (5.3 oz/150 g) stone-ground yellow cornmeal

1 cup (7 oz/200 g) granulated sugar

2 teaspoons baking powder

¼ teaspoon salt

3 large eggs

1½ cups (12.75 oz/363 g) sour cream

¾ cup (1½ sticks/6 oz/170 g) unsalted butter, melted

1 tablespoon (0.2 oz/6 g) finely grated lemon zest

1 tablespoon (15 ml) freshly squeezed lemon juice

1½ teaspoons vanilla extract

GARNISH

Confectioners' sugar for dusting

MAKE THE CAKE

1. Position a rack in the center of the oven and preheat the oven to 350°F. Grease the bottom and sides of a 9 x 3-inch springform pan. Dust the pan with flour.

2. In a large bowl, whisk together the flour, cornmeal, sugar, baking powder, and salt; set aside.

3. In a medium bowl, whisk together the eggs until blended. Add the sour cream and whisk until combined. Add the butter and whisk until blended. Add the lemon zest, lemon juice, and vanilla extract and whisk until combined. Using a rubber spatula, fold the wet ingredients into the dry ingredients, mixing just until blended. Scrape the batter into the prepared pan and smooth the top.

4. Bake the cake for 40 to 45 minutes, until the top is lightly golden and a toothpick inserted into the center comes out clean. Cool the cake completely in the pan on a wire rack.

5. Unmold the cake and dust the top with confectioners' sugar before slicing and serving.

STORE *at room temperature, covered in foil, for up to 5 days.*

CHOCOLATE GUINNESS CAKE

During a recent trip to Ireland, I was delighted to see cakes and other desserts flavored with Guinness stout on restaurant menus. The bitter, coffee-like flavor of stout marries marvelously with dark chocolate in particular, as in this ultra-moist, slightly earthy cake. Serve a slice with Brown Sugar Whipped Cream (page 341) or plain vanilla ice cream—and a pint of Guinness—on St. Patrick's (or any other) Day.

➤ MAKES ONE 9-INCH CAKE, SERVING 10

CHOCOLATE GUINNESS CAKE

1¾ cups (7.4 oz/212 g) all-purpose flour

¾ cup (2.2 oz/61 g) natural (not Dutch-processed) cocoa powder

1¾ teaspoons baking powder

½ teaspoon baking soda

½ teaspoon ground cinnamon

21 tablespoons (10.5 oz/298 g) unsalted butter, softened

2¼ cups (17.2 oz/488 g) firmly packed light brown sugar

3 large eggs

1½ teaspoons vanilla extract

1½ cups (360 ml) Guinness stout (do not include foam when measuring)

1 cup (4 oz/114 g) coarsely chopped pecans

GARNISH

Confectioners' sugar for dusting

MAKE THE CAKE

1. Position a rack in the center of the oven and preheat the oven to 325°F. Grease the bottom and sides of a 9 x 3-inch round cake pan or springform pan. Dust the pan with flour.

2. Sift together the flour, cocoa powder, baking powder, baking soda, and cinnamon into a medium bowl. Whisk to combine, and set aside.

3. In the bowl of an electric mixer, using the paddle attachment, beat the butter at medium-high speed until creamy, about 1 minute. Gradually add the brown sugar and beat at high speed until very light and creamy, about 3 minutes. Reduce the speed to medium-low and add the eggs one at a time, beating well after each addition and scraping down the sides of the bowl with a rubber spatula as necessary. Beat in the vanilla extract. Reduce the speed to low and add the dry ingredients in three additions, alternating with the stout in two additions and mixing just until blended. Add the pecans and mix just until combined. Remove the bowl from the mixer stand and stir a few times with the rubber spatula to make sure the batter is evenly blended. Scrape the batter into the prepared pan and smooth the top.

4. Bake the cake for 70 to 75 minutes, until a cake tester inserted into the center comes out clean. Cool the cake in the pan on a wire rack for 20 minutes.

5. Invert the cake onto the rack and cool completely.

6. Just before serving, dust the top of the cake lightly with confectioners' sugar.

STORE *in an airtight container at room temperature for up to a week.*

Pumpkin Walnut Cake

Moist and fragrant, with the spicy flavor of pumpkin pie, this unusual cake is quite addictive (I somehow managed to eat half a cake by myself in one session). Perfect on its own as a simple fall dessert, or with the Caramel Cream as an alternative to pumpkin pie on Thanksgiving.

➤ MAKES ONE 9-INCH SQUARE CAKE, SERVING 9

PUMPKIN WALNUT CAKE

1¾ cups (7 oz/200 g) cake flour

1 teaspoon baking soda

1 teaspoon ground cinnamon

¾ teaspoon ground ginger

¼ teaspoon freshly grated nutmeg

½ teaspoon salt

2 large eggs

¾ cup (5.3 oz/150 g) granulated sugar

¾ cup (5.7 oz/163 g) firmly packed light brown sugar

½ cup (120 ml) safflower oil or other neutral vegetable oil

1 cup (240 ml) pumpkin puree

⅓ cup (80 ml) whole milk

1 teaspoon vanilla extract

¾ cup (2.6 oz/75 g) walnuts, coarsely chopped

Caramel Cream (page 347)

MAKE THE CAKE

1. Position a rack in the center of the oven and preheat the oven to 350°F. Grease the bottom and sides of a 9-inch square baking pan.

2. Sift together the flour, baking soda, cinnamon, ginger, nutmeg, and salt into a medium bowl. Whisk to combine well, and set aside.

3. In the bowl of an electric mixer, using the whisk attachment, beat the eggs with both sugars at medium speed until pale, about 2 minutes. Add the oil, pumpkin puree, milk, and vanilla extract and mix until blended. Add the flour mixture at low speed in three additions, mixing just until blended. Remove the bowl from the mixer stand and stir in the walnuts. Pour the batter into the prepared pan and smooth the top.

4. Bake the cake for 25 to 30 minutes, until a cake tester inserted into the center comes out clean. Cool the cake completely in the pan on a wire rack.

5. To serve, cut the cake into squares, and top each with a large dollop of the cream.

STORE *at room temperature, under a cake keeper or covered with foil, for up to 5 days.*

SAUCY CHOCOLATE PUDDING CAKE

Half pudding, half cake, this is an old-fashioned dessert that will speak to the kid in you. As it bakes, the boiling water sinks to the bottom and mingles with the cocoa powder and brown sugar, forming a chocolate sauce that you then drizzle over the warm cake before serving. Serve it with Brown Sugar Whipped Cream (page 341) or your favorite ice cream.

➤ MAKES ONE 8-INCH SQUARE CAKE, SERVING 9

1 cup (4 oz/114 g) cake flour

¾ cup (5.3 oz/150 g) granulated sugar

¼ cup plus 2 tablespoons (1.2 oz/34 g) Dutch-processed cocoa powder, divided

2 teaspoons baking powder

¼ teaspoon salt

½ cup (120 ml) whole milk

2 tablespoons (1 oz/28 g) unsalted butter, melted

1½ teaspoons vanilla extract

1 teaspoon instant espresso powder, dissolved in 1 teaspoon hot water

½ cup (2 oz/57 g) coarsely chopped pecans

½ cup (3.8 oz/108 g) firmly packed light brown sugar

1½ cups (360 ml) boiling water

1. Position a rack in the center of the oven and preheat the oven to 350°F. Butter the bottom and sides of an 8-inch square baking pan.

2. In a medium bowl, whisk together the cake flour, sugar, 2 table-spoons of the cocoa powder, the baking powder, and salt. Set aside.

3. In a small bowl, combine the milk, butter, vanilla, and espresso mixture. Add, along with the pecans, to the dry ingredients and stir until blended. Scrape the batter (it will be fairly thick) into the prepared pan and smooth the top.

4. Place the brown sugar in a small bowl and use your fingers to break up any large lumps. Add the remaining ¼ cup cocoa powder and stir to blend. Sprinkle the mixture evenly on top of the batter. Slowly pour the boiling water over the top (don't stir; just let it stand as is).

5. Bake the cake for 25 to 30 minutes, until the top is set. Cool the cake in the pan on a wire rack for about 15 minutes.

6. Serve the cake warm, spooning it into bowls and drizzling a generous amount of the sauce over the cake.

STORE *in the refrigerator, covered, for up to 3 days.*

TRES LECHES CAKE

Here's a recipe for those who prefer their cake on the moist—make that *very* moist—side. This classic Latin American sweet is a light white cake soused with a rum-flavored milk and cream concoction and topped with dramatic swirls of meringue frosting. Serve squares of this indulgent cake with some of the sauce spooned around it.

➤ MAKES ONE 9-INCH SQUARE CAKE, SERVING 9

WHITE CAKE

1⅔ cups (7 oz/200 g) cake flour

1½ teaspoons baking powder

½ teaspoon ground cinnamon

¼ teaspoon salt

½ cup (1 stick/4 oz/113 g) unsalted butter, softened

⅔ cup (5 oz/143 g) firmly packed light brown sugar

¾ cup (180 ml) whole milk

1 teaspoon vanilla extract

4 large egg whites

¼ teaspoon cream of tartar

¼ cup (1.7 oz/50 g) granulated sugar

MAKE THE CAKE

1. Position a rack in the center of the oven and preheat the oven to 325°F. Grease the bottom and sides of a 9-inch square baking pan.

2. Sift together the cake flour, baking powder, cinnamon, and salt into a medium bowl. Whisk to combine, and set aside.

3. In the bowl of an electric mixer, using the paddle attachment, beat the butter and brown sugar at medium-high speed until light, about 2 minutes. In a small bowl, combine the milk and vanilla extract. At low speed, add the flour mixture to the butter mixture in three additions, alternating it with the milk mixture in two additions.

4. In a clean mixer bowl, using the whisk attachment, beat the egg whites until foamy. Add the cream of tartar and beat at medium-high speed until soft peaks begin to form. Gradually beat in the sugar and beat at high speed until stiff peaks form. Using a rubber spatula, gently fold the egg whites into the batter. Scrape the batter into the prepared pan and smooth it into an even layer.

5. Bake the cake for 30 to 35 minutes, until a toothpick inserted into the center comes out clean. Cool the cake in the pan on a wire rack for 10 minutes.

MEANWHILE, MAKE THE TRES LECHES SOAK

6. In a large glass measure or a medium bowl, combine all the ingredients. After the cake has cooled for 10 minutes, using a

¾ cup (180 ml) light cream

One 12-ounce can evaporated milk

One 14-ounce can sweetened condensed milk

3 tablespoons (45 ml) dark rum (optional)

1 teaspoon vanilla extract

MERINGUE TOPPING

3 large egg whites

1 cup (7 oz/200 g) granulated sugar

3 tablespoons (45 ml) water

Pinch of cream of tartar

¾ teaspoon vanilla extract

toothpick, poke holes all over the cake at 1-inch intervals, going all the way down to the bottom. Slowly pour all of the soak over the top of the cake, covering it completely. It will seem like a lot of liquid; the cake should be "floating." Refrigerate the cake for at least 2 hours, or overnight.

UP TO 2 HOURS BEFORE SERVING THE CAKE, MAKE THE TOPPING

7. In a medium deep metal bowl, combine the egg whites, sugar, water, and cream of tartar. With a handheld electric mixer, beat until foamy, about 1 minute.

8. Place the bowl over a saucepan of simmering water, making sure that the bottom of the bowl does not touch the water, and beat constantly on high speed until the mixture reaches 140°F, about 7 minutes. Remove the bowl from the heat, add the vanilla, and beat on high speed until the frosting holds stiff peaks, about 2 minutes.

9. Leave the cake in the pan or carefully invert it onto a cake plate or platter that has a lip (to catch the sauce that will pool around the cake). The topping can be either spread on top of the cake with a small offset metal spatula or piped through a pastry bag. To spread the topping, scrape it onto the top of the cake and pile it into dramatic swirls. To pipe the topping, place it in a pastry bag fitted with a medium star tip (such as Ateco #6), and pipe shells or rosettes over the cake, covering the top completely. Refrigerate the cake until serving.

10. To serve, cut the cake into squares and serve with some of the sauce spooned around the cake.

STORE *without the topping, in the refrigerator, covered with foil, for up to 5 days; with the meringue topping, store at room temperature for up to 2 hours.*

AFTER A GOOD DINNER, ONE CAN FORGIVE ANYBODY, EVEN ONE'S OWN RELATIONS.
—OSCAR WILDE

STICKY TOFFEE PUDDING CAKE

This British import has become very popular in American restaurants. It is a very moist brown sugar date cake that is skewered with deep holes after baking and drenched with a delightfully sweet and sticky toffee sauce. Serve this gooey cake with a scoop of top-quality vanilla ice cream or some whipped cream alongside.

➤ MAKES ONE 10-INCH BUNDT CAKE, SERVING 10 TO 12

STICKY TOFFEE SAUCE

3 cups (720 ml) half-and-half

1¼ cups (10.6 oz/300 g) firmly packed dark brown sugar

2 tablespoons (30 ml) Lyle's Golden Syrup or light corn syrup

½ cup (1 stick/4 oz/113 g) unsalted butter, cut into tablespoons

Pinch of salt

BROWN SUGAR DATE CAKE

1½ cups (360 ml) water

2 cups (10 oz/283 g) pitted dates, cut into ½-inch pieces

1 cinnamon stick

2½ cups (10.6 oz/302 g) all-purpose flour

1 tablespoon baking powder

1¾ teaspoons baking soda

⅛ teaspoon salt

1 cup (2 sticks/8 oz/227 g) unsalted butter, softened

¾ cup (6.3 oz/180 g) firmly packed dark brown sugar

MAKE THE SAUCE

1. In a medium saucepan, combine all the ingredients and bring to a boil over medium heat, stirring constantly with a wooden spoon. Reduce to a simmer and cook, stirring constantly, for another minute. Remove from the heat and set aside. (The sauce can be made ahead and refrigerated, covered, for up to a day. Reheat before using.)

MAKE THE CAKE

2. Position a rack in the center of the oven and preheat the oven to 350°F. Generously grease the inside of a 10-inch Bundt pan.

3. In a medium saucepan, combine the water, dates, and cinnamon stick. Bring to a boil over medium-high heat, then remove from heat and set aside to cool completely. Remove the cinnamon stick when the sauce is cool.

4. Sift together flour, baking powder, baking soda, and salt into a medium bowl. Whisk to combine, and set aside.

5. In the bowl of an electric mixer, using the paddle attachment, beat the butter at medium-high speed until creamy, about 1 minute. Gradually add the brown sugar and beat at high speed until light, about 3 minutes. Beat in the eggs one a time, beating well after each addition and scraping down the sides of the bowl with a rubber spatula as necessary. Beat in the vanilla extract. Reduce the speed to low and add the flour mixture in three additions, alternating it with the cooled date mixture in two additions

4 large eggs

1 tablespoon (15 ml) vanilla extract

GARNISH

Confectioners' sugar for dusting

and mixing just until blended. Scrape the batter into the prepared pan and smooth the top with a rubber spatula.

6. Bake the cake for 30 to 40 minutes, until it is golden brown and a toothpick inserted into the cake comes out clean.

7. Using a bamboo skewer, poke holes all over top of cake at 1-inch intervals. (Leave the oven on.) Pour about 2 cups of the sticky toffee sauce onto the top of the cake, distributing it evenly (reserve the remaining sauce for serving). Return the cake to the oven and bake for another 5 to 10 minutes, until the sauce is bubbling. Transfer the pan to a wire rack and cool for about 30 minutes. There should still be some sauce on top of the cake.

8. Invert a large cake plate (preferably with a lip on it to contain any dripping sauce) over the cake. Very carefully, using pot holders if the pan is still hot, invert the cake onto the plate. Sprinkle the top of the cake with a dusting of confectioners' sugar.

9. Reheat the reserved sticky toffee sauce. Serve slices of cake drizzled with the warm sauce.

STORE *at room temperature, covered, for up to 3 days, or refrigerate for up to 5 days.*

LET US EAT AND DRINK; FOR TOMOR-ROW WE SHALL DIE.
—ISAIAH 22:13

Sour Cream Poppy Seed Cake with Whipped White Chocolate Lemon Ganache

This moist, lemony cake is punctuated by the crunch of poppy seeds and topped with a creamy whipped white chocolate and lemon ganache. Because of its sophisticated flavor, this seemingly down-home cake works as well at an elegant dinner as it does for a casual lunch or tea.

➤ Makes one 9 x 13-inch cake, serving 20

SOUR CREAM POPPY SEED CAKE

2¼ cups (9.6 oz/272 g) cake flour

1¼ teaspoons baking powder

½ teaspoon baking soda

½ teaspoon salt

¾ cup (3.9 oz/112 g) poppy seeds

14 tablespoons (7 oz/198 g) unsalted butter, softened

1½ cups (10.5 oz/300 g) granulated sugar

3 large eggs

1 tablespoon (15 ml) finely grated lemon zest

¼ cup (60 ml) freshly squeezed lemon juice

½ teaspoon vanilla extract

1 cup (8.5 oz/242 g) sour cream

Whipped White Chocolate Lemon Ganache (page 318)

MAKE THE CAKE

1. Position a rack in the center of the oven and preheat the oven to 350°F. Grease the bottom and sides of a 9 x 13-inch baking pan. Dust the pan with flour.

2. Sift together the flour, baking powder, baking soda, and salt into a medium bowl. Add the poppy seeds and whisk to combine; set aside.

3. In the bowl of an electric mixer, using the paddle attachment, beat the butter at medium speed until creamy, about 30 seconds. Gradually add the sugar and beat at high speed until well blended and light, about 2 minutes. Scrape down the sides of the bowl with a rubber spatula. Reduce the speed to medium and add the eggs one at a time, beating well after each addition and mixing until blended. Beat in the lemon zest, lemon juice, and vanilla extract until blended. Reduce the speed to low and add the flour mixture in three additions, alternating it with the sour cream in two additions and mixing just until blended. Scrape the batter into the prepared pan and smooth the top with a rubber spatula.

4. Bake the cake for 25 to 30 minutes, until it is golden brown and a toothpick inserted into the center comes out clean. Cool the cake in the pan on a wire rack for 15 minutes.

5. Invert the cake onto the rack and cool completely.

FROST THE CAKE

6. Transfer the cake, still upside down, to a serving plate or platter. Frost the top of the cake with the ganache. Cut the cake into squares to serve.

STORE *unfrosted, at room temperature, covered in foil, for up to 5 days; once frosted, refrigerate for up to 3 days.*

SOUR CREAM FUDGE CAKE WITH PEANUT BUTTER FROSTING

This is what I call a "pan-cake," because it's served in the pan in which it's baked. This particular pan-cake is a rich, fudgy cake embellished with a thick layer of creamy peanut butter frosting and a sprinkle of crunchy sugared peanuts. For a double fudge infusion, frost it with Fudgy Chocolate Frosting (page 314) instead.

➤ MAKES ONE 9 X 13-INCH CAKE, SERVING 20

SOUR CREAM FUDGE CAKE

2¼ cups (9 oz/256 g) cake flour

1½ teaspoons baking soda

½ teaspoon salt

3 ounces (85 g) unsweetened chocolate, chopped

¾ cup (1½ sticks/6 oz/170 g) unsalted butter, softened

2¼ cups (15.9 oz/450 g) granulated sugar

3 large eggs

2 teaspoons vanilla extract

¾ cup (6.3 oz/181 g) sour cream

¾ cup (180 ml) hot water

Creamy Peanut Butter Frosting (page 313)

Sugared Peanuts (page 337)

MAKE THE CAKE

1. Position a rack in the center of the oven and preheat the oven to 325°F. Grease the bottom and sides of a 9 x 13-inch baking pan. Dust the pan with flour.

2. Sift together the cake flour, baking soda, and salt into a medium bowl. Whisk to combine, and set aside.

3. Put the chocolate in a medium stainless steel bowl and place over a pot of barely simmering water. Heat, stirring frequently, until the chocolate is completely melted. Remove the bowl from the pot and set the chocolate aside to cool until tepid.

4. In the bowl of an electric mixer, using the paddle attachment, beat the butter at medium-high speed until creamy, about 1 minute. Gradually add the sugar and beat at high speed until well blended and light, about 3 minutes. At medium speed, add the eggs one at a time, beating well after each addition and scraping down the sides of the bowl with a rubber spatula as necessary. Beat in the vanilla extract until blended. Add the chocolate in two additions, mixing until blended. At low speed, add the flour mixture in three additions, alternating it with the sour cream in two additions and mixing just until blended. Add the hot water one-third at a time, mixing until blended. Remove the bowl from the mixer stand and, using a rubber spatula, stir the batter a few times to ensure that it is evenly blended. Scrape the batter into the prepared pan.

5. Bake the cake for 45 to 55 minutes, until a toothpick inserted into the center comes out clean. Cool the cake completely in the pan on a wire rack.

FROST THE CAKE

6. Frost the top of the cake with the peanut butter frosting, making dramatic swirls with a small offset metal spatula. Serve the cake from the pan, cutting it into squares and sprinkling each piece with some sugared peanuts.

STORE *in the refrigerator for up to 5 days.*

Individual Glazed Chocolate Buttermilk Cakes

These unforgettable little cakes are packed with chocolate flavor. A good amount of cocoa powder gives them a deep chocolate flavor, while slivers of bittersweet chocolate ratchet up the chocolate intensity. The coup de grâce is the coating of rich chocolate glaze, which makes them shine like little chocolate jewels. I recommend that you serve the cakes with vanilla ice cream or whipped cream, to cut through all that chocolate-ness.

➤ Makes 6 individual cakes
➤ Special Equipment: one 6-cake Bundtlette pan

CHOCOLATE BUTTERMILK CAKES

1 cup (4 oz/114 g) cake flour

½ cup (1.6 oz/46 g) Dutch-processed cocoa powder

1 teaspoon baking powder

¼ teaspoon salt

¾ cup (1½ sticks/6 oz/170 g) unsalted butter, softened

1¼ cups (8.8 oz/250 g) granulated sugar

2 large eggs

¾ cup (180 ml) buttermilk

2 tablespoons (30 ml) Kahlúa (optional)

1 teaspoon vanilla extract

4 ounces (113 g) bittersweet chocolate, finely chopped, or ¾ cup miniature semisweet chocolate morsels

1⅓ cups Bittersweet Chocolate Glaze (page 306)

1. Position a rack in the center of the oven and preheat the oven to 350°F. Generously grease the molds of a 6-cake Bundtlette pan. Dust the molds with flour.

2. Sift together the flour, cocoa powder, baking powder, and salt into a medium bowl. Whisk to combine, and set aside.

3. In the bowl of an electric mixer, using the paddle attachment, beat the butter at medium speed until very creamy, about 2 minutes. Gradually beat in the sugar, increase the speed to medium-high, and beat until the mixture is well blended and light, about 3 minutes. At medium speed, beat in the eggs one at a time, mixing well after each addition and scraping down the sides of the bowl as necessary.

4. In a small bowl, stir together the buttermilk, Kahlúa, if using, and vanilla extract. If your mixer has a splatter shield attachment, attach it now. At low speed, add the dry ingredients to the butter mixture in three additions, alternating with the buttermilk mixture in two additions and mixing just until blended. Remove the bowl from the mixer stand and stir in the finely chopped chocolate or semisweet morsels. Scrape the batter into the prepared cake molds, dividing it evenly and smoothing the tops.

5. Bake the cakes for 25 to 30 minutes, until a cake tester inserted into the center of a cake comes out clean. Cool the cakes in the pan on a wire rack for 10 minutes.

6. Invert the cakes onto the rack and cool completely.

GLAZE THE CAKES

7. Trim off any crusty bottom edges of the cakes with a serrated knife. Make sure there is a hole in the center of each cake: if the batter has baked over the hole, poke the cake covering it out with your finger. Arrange the cakes about 1 inch apart on the wire rack. Place the rack over a baking sheet. Pour the glaze over the cakes, covering them completely. Refrigerate the cakes on the rack for 5 minutes to set the glaze. Leave the baking pan with the excess glaze on it at room temperature.

8. Scrape up the excess glaze from the baking sheet and place it into a small sealable plastic bag. Seal the bag and, using scissors, snip a tiny hole in one of the bottom corners. Drizzle lines of glaze from the top to the base of each cake, using all of the glaze.

STORE *in an airtight container at room temperature for up to 5 days.*

CHOCOLATE COCONUT CUPCAKES

My favorite chocolate bar from childhood was the Mounds Bar (Almond Joy was a close second). The rich, deep flavor of dark chocolate counterbalances the nutty sweetness of coconut in the candy bar, just as it does in these moist cupcakes. Your choice of frostings will determine how rich the finished cupcakes will be. If you use the Fluffy White Frosting, which is not as rich as the ganache, pile it high on top of the cupcakes.

These cupcakes can also be baked in standard muffin cups, making 27 standard cupcakes. Bake them for 18 to 22 minutes.

▶ MAKES 12 JUMBO CUPCAKES

CHOCOLATE COCONUT CUPCAKES

1¾ cups (7.4 oz/212 g) all-purpose flour

¼ cup (0.7 oz/20 g) natural (not Dutch-processed) cocoa powder

1¼ teaspoons baking powder

½ teaspoon baking soda

½ teaspoon salt

4 ounces (113 g) unsweetened chocolate, chopped

1 cup (2 sticks/8 oz/227 g) unsalted butter, softened

2 cups (14 oz/400 g) granulated sugar

4 large eggs

2 teaspoons vanilla extract

1 cup (8.5 oz/242 g) sour cream

½ cup (120 ml) whole milk

1 cup (2.8 oz/80 g) sweetened flaked coconut

MAKE THE CUPCAKES

1. Position a rack in the center of the oven and preheat the oven to 350°F. Grease 12 jumbo (7-ounce) muffin cups. Dust the cups with flour.

2. Sift together the flour, cocoa powder, baking powder, baking soda, and salt into a medium bowl. Whisk to combine, and set aside.

3. Put the chocolate in a medium stainless steel bowl and place over a pot of barely simmering water. Heat, stirring frequently, until the chocolate is completely melted. Remove the bowl from the pot and set the chocolate aside to cool until tepid.

4. In the bowl of an electric mixer, using the paddle attachment, beat the butter at medium-high speed until creamy, about 1 minute. Gradually add the sugar and beat at high speed until well blended and light, about 3 minutes. At medium speed, add the eggs one at a time, beating well after each addition and scraping down the sides of the bowl with a rubber spatula as necessary. Beat in the vanilla extract until blended. Add the chocolate in two additions, mixing until blended.

5. In a small bowl, whisk together the sour cream and milk. At low speed, add the flour mixture to the butter mixture in three additions, alternating it with the sour cream mixture in two addi-

**Milk Chocolate Coconut Ganache
(page 316) or Fluffy White
Frosting (page 312)**

1¼ cups (3.5 oz/100 g) natural or
sweetened flaked coconut (natural flaked coconut is available at
gourmet and health food stores)

tions and mixing just until blended. Remove the bowl from the
mixer stand and, using a rubber spatula, stir in the flaked coconut.
Spoon the batter into the prepared muffin cups, dividing it evenly.

6. Bake the cupcakes for 25 to 30 minutes, until a toothpick
inserted into the center of a cupcake comes out clean. Cool the cupcakes in the pan on a wire rack for 15 minutes.

7. Unmold the cupcakes and stand them upright on the wire rack.
Cool completely.

FROST THE CUPCAKES

8. Using a small offset metal spatula, frost the tops of the cupcakes
with the ganache or the white frosting. Sprinkle the cupcakes with
enough coconut to cover.

STORE *unfrosted, in an airtight container at room temperature for up to 5 days; once
frosted, refrigerate in an airtight container for up to 3 days. Bring to room temperature
before serving.*

SOLID GOLD CARROT CAKE

To maximize moistness and flavor, this tall, lavish cake is made with a combination of vegetable oil and melted butter and lots of shredded carrots, spices, and chopped walnuts. The White Chocolate Cream Cheese Frosting (page 311) is a lush accompaniment, just a little richer than the standard version.

➤ MAKES ONE 9-INCH CAKE, SERVING 10

CARROT CAKE

2 cups (8.5 oz/242 g) all-purpose flour

2 teaspoons baking powder

1 teaspoon baking soda

¾ teaspoon salt

1½ teaspoons ground cinnamon

½ teaspoon freshly grated nutmeg

½ teaspoon ground cloves

4 large eggs

1 cup (7 oz/200 g) granulated sugar

1¼ cups (9.6 oz/271 g) firmly packed light brown sugar

1 cup (240 ml) safflower or other neutral vegetable oil

½ cup (1 stick/4 oz/113 g) unsalted butter, melted

¼ cup (60 ml) whole milk

1 tablespoon (15 ml) vanilla extract

2 tablespoons (0.7 oz/20 g) finely chopped crystallized ginger

1 tablespoon (0.2 oz/6 g) finely grated orange zest

MAKE THE CAKE

1. Position a rack in the center of the oven and preheat the oven to 350°F. Butter the bottom and sides of two 9-inch round cake pans. Dust the pans with flour.

2. Sift together the flour, baking powder, baking soda, salt, cinnamon, nutmeg, and cloves into a medium bowl. Whisk together the dry ingredients until blended, and set aside.

3. In the bowl of an electric mixer, using the paddle attachment, beat the eggs, granulated sugar, and light brown sugar at medium speed until well combined, about 2 minutes. At low speed, add the oil, melted butter, milk, vanilla extract, ginger, and orange zest and mix until blended, scraping down the sides of the bowl with a rubber spatula as necessary. Add the flour mixture in three additions, mixing just until blended. Add the carrots and walnuts and mix until blended. Scrape the batter into the prepared pans, dividing it evenly.

4. Bake the cakes for 25 to 30 minutes, until they are dark golden brown and a cake tester inserted in the center comes out clean. Cool the cakes in the pans on wire racks for 15 minutes.

5. Invert the cakes onto the racks and cool completely.

FROST THE CAKE

6. Place one of the cake layers right side up on a serving plate or cardboard cake round. Spread the top of the cake with about 1 cup

3 cups (10.5 oz/300 g) firmly packed shredded carrots

1 cup (3.5 oz/100 g) walnuts, chopped

White Chocolate Cream Cheese Frosting (page 311)

of the frosting. Top with the other cake layer, upside down. Frost the top and sides of the cake with the remaining frosting. Serve the cake immediately, or refrigerate; bring to room temperature before serving.

STORE, *unfrosted, at room temperature, wrapped in foil, for up to 5 days; once frosted, refrigerate for up to 5 days.*

TO DREAM OF CAKE FORETELLS ADVANCEMENT FOR THE LABORER AND ENHANCEMENT FOR THE INDUSTRIOUS . . .
—BALLANTYNE AND COELI

"SEVEN LAYER" CAKE

My mother is a great cook, but she didn't always have time to make dessert for family meals (I have four siblings, so she deserved some slack here). Occasionally, though, she'd surprise us with a Seven Layer Cake from the bakery, ultrathin layers of yellow cake sandwiched with dark chocolate filling and frosted with a silky chocolate buttercream. Here's my version of the family favorite, though it is actually made of eight, not seven, layers. The eighth is a bonus: one more layer of really good stuff.

➤ MAKES ONE 3¾ X 11-INCH CAKE, SERVING 8

BUTTERY SHEET CAKE

2 cups (8 oz/228 g) cake flour

1¾ teaspoons baking powder

¼ teaspoon salt

¾ cup (1½ sticks/6 oz/170 g) unsalted butter, softened

1½ cups (10.6 oz/300 g) granulated sugar, divided

4 large eggs, separated

1 teaspoon vanilla extract

¾ cup (180 ml) whole milk

¼ teaspoon cream of tartar

Silky Chocolate Buttercream (page 326) or Fudgy Chocolate Frosting (page 314)

MAKE THE CAKE

1. Position a rack in the center of the oven and preheat the oven to 350°F. Grease the bottom and sides of an 11½ x 17½ jelly-roll pan (also known as a half sheet pan). Line the bottom of the pan with parchment paper and grease the paper.

2. Sift together the flour, baking powder, and salt into a medium bowl. Whisk to combine, and set aside.

3. In the bowl of an electric mixer, using the paddle attachment, beat the butter at medium speed until creamy, about 1 minute. Gradually add 1¼ cups of the sugar; increase the speed to high, and beat until well blended and light, about 3 minutes. Reduce the speed to medium and add the egg yolks one at a time, beating well after each addition and scraping down the sides of the bowl with a rubber spatula as necessary. Beat in the vanilla extract. Reduce the speed to low and add the flour mixture in three additions, alternating it with the milk in two additions and mixing just until blended. Remove the bowl from the mixer stand.

4. In a clean mixer bowl, using the whisk attachment, beat the egg whites at medium speed until frothy. Add the cream of tartar and beat at medium-high speed until the whites begin to form soft peaks. Gradually add the remaining ¼ cup sugar and beat at high speed until the whites form stiff, glossy peaks. Using a rubber spatula, gently fold one-quarter of the beaten whites into the batter.

Fold in the remaining whites in two additions. Scrape the batter into the prepared pan and spread it into an even layer.

5. Bake the cake for 18 to 22 minutes, until it is golden and springs back when lightly touched. Cool the cake in the pan on a wire rack for 15 minutes.

6. Invert the pan onto the rack, peel off the paper, and let cool completely.

7. Using a long serrated knife, trim about ⅛ inch off each side of the cake. Cut the cake crosswise into four equal strips, each measuring about 3¾ x 11 inches. Cut each strip lengthwise in half to form eight very thin strips. (If you have not made the frosting yet, stack the strips on top of one another and cover with plastic wrap or foil while you prepare it.)

ASSEMBLE AND FROST THE CAKE

8. Place one of the cake strips on a long serving platter. Spread it with a thin layer of frosting (a scant ¼ cup). Top with another strip, and continue layering the strips with frosting until they are all used. Spread the sides and top of the cake with frosting, reserving ½ cup, if possible, for garnish. Place the reserved frosting in a pastry bag fitted with a small star tip (such as Ateco #3), and pipe a row of shells down the center of the cake. Serve the cake or refrigerate; bring to room temperature before serving.

STORE *in the refrigerator, loosely covered, for up to 3 days; bring to room temperature before serving.*

SACHER TORTE

People make quite a fuss about this legendary Viennese cake, probably because it's considered a national treasure in Austria. On its own the cake is a little dry, but once it's soaked with a generous amount of rum syrup and glazed with preserves and chocolate, it becomes downright moist. I like to make it with raspberry preserves, though in Austria that is verboten; there, only apricot preserves will do. Serve with a healthy dollop of whipped cream.

➤ MAKES ONE 9-INCH CAKE, SERVING 10

CHOCOLATE TORTE

4 ounces (113 g) bittersweet chocolate, chopped

10 tablespoons (1¼ sticks/ 5 oz/142 g) unsalted butter, softened

½ cup (2 oz/57 g) confectioners' sugar

6 large eggs, separated, at room temperature

1 teaspoon vanilla extract

⅛ teaspoon salt

⅛ teaspoon cream of tartar

½ cup (3.5 oz/100 g) superfine sugar

¾ cup (3 oz/85 g) cake flour

RUM SYRUP

⅓ cup (2.3 oz/66 g) granulated sugar

⅓ cup (80 ml) water

3 tablespoons (45 ml) dark rum

MAKE THE TORTE

1. Position a rack in the center of the oven and preheat the oven to 325°F. Grease the bottom and sides of a 9 x 3-inch springform pan. Line the bottom of the pan with a circle of parchment paper and grease the paper.

2. Put the chocolate in a medium stainless steel bowl and place over a pot of barely simmering water. Heat, stirring frequently, until the chocolate is completely melted. Remove the bowl from the pot and set aside to cool.

3. In the bowl of an electric mixer, using the paddle attachment, beat the butter at medium-high speed until creamy, about 1 minute. Gradually add the confectioners' sugar and beat at high speed until light, about 2 minutes. Reduce the speed to medium-low and add the egg yolks one at a time, beating well after each addition and scraping down the sides of the bowl with a rubber spatula as needed. Add the cooled melted chocolate and vanilla extract and mix until blended.

4. In a clean mixer bowl, using the whisk attachment, beat the egg whites with the salt at medium speed until foamy. Add the cream of tartar and beat at medium-high speed until the whites just begin to form soft peaks. While continuing to beat, add the superfine sugar 1 tablespoon at a time, then beat at high speed until medium stiff peaks form.

1 cup (240 ml) apricot or seedless raspberry preserves

2 tablespoons (30 ml) water

1⅓ cups Bittersweet Chocolate Glaze (page 306)

5. Using a rubber spatula, gently fold half of the beaten whites into the chocolate mixture. Sift half of the flour over the batter and fold it in. Sift over the remaining flour and fold it in until it is almost but not completely blended. Scrape over the remaining whites and gently fold them in until blended. Scrape the batter into the prepared pan and smooth it into an even layer.

6. Bake the torte for 40 to 45 minutes, until a tester inserted into the center comes out clean. Cool the cake completely in the pan on a wire rack.

MAKE THE SYRUP

7. Combine the sugar and water in a small saucepan and bring to a boil over medium heat, stirring to dissolve the sugar. Remove the pan from the heat and let the syrup cool to room temperature, then stir in the rum. (The syrup can be prepared ahead and stored in an airtight container in the refrigerator for up to a month.)

PREPARE THE FILLING

8. In a small saucepan, combine the preserves and water and cook over medium heat, stirring constantly, until the mixture begins to bubble. Pour the mixture through a fine-mesh sieve into a bowl, pressing it through with a rubber spatula.

ASSEMBLE THE CAKE

9. Run a thin knife around the edge of the pan to loosen the cake. Remove the side of the pan. Invert the cake onto a cardboard cake round and remove the bottom of the pan and the paper. Using a serrated knife, cut the cake horizontally into 2 even layers. Set the top layer aside.

10. Brush the bottom layer generously with half of the rum syrup. Once the syrup is absorbed, spread one-third of the strained preserves over the layer. Top with the remaining cake layer. Brush it with the remaining syrup. Spread the remaining preserves over the top and sides of the cake. Refrigerate the cake while you make the glaze.

GLAZE THE CAKE

11. Place the chilled cake, still on the cake round, on a wire rack set over a baking sheet. Slowly pour the glaze onto the center of the cake. Using a small offset metal spatula, smooth the glaze over the top and sides of the cake, letting the excess glaze drip onto the baking sheet.

12. If you are a proficient piper, pipe the name "SACHER" on top of the cake: Scrape the extra glaze from the baking sheet and put it into a small parchment paper cone or sealable plastic bag (if using a bag, seal it and cut a tiny hole in one of the bottom corners), and use it for piping the name. Let the cake stand for at least 1 hour before serving.

STORE *in the refrigerator for up to 5 days; bring to room temperature before serving.*

GERMAN CHOCOLATE CAKE

This popular American classic did not originate in the land of sauerkraut and Weiner schnitzel; rather, it's named for Sam German, the man who developed German's sweet baking chocolate, which was used in the original recipe. Typically this cake is presented with just a coconut pecan filling sandwiching the layers and topping the cake, but I've turned this homespun layer cake into a show-stopper by adding a chocolate frosting for the sides. You can skip this extra adornment if you like, though, and make the classic version.

➤ MAKES ONE 9-INCH CAKE, SERVING 12

GERMAN CHOCOLATE CAKE

2 cups (8 oz/228 g) cake flour

⅓ cup (1 oz/27 g) natural (not Dutch-processed) cocoa powder

1 teaspoon baking soda

½ teaspoon salt

4 ounces (113 g) bittersweet chocolate, finely chopped

½ cup (120 ml) boiling water

1 cup (8.5 oz/242 g) sour cream

2 teaspoons vanilla extract

1 cup (2 sticks/8 oz/227 g) unsalted butter, softened

2 cups (14 oz/400 g) granulated sugar, divided

4 large eggs, separated, at room temperature

¼ teaspoon cream of tartar

CHOCOLATE FROSTING

3 ounces (85 g) bittersweet chocolate, chopped

MAKE THE CAKE

1. Position a rack in the center of the oven and preheat the oven to 350°F. Grease the bottom and sides of two 9-inch round cake pans. Dust the pans with flour.

2. Sift together the cake flour, cocoa powder, baking soda, and salt into a medium bowl. Whisk to combine, and set aside.

3. Combine the chocolate and boiling water in a bowl and whisk until the chocolate is completely melted and the mixture is smooth. Set aside to cool until tepid.

4. In a small bowl, stir together the sour cream and vanilla extract; set aside.

5. In the bowl of an electric mixer, using the paddle attachment, beat the butter at medium speed until creamy, about 1 minute. Gradually add 1½ cups of the sugar and beat at high speed until well blended and light, about 3 minutes. Reduce the speed to medium and add the egg yolks one at a time, beating well after each addition and scraping down the sides of the bowl as necessary. Add the tepid chocolate and mix until blended. If your mixer has a splatter shield attachment, attach it now. Reduce the speed to low and add the flour mixture in three additions, alternating it with the sour cream in two additions and mixing just until blended. Remove the bowl from the mixer stand and set aside.

½ cup (1 stick/4 oz/113 g) unsalted butter, softened

1 cup (4 oz/113 g) confectioners' sugar

1 teaspoon vanilla extract

Coconut Pecan Filling (page 309)

6. In a clean mixer bowl, using the whisk attachment, beat the egg whites at low speed until frothy. Add the cream of tartar and mix just until blended. Increase the speed to medium and beat until the whites are fluffy and begin to form soft peaks. Gradually add the remaining ½ cup sugar, about 1 tablespoon at a time. Then increase the speed to high and whip the whites until they are glossy and smooth and form stiff peaks. Using a rubber spatula, gently fold the whites into the chocolate batter one-third at a time. Scrape the batter into the prepared pans and smooth the tops.

7. Bake the cakes for 30 to 35 minutes, until a toothpick inserted into the center comes out clean. Cool the cakes in their pans on wire racks for 20 minutes.

8. Run a small knife around the edge of each pan to loosen the cake. Invert each cake onto a wire rack and cool completely.

MAKE THE FROSTING

9. Put the chocolate in a medium stainless steel bowl and place the bowl over a pot of barely simmering water. Heat, stirring frequently, until the chocolate is completely melted. Remove the bowl from over the pot and set the chocolate aside to cool until tepid.

10. In the bowl of an electric mixer, using the paddle attachment, beat the butter at medium speed until creamy, about 30 seconds. Gradually add the confectioners' sugar and beat at high speed until light and creamy, about 2 minutes. Beat in the vanilla extract. Add the tepid chocolate at low speed, mixing until blended and scraping down the sides of the bowl as necessary. Increase the speed to high and beat until the frosting is slightly aerated, about 1 minute. Use the frosting immediately, or cover tightly and set aside at room temperature for up to 3 hours.

ASSEMBLE THE CAKE

11. If necessary, using a serrated knife, trim the sides of each cake layer, so that it is straight, not sloped. Place one of the layers upside down on a cardboard cake round or serving platter. Spread the cake with about 1½ cups of the filling. Top with the other cake layer, bottom (smooth) side up.

12. Using a small offset metal spatula, spread the frosting over the sides of the cake in a smooth layer, filling in any gaps between the layers (there will be plenty of frosting for this; if you have any frosting left over, you can put it into a pastry bag fitted with a medium star tip (such as Ateco #6) and pipe a row of rosettes around the top edge of the cake). Spread the remaining filling on top of the cake. Serve the cake, or refrigerate; bring to room temperature before serving.

STORE *in the refrigerator for up to 3 days; bring to room temperature before serving.*

BANANA CAKE WITH CARAMEL ESPRESSO FROSTING

I 've never been very good at banana management—I tend to buy a bunch, eat a few, and then watch the rest turn black. Here's a cake to use up those overripe, mismanaged bananas. It's moist, surprisingly light, and full of banana flavor, with a hint of spice and some chopped pecans for crunch. The caramel-espresso buttercream is not overly sweet and blends nicely with the earthy notes of this delicious cake.

➤ MAKES ONE 9-INCH CAKE, SERVING 10

BANANA CAKE

2½ cups (10 oz/285 g) cake flour

1½ teaspoons baking soda

¼ teaspoon salt

2 teaspoons ground cinnamon

¼ teaspoon ground cardamom

1½ cups (360 ml) pureed or well-mashed very ripe bananas (about 3 large bananas)

½ cup (4.2 oz/121 g) sour cream

11 tablespoons (5.5 oz/156 g) unsalted butter, softened

6 tablespoons (90 ml) safflower or other neutral vegetable oil

1 cup (7 oz/200 g) granulated sugar

½ cup (4.2 oz/120 g) firmly packed dark brown sugar

3 large eggs

1½ teaspoons vanilla extract

1 cup (4 oz/114 g) coarsely chopped pecans

MAKE THE CAKE

1. Position a rack in the center of the oven and preheat the oven to 350°F. Grease the bottom and sides of two 9-inch round cake pans. Dust the pans with flour.

2. Sift together the cake flour, baking soda, salt, cinnamon, and cardamom into a medium bowl. Whisk to combine, and set aside.

3. In a small bowl, combine the bananas with the sour cream; set aside.

4. In the bowl of an electric mixer, using the paddle attachment, beat the butter at medium-high speed until creamy, about 30 seconds. Add the safflower oil, granulated sugar, and brown sugar and beat at high speed until creamy and light, about 3 minutes. At medium speed, add the eggs one at a time, beating well after each addition and scraping down the sides of the bowl as necessary. Beat in the vanilla extract. At low speed, add the flour mixture in three additions, alternating it with the banana mixture in two additions and mixing just until blended.

5. Remove the bowl from the mixer stand and stir in the pecans by hand. Scrape the batter into the prepared pans, dividing it evenly.

6. Bake the cakes for 25 to 30 minutes, until a toothpick inserted into the center of the cake comes out clean. Cool the cakes in the pans on wire racks for 10 minutes.

Caramel Espresso Buttercream
(page 328)

Sugared Pecans (page 337)

7. Invert the cakes onto the racks and let cool completely.

ASSEMBLE THE CAKE

8. Set aside about ⅔ cup (160 ml) of the buttercream for garnishing. Place one of the cake layers upside down on a cardboard cake round or cake plate. Using a small offset metal spatula, spread 1 cup of the buttercream over the top of the layer. Top with the other cake layer, upside down. Spread the remaining buttercream over the sides and top of the cake. Place the reserved buttercream in a pastry bag fitted with a medium star tip (such as Ateco #6), and pipe rosettes or shells around the edge of the top of the cake. Garnish with the pecans.

STORE *unfrosted, at room temperature, covered with foil, for up to 5 days; once frosted, store in the refrigerator, loosely covered with foil, for up to 5 days. Bring to room temperature before serving.*

BROOKLYN BLACKOUT CAKE 2003

My version of this famous chocolate cake is named for the blackout that hit New York in August 2003, a sweltering evening that I spent at home in Brooklyn lighting candles and searching for batteries (all baking was obviously suspended). This rendition is everything a blackout cake should be: a really moist, chocolaty cake with a fudgy pudding filling, dark chocolate frosting, and lots of chocolate crumbs covering the whole thing. The perfect cake to make when the lights finally come on (as they did the next morning).

➤ MAKES ONE 9-INCH CAKE, SERVING 10 TO 12

CHOCOLATE BLACKOUT CAKE

1½ cups (6.4 oz/181 g) all-purpose flour

1 cup (2.9 oz/85 g) natural (not Dutch-processed) cocoa powder

1½ teaspoons baking powder

1½ teaspoons baking soda

1 teaspoon salt

2 cups (14 oz/400 g) granulated sugar

2 large eggs

1 large egg yolk

1 cup (240 ml) buttermilk

½ cup (1 stick/4 oz/113 g) unsalted butter, melted

2 teaspoons vanilla extract

1 cup (240 ml) hot brewed coffee

MAKE THE CAKE

1. Position a rack in the center of the oven and preheat the oven to 350°F. Grease the bottom and sides of two 9-inch round cake pans. Dust the pans with flour.

2. Sift together the flour, cocoa powder, baking powder, baking soda, and salt into the bowl of an electric mixer. Add the granulated sugar and, using the paddle attachment, mix at low speed until blended.

3. In a medium bowl, whisk together the eggs, egg yolk, buttermilk, melted butter, and vanilla extract. At low speed, add the egg mixture to the dry ingredients in a steady steam. Scrape down the sides of the bowl with a rubber spatula, then beat at medium speed until well blended, about 1 minute. Add the hot coffee, mixing just until blended. Remove the bowl from the mixer stand and stir the batter up from the bottom of the bowl a few times to thoroughly blend it. Scrape the batter into the prepared pans, dividing it evenly and smoothing the tops.

4. Bake the cakes for 30 to 35 minutes, until a cake tester inserted into the center comes out clean. Cool the cakes in the pans on wire racks for 10 minutes.

5. Invert the cakes onto the racks and cool completely.

CHOCOLATE PUDDING FILLING

4 large egg yolks

²⁄₃ cup (4.6 oz/132 g) granulated sugar

2 tablespoons plus ½ teaspoon cornstarch

⅛ teaspoon salt

1 cup (240 ml) water

²⁄₃ cup (160 ml) heavy cream

3 ounces (85 g) semisweet or bittersweet chocolate, finely chopped

1 teaspoon vanilla extract

FUDGY CHOCOLATE FROSTING

4 ounces (113 g) unsweetened chocolate, coarsely chopped

11 tablespoons (5.5 oz/156 g) unsalted butter, softened

1²⁄₃ cups (6.7 oz/191 g) confectioners' sugar

2 teaspoons vanilla extract

MAKE THE FILLING

6. In the bowl of an electric mixer, using the paddle attachment, beat the egg yolks, sugar, cornstarch, and salt at medium speed until pale, about 1 minute.

7. In a medium heavy saucepan, combine the water and cream and bring to a boil over medium heat. Remove the pan from the heat and whisk about half of the hot cream mixture into the yolk mixture. Whisk this mixture back into the remaining cream mixture in the saucepan. Cook over medium heat, whisking constantly, until the mixture comes to a boil. Continue to boil, whisking, for 1 minute. Remove the pan from the heat and whisk in the chocolate until completely melted.

8. Pass the filling through a fine-mesh sieve into a small bowl. Stir in the vanilla extract. Cover the surface of the pudding with plastic wrap and refrigerate for at least 2 hours, until chilled.

MAKE THE FROSTING

9. Put the chocolate in a medium stainless steel bowl and place over a pot of barely simmering water. Heat, stirring frequently, until the chocolate is completely melted. Remove the bowl from the pot and set the chocolate aside to cool until tepid.

10. In the bowl of an electric mixer, using the paddle attachment, beat the butter at medium speed until creamy, about 1 minute. Add the confectioners' sugar and beat at medium-high speed for 2 minutes, scraping down the sides of the bowl as necessary. Beat in the vanilla extract and melted chocolate, then beat until well-blended and creamy, about 1 minute.

ASSEMBLE THE CAKE

11. Using a long serrated knife, cut each cake layer in half horizontally, to make 4 layers. Reserve one layer. Place another cake layer, cut side up, on a serving plate. Whisk the chilled filling until smooth. Using a small offset metal spatula, spread half of the filling over the layer. Top with another cake layer and spread it with the remaining filling. Top with a third cake layer, smooth side up.

12. Break half of the reserved cake layer into large pieces and place them in the bowl of a food processor (save the remainder of the cake layer for snacking). Process the cake to fine crumbs, and set aside.

13. Using a narrow metal spatula, frost the top and sides of the cake with the frosting. Pat a generous amount of cake crumbs onto the sides of the cake, pressing them lightly into the frosting. Sprinkle the remaining cake crumbs over the top of the cake. Serve at room temperature or slightly chilled.

STORE *in the refrigerator, loosely covered, for up to 2 days.*

CHOCOLATE WALNUT TORTE WITH COGNAC CREAM

🍫 🍫 🍫 🍫

This rich chocolate-walnut torte is generously imbibed with a Cognac syrup and topped with a Cognac-fueled whipped cream. Be sure to buy a fine Cognac for this cake—it won't be cheap, but it will make all the difference, and you'll have the rest of the bottle to enjoy for quite a while (in theory at least).

➤ MAKES ONE 9-INCH CAKE, SERVING 10

CHOCOLATE WALNUT TORTE

9 ounces (255 g) bittersweet chocolate, coarsely chopped

¼ cup (60 ml) Cognac

2 tablespoons (30 ml) water

½ cup (1.8 oz/50 g) walnuts

⅓ cup (1.3 oz/38 g) confectioners' sugar

¾ cup (3 oz/85 g) cake flour

¼ cup (0.7 oz/20 g) natural (not Dutch-processed) cocoa powder

¼ teaspoon salt

15 tablespoons (7.5 oz/213 g) unsalted butter, softened

¾ cup (5.25 oz/150 g) granulated sugar, divided

5 large eggs, separated, at room temperature

1½ teaspoons vanilla extract

¼ teaspoon cream of tartar

MAKE THE TORTE

1. Position a rack in the center of the oven and preheat the oven to 350°F. Grease the bottom and sides of a 9 x 3-inch springform pan. Line the bottom of the pan with a circle of parchment paper. Dust the sides of the pan with flour.

2. Put the chocolate, Cognac, and water in a medium stainless steel bowl and place the bowl over a pot of barely simmering water. Heat, stirring frequently, until the chocolate is completely melted and the mixture is smooth. Remove the bowl from the pot and set aside to cool.

3. Place the walnuts and confectioners' sugar in the bowl of a food processor and process until the walnuts are finely ground (the mixture should be powdery, but don't let it form a paste). Transfer to a medium bowl. Sift the cake flour, cocoa powder, and salt over the nut mixture and whisk to combine. Set aside.

4. In the bowl of an electric mixer, using the paddle attachment, beat the butter at medium-high speed until creamy, about 1 minute. Gradually add ½ cup of the granulated sugar and beat at high speed until light and creamy, about 2 minutes. Reduce the speed to medium-low and beat in the egg yolks one at a time, mixing well after each addition and scraping down the sides of the bowl with a rubber spatula as necessary. Beat in the vanilla extract and melted chocolate mixture.

3 tablespoons (1.3 oz/37 g) granulated sugar

3 tablespoons (45 ml) water

2 tablespoons (30 ml) Cognac

1¼ cups (300 ml) heavy cream

3 tablespoons (0.7 oz/21 g) confectioners' sugar

1 tablespoon (15 ml) Cognac

½ teaspoon vanilla extract

Confectioners' sugar for dusting

Walnut Praline Powder (page 334)

5. In a clean mixer bowl, using the whisk attachment, beat the egg whites at medium speed until foamy. Add the cream of tartar and beat at medium-high speed until the whites just begin to form soft peaks. Gradually add the remaining ¼ cup granulated sugar, about 1 tablespoon at a time, then beat at high speed until stiff, glossy peaks form. Fold one-third of the egg whites and one-third of the flour mixture into the chocolate batter. Gently fold in the remaining whites and flour mixture in two additions each. Scrape the batter into the prepared pan and smooth it into an even layer.

6. Bake the cake for 35 to 40 minutes, until a toothpick inserted into the center comes out with a few moist crumbs clinging to it. Cool the cake in the pan on a wire rack for 30 minutes.

7. Run a thin-bladed knife around the edge of the pan to loosen the cake and remove the side of the pan. Carefully invert the torte onto a cardboard cake round or a cake plate. Peel off the parchment paper and let the cake cool completely (it will fall slightly as it cools).

MAKE THE SYRUP AND IMBIBE THE CAKE

8. Combine the sugar and water in a small saucepan and bring to a boil over medium heat, stirring to dissolve the sugar. Remove the pan from the heat and let the syrup cool to room temperature, then stir in the Cognac. (The syrup can be prepared ahead and stored in an airtight container in the refrigerator for up to a month.)

9. Brush the top of the cooled cake with all of the syrup.

MAKE THE CREAM TOPPING

10. In the bowl of an electric mixer, using the whisk attachment, beat the heavy cream with the confectioners' sugar, Cognac, and vanilla extract at high speed until firm peaks form. (The cream topping can be prepared up to an hour before serving the cake. Cover and refrigerate; whisk the cream a few times if necessary before using.)

Garnish the Cake

1 1. Dust the top edge and sides of the cake with sifted confectioners' sugar. Scrape the Cognac cream on top of the cake and, using a metal spatula, spread it into dramatic swirls. Sprinkle some praline powder over the topping (you won't need it all). Serve the cake immediately, or refrigerate and serve within 2 hours. Use a thin-bladed knife to cut the cake into wedges.

STORE *unfrosted, at room temperature, covered in foil, for up to 3 days; once frosted, refrigerate for up to 2 hours.*

LEMON LUST CAKE

Lemon lovers are a special breed. They are shamelessly devoted to their favorite flavor, and they like it to be assertive and bold, as it is in this zesty layer cake. The tangy lemon curd, the base for both the filling and frosting, can be made up to three weeks in advance and stored in the refrigerator.

➤ MAKES ONE 9-INCH CAKE, SERVING 12

LEMON CAKE

3 cups (12 oz/342 g) cake flour

2½ teaspoons baking powder

½ teaspoon salt

1 cup (2 sticks/8 oz/227 g) unsalted butter, softened

1¾ cups (12.3 oz/350 g) granulated sugar

4 large eggs

2 teaspoons finely grated lemon zest

¼ cup (60 ml) strained freshly squeezed lemon juice

⅔ cup (160 ml) whole milk

LEMON CREAM CHEESE FILLING

¾ cup (180 ml) heavy cream

4 ounces (113 g) cream cheese, softened

½ teaspoon vanilla extract

1 cup (240 ml) Lemon Curd (page 353)

MAKE THE CAKE

1. Position a rack in the center of the oven and preheat the oven to 350°F. Grease the bottom and sides of two 9-inch round cake pans. Dust the pans with flour and tap out the excess.

2. Sift together the cake flour, baking powder, and salt into a medium bowl. Whisk to combine, and set aside.

3. In the bowl of an electric mixer, using the paddle attachment, beat the butter at medium speed until creamy, about 30 seconds. Gradually add the sugar and beat at high speed until well blended and light, about 3 minutes. Scrape down the sides of the bowl with a rubber spatula. Reduce the speed to medium and add the eggs one at a time, beating well after each addition and mixing until blended. Beat in the lemon zest and lemon juice until blended. Reduce the speed to low and add the flour mixture in three additions, alternating it with the milk in two additions and mixing just until blended. Scrape the batter into the prepared pans, dividing it evenly, and smooth the tops with a rubber spatula.

4. Bake the cakes for 22 to 25 minutes, until they are golden brown around the edges and a toothpick inserted into the center comes out clean. Cool the cakes in the pans on wire racks for 15 minutes.

5. Invert the cakes onto the wire racks and let cool completely.

⅓ cup (80 ml) water

¼ cup (60 ml) freshly squeezed lemon juice

½ cup (3.5 oz/100 g) granulated sugar

LEMON BUTTERCREAM

1½ cups (3 sticks/12 oz/340 g) unsalted butter, softened

1 cup (240 ml) Lemon Curd (page 353)

Pinch of salt

MAKE THE FILLING

6. In the bowl of an electric mixer, using the whisk attachment, beat the heavy cream at high speed until firm peaks form. Transfer the whipped cream to a smaller bowl, cover, and refrigerate.

7. In the same mixer bowl (no need to wash it), using the paddle attachment, beat the cream cheese at medium speed until very creamy, about 2 minutes. On low speed, beat in the vanilla extract. Add the lemon curd and beat at medium speed until well blended and smooth, about 1 minute. Remove the bowl from the mixer stand and, using a rubber spatula, gently fold in the whipped cream until almost completely blended. Cover the bowl and refrigerate while you make the syrup and buttercream. (The filling can be made ahead and refrigerated for up to a day.)

MAKE THE SYRUP

8. In a small saucepan, combine the water, lemon juice, and sugar and bring to a boil over medium-high heat, stirring occasionally to dissolve the sugar. Remove the pan from the heat and set aside at room temperature.

MAKE THE BUTTERCREAM

9. In the bowl of an electric mixer, using the paddle attachment, beat the butter at medium speed until creamy and light, about 2 minutes. At medium speed, gradually add the lemon curd, a large spoonful at a time, then add the salt and beat at medium-high speed until creamy and light, about 1½ minutes. Set aside at room temperature while you assemble the cake.

ASSEMBLE THE CAKE

10. Using a long serrated knife, trim off the domed tops of the cakes so that they are even (save any cake pieces and crumbs for snacking). Cut each cake horizontally into 2 layers. Reserve one of the flat bottom layers for the top of the cake. Place another layer cut side up on a cardboard cake round or flat serving plate. Generously brush with some of the lemon syrup. Spoon a scant cup of the filling onto the cake and, using a small offset metal spatula, spread it into an even layer, leaving a ½-inch border around the edge of the cake. Top with another cake layer and brush it with more syrup. Top with another scant cup of filling. Repeat with another layer, more syrup, and the remaining filling. Brush the cut side of the reserved cake layer with the remaining syrup. Place the layer cut side down on top of the cake.

11. Frost the sides and top of the cake with the buttercream. Serve the cake or refrigerate it. If it has been refrigerated, let stand at room temperature for about 45 minutes before serving.

STORE *in the refrigerator for up to 3 days; bring to room temperature before serving.*

ORANGE GROVE CAKE

The fresh citrus flavor of this gorgeous layer cake is like a little shot of sunshine. Make it in the dead of winter, when you need a trip to Florida but can't get away. It won't give you a tan, but it *will* perk you up. The components of the cake can be made in stages: The cake layers can be made up to five days ahead, the filling and buttercream three days ahead, and the syrup up to a month ahead.

➤ MAKES ONE 9-INCH CAKE, SERVING 12

ORANGE LAYER CAKE

3 cups (12 oz/342 g) cake flour

2½ teaspoons baking powder

½ teaspoon salt

1 cup (2 sticks/8 oz/227 g) unsalted butter, softened

1¾ cups (12.3 oz/350 g) granulated sugar

4 large eggs

2 teaspoons finely grated orange zest

⅓ cup (80 ml) strained freshly squeezed orange juice

⅔ cup (160 ml) whole milk

ORANGE FILLING

½ cup (3.5 oz/100 g) granulated sugar

1 tablespoon plus 2 teaspoons (0.7 oz/20 g) cornstarch

⅛ teaspoon salt

1 teaspoon finely grated orange zest

MAKE THE CAKE

1. Position a rack in the center of the oven and preheat the oven to 350°F. Grease the bottom and sides of two 9-inch round cake pans. Dust the pans with flour.

2. Sift together the cake flour, baking powder, and salt into a medium bowl. Whisk to combine, and set aside.

3. In the bowl of an electric mixer, using the paddle attachment, beat the butter at medium speed until creamy, about 30 seconds. Gradually add the sugar and beat at high speed for 3 minutes, until well blended and light. Scrape down the sides of the bowl with a rubber spatula. Reduce the speed to medium and add the eggs one at a time, beating well after each addition and mixing until blended. Beat in the orange zest and orange juice until blended. Reduce the speed to low and add the flour mixture in three additions, alternating it with the milk in two additions and mixing just until blended. Scrape the batter into the prepared pans, dividing it evenly, and smooth the tops with a rubber spatula.

4. Bake the cakes for 22 to 25 minutes, until they are golden brown around the edges and a toothpick inserted into the center comes out clean. Cool the cakes in the pans on wire racks for 15 minutes.

5. Invert the cakes onto wire racks and let cool completely.

⅔ cup (160 ml) strained freshly squeezed orange juice

2 tablespoons (30 ml) strained freshly squeezed lemon juice

2 tablespoons (30 ml) water

3 large egg yolks

ORANGE SOAKING SYRUP

⅓ cup (80 ml) water

¼ cup (60 ml) strained freshly squeezed orange juice

½ cup (3.5 oz/100 g) granulated sugar

1 tablespoon (15 ml) Grand Marnier or Cointreau

ORANGE BUTTERCREAM

¾ cup (5.3 oz/150 g) granulated sugar

4 large egg whites

2 tablespoons (30 ml) water

1½ cups (3 sticks/12 oz/340 g) unsalted butter, slightly softened

½ teaspoon vanilla extract

½ teaspoon orange oil,
¼ teaspoon Fiori di Sicilia (see Sources, page 366) or orange extract

1 tablespoon (15 ml) Grand Marnier or Cointreau

MAKE THE FILLING

6. In a medium saucepan, stir together all the ingredients. Place over medium-high heat and cook, stirring constantly, until the mixture thickens and comes to a boil. Let boil, stirring, for 1 minute. Remove the pan from the heat and scrape the filling into a small bowl. Cover the surface with plastic wrap and refrigerate until chilled, about 1 hour.

MAKE THE SYRUP

7. In a small saucepan, combine the water, orange juice, and sugar and bring to a boil over medium-high heat, stirring occasionally to dissolve the sugar. Remove the pan from the heat and stir in the orange liqueur. Set aside at room temperature.

MAKE THE BUTTERCREAM

8. Pour ½ inch water into a large skillet and bring the water to a simmer; reduce the heat to medium-low to maintain a simmer.

9. In the bowl of an electric mixer, combine the sugar, egg whites, and water. Place the bowl in the skillet of water and whisk gently until the mixture registers 160°F on an instant-read thermometer. Transfer the bowl to the mixer stand and, using the whisk attachment, beat at medium-high speed until the meringue is cool and forms stiff, shiny peaks, about 5 minutes.

10. Reduce the speed to medium and beat in the butter 1 tablespoon at a time. Beat in the vanilla extract, orange oil, and orange liqueur and beat at high speed until the buttercream is smooth, about 1 minute.

ASSEMBLE THE CAKE

11. Using a long serrated knife, trim off the domed tops of the cakes so that they are even (save any cake pieces and crumbs for snacking). Cut each cake horizontally into 2 layers. Reserve one of the flat bottom layers for the top of the cake. Arrange another cake layer cut side up on a cardboard cake round or flat serving plate. Generously brush the cake with some of the orange syrup. Spread ½ cup of the buttercream over the cake layer. Spread one-third of the

filling (just under ⅓ cup) on top of the buttercream. Top with another cake layer and brush it with syrup. Spread the layer with buttercream and filling as before, and top with another cake layer. Repeat and top with the reserved cake layer. Soak this layer with the remaining syrup. Frost the top and sides of the cake with the remaining buttercream, making it as smooth as possible.

STORE *in the refrigerator for up to 3 days. Bring to room temperature before serving.*

CREAMY COCONUT CAKE

A creamy coconut custard made with coconut-infused whole milk forms the base for the filling and frosting of this tall layer cake. A rum-spiked soaking syrup adds some punch to the white coconut cake layers as it offsets the richness of the coconut.

➤ MAKES ONE 9-INCH CAKE, SERVING 12 TO 16

COCONUT CUSTARD

1½ cups (360 ml) whole milk, or as needed

1 cup (2.8 oz/80 g) sweetened flaked coconut

4 large egg yolks

⅓ cup (2.3 oz/66 g) granulated sugar

3 tablespoons (0.8 oz/22 g) cornstarch

1 tablespoon (15 ml) Malibu coconut rum or dark rum

1 teaspoon vanilla extract

RUM SOAKING SYRUP

½ cup (120 ml) water

½ cup (3.5 oz/100 g) granulated sugar

2 tablespoons (30 ml) dark rum

COCONUT CREAM FILLING

¾ cup (180 ml) Coconut Custard (above)

¾ cup (180 ml) heavy cream

MAKE THE CUSTARD

1. Combine the milk and coconut in a medium saucepan, and heat over medium heat until the milk is just under a boil. Remove the pan from the heat and set aside to steep for 1 hour.

2. Strain the milk through a sieve, pressing down on the coconut with a spoon to extract as much liquid as possible. Measure the milk; you should have 1⅓ cups. If you have less, add a little more milk to make up the difference.

3. In a medium bowl, whisk together the yolks, sugar, and cornstarch; set aside.

4. Return the coconut-infused milk to the saucepan and bring it to a gentle boil. Remove the pan from the heat and whisk about ⅓ cup of the hot milk into the yolk mixture. Return the mixture to the saucepan, place over medium-high heat, and bring to a boil, whisking constantly. Boil, whisking constantly, for 1 minute. Remove the pan from the heat, scrape the bottom of the pan with a spatula, and whisk until smooth. Quickly strain the custard through a fine-mesh sieve into a medium bowl. Whisk in the rum and vanilla extract.

5. Set the bowl containing the coconut mixture in a larger bowl filled about one-third of the way with ice water (be careful that the water doesn't splash into the coconut mixture). Stir the custard frequently until it is slightly chilled, about 15 minutes.

1½ cups (3 sticks/12 oz/340 g) unsalted butter, softened

⅓ cup (1.3 oz/38 g) confectioners' sugar

¾ cup (180 ml) Coconut Custard (above)

1 teaspoon vanilla extract

Pinch of salt

Coconut Cake Layers (page 119)

GARNISH

1 cup (2.8 oz/80 g) natural shredded coconut (available at gourmet and health food stores)

MAKE THE SYRUP

6. In a small saucepan, combine the water and sugar and bring to a boil over medium-high heat, stirring occasionally to dissolve the sugar. Remove the pan from the heat and stir in the rum. Set aside at room temperature.

MAKE THE FILLING

7. In the bowl of an electric mixer, using the whisk attachment, beat the ¾ cup coconut custard with the heavy cream at high speed until the mixture is light and forms soft peaks. Cover the bowl with plastic wrap and refrigerate until ready to use.

MAKE THE BUTTERCREAM

8. In a clean mixer bowl, using the paddle attachment, beat the butter and confectioners' sugar at high speed until very light and creamy, about 4 minutes. Add the ¾ cup coconut custard, vanilla extract, and salt and beat at medium speed until blended and smooth.

ASSEMBLE THE CAKE

9. Using a long serrated knife, trim off the domed tops of the cakes so that they are even (save any cake pieces and crumbs for snacking). Cut each cake horizontally into 2 layers. Reserve one of the flat bottom layers for the top of the cake. Place another cake layer cut side up on a cardboard cake round or flat serving plate. Generously brush the cake with some of the soaking syrup. Spoon one-third of the filling onto the cake and, using a small offset metal spatula, spread it into an even layer, leaving a ½-inch border around the edge of the cake. Top with another cake layer and brush it with more syrup. Top with another one-third of the filling. Repeat with another layer, more syrup, and the remaining filling. Brush the cut side of the reserved cake layer with the remaining syrup. Place the layer cut side down on top of the cake.

10. Frost the sides and top of the cake with the buttercream. Pat the coconut onto the sides of the cake.

STORE *in the refrigerator, loosely covered, for up to 3 days. Bring to room temperature before serving.*

9

FRUIT-BASED

CAKES

LEMON SOUFFLÉ CAKE • APPLE CAKE WITH MAPLE FROSTING • BANANA WALNUT CAKE • CLASSIC APPLE CHARLOTTE • DATE, FIG, AND GOLDEN RAISIN CAKE WITH BOURBON • FIG AND MARSALA WINE CAKE • JASMINE AND GINGER PLUM UPSIDE-DOWN CAKE • PEACH TATIN CAKE • RUM-SOPPED FRUITCAKE • STRAWBERRY SHORTCAKE • WHITE CHOCOLATE RASPBERRY ALMOND CAKE • BLACK FOREST CAKE

T his chapter is a departure from the others in this book, in that the recipes are categorized by ingredient, not method. It wouldn't be inaccurate to consider this chapter an homage to fruit. For every fruit—fresh, dried, candied, or preserved—there is a fruit-based cake for every method of cake making and for every conceivable occasion. These are flexible recipes that reflect the versatility of fruit.

Whether you choose a layer cake, loaf cake, upside-down cake, or some fancy French classic, all of the recipes in this chapter rely on fruit for their showstopping flavors. Happily, fruit is always willing and able to share center stage with a range of supporting players: chocolate, liquors, a variety of herbs and spices, and any nut you choose.

Or if, like Truman Capote and generations of Southerners before him, the most famous of fruit-based cakes—the fruitcake—is what you crave, then rejoice. Since the Greeks deemed fruitcake "the food of the gods," it would be pure blasphemy not to include my favorite version here. Scented with molasses and classic Christmas spices such as nutmeg, cinnamon, and clove; packed full of candied orange peel, crystallized ginger, and plump raisins; and soaked in rum—this fruitcake is likely to convert even the most cynical.

Perhaps best of all, with this or any fruit-based cake, if you want to swap one flavor for another, feel free. If you want more (or less) candied or dried fruit, or if you prefer a different fresh fruit from the one I like best, this is the one time when you're encouraged to play with your food.

LEMON SOUFFLÉ CAKE

This old-fashioned dessert, half cake, half soufflé, has a fresh lemon flavor and an intriguing texture. Serve it on its own, or with a little whipped cream and Red Berry Sauce (page 350) or Gingered Berry Compote (page 351).

➤ MAKES ONE 8-INCH SQUARE CAKE, SERVING 9

1 cup (7 oz/200 g) granulated sugar

¼ cup (1 oz/30 g) all-purpose flour

¼ teaspoon salt

3 large eggs, separated

1 cup (8.5 oz/242 g) sour cream

2 tablespoons (1 oz/28 g) unsalted butter, melted

2 teaspoons finely grated lemon zest

¼ cup (60 ml) freshly squeezed lemon juice

1. Position a rack in the center of the oven and preheat the oven to 325°F. Butter the bottom and sides of an 8-inch square baking pan.

2. In a medium bowl, stir together the sugar, flour, and salt; set aside.

3. In another medium bowl, whisk together the egg yolks, sour cream, melted butter, lemon zest, and lemon juice until blended. Pour this mixture over the dry ingredients and stir until blended.

4. In the bowl of an electric mixer, using the whisk attachment, beat the egg whites at medium-low speed until frothy. Gradually increase the speed to high and beat until the whites just form stiff peaks; do not overbeat. Gently fold the beaten whites into the batter. Scrape the batter into the prepared pan.

5. Place the baking pan in a roasting pan or larger baking pan. Pour enough hot water into the roasting pan so that it comes ¾ inch up the sides of the square pan.

6. Bake the cake for 30 to 35 minutes, until it is puffed and set in the center. Remove the pan from the water bath and place it on a wire rack. Let the cake cool for 10 minutes before serving.

7. To serve, cut the cake into squares. Scoop each square onto a plate and serve immediately.

STORE: *This cake is best served the day it's made.*

APPLE CAKE WITH MAPLE FROSTING

As this cake bakes, it will fill your house with the warm scent of cinnamon, ginger, cloves, and sweet baked apple. It is a moist, unpretentious cake, perfect as a simple fall dessert or snack.

➤ MAKES ONE 9-INCH SQUARE CAKE, SERVING 12

APPLE CAKE

1½ cups (6.4 oz/181 g) all-purpose flour

1 teaspoon baking powder

1 teaspoon ground cinnamon

¼ teaspoon ground cloves

¼ teaspoon ground ginger

¼ teaspoon baking soda

¼ teaspoon salt

½ cup (1 stick/4 oz/113 g) unsalted butter, softened

1 cup (7.6 oz/217 g) firmly packed light brown sugar

1 teaspoon vanilla extract

2 large eggs

⅔ cup (160 ml) buttermilk

2 cups (4.2 oz/120 g) peeled and chopped (⅓-inch pieces) Granny Smith apples (about 2 apples)

½ cup (2 oz/57 g) coarsely chopped walnuts

Cream Cheese Maple Frosting (page 310)

1. Position a rack in the center of the oven and preheat the oven to 350°F. Grease the bottom and sides of a 9-inch square baking pan. Dust the pan with flour.

2. In a medium bowl, whisk together the flour, baking powder, cinnamon, cloves, ginger, baking soda, and salt; set aside.

3. In the bowl of an electric mixer, using the paddle attachment, beat the butter at medium speed until creamy, about 1 minute. Gradually add the sugar and beat at medium-high speed until well blended and light, about 2 minutes. Add the vanilla extract, then add the eggs one at a time, beating well after each addition and scraping down the sides of the bowl with a rubber spatula as needed. Reduce the speed to low and add the flour mixture in three additions, alternating it with the buttermilk in two additions and mixing just until blended. Remove the bowl from the mixer stand and stir in the chopped apples and walnuts.

4. Scrape the batter into the prepared pan and smooth the top. Bake the cake for 25 to 30 minutes, until it is golden and a toothpick inserted into the center of the cake comes out clean. Cool the cake completely in the pan on a wire rack.

5. Frost the top of the cooled cake with the maple frosting. Cut the cake into squares and serve it directly from the pan.

STORE *in the refrigerator, loosely covered, for up to 3 days; bring the cake to room temperature before serving.*

BANANA WALNUT CAKE

Asimple, fragrant cake with a light texture and the flavor of toasted walnut and musky banana. A topping of spiced cream cheese frosting adds a sweet finish. For peak flavor, use a very ripe banana and serve the cake at room temperature.

➤ MAKES ONE 9-INCH CAKE, SERVING 8

BANANA WALNUT CAKE

1½ cups (6.4 oz/181 g) all-purpose flour

½ teaspoon baking powder

½ teaspoon baking soda

½ teaspoon ground cinnamon

½ teaspoon salt

13 tablespoons (6.5 oz/182 g) unsalted butter, softened

¾ cup (5.3 oz/150 g) granulated sugar

½ cup (3.8 oz/108 g) firmly packed light brown sugar

2 large eggs

1 teaspoon vanilla extract

½ cup (4.3 oz/121 g) sour cream

½ cup (4 oz/113 g) mashed ripe banana (about 1 large banana)

½ cup (2 oz/57 g) chopped toasted (see page 37) walnuts

Cream Cheese Spice Frosting (page 310)

---

1. Position a rack in the center of the oven and preheat oven to 325°F. Grease the bottom and sides of a 9 x 3-inch springform pan. Dust the pan with flour.

2. Sift together the flour, baking powder, baking soda, ground cinnamon, and salt into a medium bowl. Whisk until blended, and set aside.

3. In the bowl of an electric mixer, using the paddle attachment, beat the butter at medium speed until creamy, about 1 minute. Gradually add the sugars, about 1 tablespoon at a time, and beat at high speed until light and aerated, about 2 minutes. Add the eggs one at a time, beating well after each addition and scraping down the sides of the bowl as necessary. Add the vanilla extract, then the sour cream and mashed banana, mixing until blended. Add the dry ingredients at low speed, mixing just until blended. Remove the bowl from the mixer stand and stir in the walnuts by hand.

4. Scrape the batter into the prepared pan and smooth the top with a rubber spatula. Bake for 35 to 40 minutes, until the cake is lightly browned and a toothpick inserted into the center comes out clean. Cool the cake in the pan on a wire rack for about 10 minutes.

5. Carefully unclasp and remove the side of the pan. Invert the cake onto the rack, remove the bottom, and cool completely, still upside down.

6. Frost the top (which is really the bottom) of the cake. Serve at room temperature.

STORE *in an airtight container at room temperature for up to 2 days, or refrigerate for up to a week. Bring to room temperature before serving.*

CLASSIC APPLE CHARLOTTE

This is another recipe from Carole Harlam. Carole's Apple Charlotte is a rustic dessert composed of sweet, buttery rectangles of toast encasing a rum-laced spiced apple filling. For the filling to have the proper consistency, be sure to use a firm-textured, dry apple such as Rome Beauty. It's also important to overlap the bread slices as directed, which will prevent the charlotte from collapsing. Serve the dessert with sweetened whipped cream, vanilla ice cream, or a crème anglaise (page 355).

➤ MAKES ONE 7 X 4-INCH CHARLOTTE, SERVING 8
➤ SPECIAL EQUIPMENT: ONE 2-QUART CHARLOTTE MOLD

APPLE FILLING

4½ pounds (2 kg) Rome Beauty, Granny Smith, Jonagold, or McIntosh apples

2 tablespoons (30 ml) freshly squeezed lemon juice

4 tablespoons (2 oz/57 g) unsalted butter

¼ cup (60 ml) dark rum

¾ cup (5.7 oz/163 g) firmly packed light brown sugar

½ teaspoon freshly grated nutmeg

½ teaspoon ground cinnamon

¼ teaspoon salt

Grated zest of 1 lemon

½ cup (2.5 oz/72 g) golden raisins

BREAD CRUST

1 cup (2 sticks/8 oz/227 g) unsalted butter, at room temperature, divided

2 tablespoons (0.88 oz/25 g) granulated sugar

MAKE THE FILLING

1. Peel, halve, and core the apples. Cut each half in half again, then cut the quarters crosswise into thin slices. As you slice the apples, place them in a large bowl and toss them with a little bit of the lemon juice.

2. In a large pot, melt the butter over medium-low heat. Add the apples and rum, cover, and cook, stirring occasionally, until the apples are completely soft, 20 to 25 minutes.

3. Stir in the sugar, nutmeg, cinnamon, and salt, increase the heat to medium-high, and cook, uncovered, stirring and mashing the apples frequently, until the liquid has completely evaporated and the apples form a coarse thick dry puree, about 10 minutes. Remove the pan from the heat and stir in the lemon zest and raisins. Set aside to cool while you make the crust.

MAKE THE CRUST AND ASSEMBLE THE CHARLOTTE

4. Position a rack in the lower third of the oven and preheat the oven to 425°F. Grease the bottom and sides of a 2-quart charlotte mold with 2 tablespoons of the butter. Dust the mold with the sugar and tap out the excess.

5. In a small saucepan, melt the remaining 14 tablespoons butter over low heat; set aside.

18 slices firm-textured white bread (including the heels, or end slices), such as Pepperidge Farm

GLAZE

½ cup (5.4 oz/154 g) apricot jam

1 tablespoon (15 ml) freshly sqeezed lemon juice

1 tablespoon (15 ml) dark rum

6. Using a serrated knife, remove the crusts from the bread (except from the heels), then trim the slices, including the heels, into 3½-inch squares; reserve the crusts and trimmings. Form a square with 4 slices of the bread. Center the bottom of the charlotte mold over the bread square and, using a paring knife, cut around the mold to make a circle; reserve the trimmings. Cut each bread "quadrant" diagonally in half so that you have 8 rounded triangles of equal size. These pieces will line the bottom of the mold. Repeat this process with 4 more bread squares, but this time center the top of the mold over the bread square; these triangular pieces will be used to cover the top of the mold. Set them aside.

7. Dip one side of each of the triangles for the bottom of the mold in the melted butter. Line the bottom of the mold with the triangles, buttered side down. Cut the remaining bread slices lengthwise in half into strips. Dip one side of each strip in the melted butter and arrange the strips, upright, around the inside of the mold, placing the buttered sides against the mold and overlapping each one by about ¾ inch to line the mold completely (include the heels of the bread, placing the white sides facing out).

8. Put the reserved bread trimmings and crusts in the bowl of a food processor and pulse to fine crumbs. Stir ½ cup of the crumbs into the cooled apple puree (save the extra crumbs for another use). Spoon the filling into the bread-lined mold, packing it down (the mold should be very full, but you may end up with a little extra filling).

9. Dip one side of each reserved bread triangle in the butter and arrange on top of the filling, buttered side up. Press down lightly.

10. Bake the charlotte for 30 minutes. Cover the top loosely with aluminum foil and bake for another 10 to 20 minutes, until the bread slices on the sides of the mold are golden brown (slide a thin-bladed knife between the bread and the side of the mold to check their color). Remove the charlotte from the oven and cool in the pan on a wire rack for 45 minutes.

11. Run a thin-bladed knife around the sides of the mold, and invert the charlotte onto a serving plate.

GLAZE THE CHARLOTTE

12. In a small saucepan, combine the apricot jam, lemon juice, and rum and cook over low heat, stirring constantly, until the jam is completely melted. Bring to a boil, then remove from the heat. Using a pastry brush, brush the charlotte all over with the glaze.

13. Serve the charlotte warm or at room temperature. Use a serrated knife to slice it into 8 wedges.

STORE *in the refrigerator, loosely covered, for up to 2 days.*

Date, Fig, and Golden Raisin Cake with Bourbon

Rich, ultra-moist, and loaded with dates, raisins, figs, and flaked coconut, this holiday cake, contributed by Lisa Yockelson, is likely to convert even the staunchest fruitcake detractor. Bourbon and pineapple juice provide just the right amount of moisture in the batter, and orange marmalade adds a subtle tang. For a more spirited version, reduce the pineapple juice to 1 cup and increase the bourbon to 1¼ cups.

➤ MAKES ONE 10-INCH CAKE, SERVING 20

BOURBON-SOAKED FRUIT

1 pound (454 g) pitted dates, finely diced

12 ounces (340 g) golden raisins

9 ounces (255 g) dried Black Mission figs, stemmed and finely diced

8 ounces (227 g) dried Calimyrna figs, stemmed and finely diced

1 cup (240 ml) good-quality bourbon

SPICED CAKE

2¾ cups (11 oz/313 g) cake flour

¾ teaspoon baking powder

1 teaspoon salt

2 teaspoons ground cinnamon

1½ teaspoons ground ginger

1¼ teaspoons freshly grated nutmeg

¾ teaspoon ground allspice

¾ teaspoon ground cardamom (optional)

MARINATE THE FRUIT

1. Up to 2 days before you plan to make the cake, place the dates, raisins, and figs in a large glass or porcelain bowl. Pour over the bourbon and toss well. Cover with plastic wrap and let stand in a cool place overnight, or up to 48 hours, stirring the fruit from time to time.

MAKE THE CAKE

2. Position a rack in the center of the oven and preheat the oven to 275°F. Grease the inside of a 10-inch tube pan, including the center tube. Line the bottom of the pan with a ring of wax paper and grease the paper heavily. Dust the inside of the pan with flour and tap out any excess flour. (The pan must be well greased and floured, or the fruit may stick.)

3. Sift together the flour, baking powder, salt, cinnamon, ginger, nutmeg, allspice, cardamom (if using), mace, and cloves into a medium bowl. Whisk to combine, and set aside.

4. In the bowl of an electric mixer, using the paddle attachment, beat the butter at medium speed until very creamy, about 5 minutes. Add the sugar in two additions, beating for 2 minutes after each one. The mixture should be light. Beat in the eggs one at a time, mixing well after each addition and scraping down the sides of the bowl as necessary. Beat in the vanilla extract and orange marmalade. At low speed, add the sifted mixture in three additions,

½ teaspoon ground mace

½ teaspoon ground cloves

1 pound (4 sticks/454 g) unsalted butter, softened

1¼ cups (10.5 oz/300 g) firmly packed dark brown sugar

5 large eggs

2 teaspoons vanilla extract

½ cup (5.4 oz/154 g) orange marmalade

1¼ cups (300 ml) pineapple juice

2 cups (5.6 oz/160 g) sweetened flaked coconut

alternating it with the pineapple juice in two additions, scraping the mixing bowl thoroughly after each addition. Beat for 45 seconds longer.

5. Scatter the coconut over the macerated fruit and toss well. Scrape the batter into a very large bowl. Spoon over the fruit mixture and stir in. Spoon the batter evenly into the prepared pan.

6. Bake the cake for 2½ hours to 2 hours and 45 minutes, or until it is risen and set and a long wooden pick or skewer comes out clean or with a few moist crumbs attached. Cool the cake in the pan on a rack for 30 minutes.

7. Slip a long flexible metal spatula around the sides and tube of the cake pan. Carefully invert the cake onto another rack, peel away the wax paper, and then invert again. Let cool completely.

8. Place the cake in an airtight cake keeper or wrap tightly in plastic and let it mellow for at least 1 day before serving.

9. To serve, cut the cake into slices using a serrated knife.

STORE *at room temperature, under a cake keeper or wrapped in foil, for up to 2 weeks.*

BOURBON DOES FOR ME WHAT THE PIECE OF CAKE DID FOR PROUST.
—WALKER PERCY

FIG AND MARSALA WINE CAKE

Though not typical, this is probably my favorite holiday fruitcake. The sweet, smoky flavor of Sicilian Marsala wine infuses nuggets of Black Mission figs in a rich, sour cream–enhanced Bundt cake. The shiny glaze made from raspberry jam and Marsala is a pretty finishing touch.

➤ MAKES ONE 10-INCH BUNDT CAKE, SERVING 12

FIG AND MARSALA CAKE

10 ounces (283 g) dried Black Mission figs, stemmed and cut into ½-inch pieces (about 2 cups)

¼ cup (60 ml) sweet Marsala wine

3 cups (12.8 oz/363 g) all-purpose flour

¾ teaspoon baking powder

¼ teaspoon baking soda

½ teaspoon salt

1 cup (2 sticks/8 oz/227 g) unsalted butter, softened

2⅓ cups (16.4 oz/466 g) granulated sugar

4 large eggs

2 teaspoons vanilla extract

1 cup (8.5 oz/242 g) sour cream

MARSALA GLAZE

¼ cup (2.7 oz/77 g) raspberry jam

1 tablespoon (15 ml) sweet Marsala wine

MAKE THE CAKE

1. Place the figs in a medium bowl and set aside.

2. In a small saucepan, heat the Marsala over medium-high heat until just beginning to bubble. Pour the hot wine over the figs and toss to coat them. Let the figs macerate for 1 hour, or until most of the wine has been absorbed.

3. Position a rack in the center of the oven and preheat the oven to 350°F. Grease the inside of a 10-inch Bundt pan. Dust the pan with flour.

4. Sift together the flour, baking powder, baking soda, and salt into a medium bowl. Whisk to combine, and set aside.

5. In the bowl of an electric mixer, using the paddle attachment, beat the butter at medium-high speed until creamy, about 1 minute. Gradually add the sugar and beat at high speed until light and very creamy, about 4 minutes. Beat in the eggs one at a time, beating well after each addition and scraping down the sides of the bowl with a rubber spatula as necessary. Blend in the vanilla extract. Add the flour mixture at low speed in three additions, alternating it with the sour cream in two additions and mixing just until the flour is incorporated.

6. Remove the bowl from the mixer stand and, using a rubber spatula, gently fold in the figs (along with any wine that has not been absorbed). Scrape the batter into the prepared pan and smooth the top.

7. Bake the cake for 50 to 60 minutes, until a cake tester inserted into the cake comes out clean. Cool the cake in the pan on a wire rack for 10 to 12 minutes.

8. Place another cooling rack on top and carefully invert the cake, then lift off the Bundt pan. Let cool completely.

GLAZE THE CAKE

9. In a small saucepan, heat the raspberry jam over medium heat, stirring, until melted and liquefied. Remove the pan from the heat and stir in the Marsala. Using a pastry brush, brush the entire cake with the glaze.

10. To serve, cut the cake into slices using a serrated knife.

STORE *under a cake keeper at room temperature for up to 3 days, or refrigerate for up to a week.*

JASMINE AND GINGER PLUM UPSIDE-DOWN CAKE

Aromatic jasmine tea and pungent ginger provide the backnote flavors in this pretty plum-topped cake. I like it warm, with a scoop of caramel or vanilla bean ice cream alongside.

➤ MAKES ONE 9-INCH CAKE, SERVING 10

BROWN SUGAR–GINGER PLUM TOPPING

5 (1 lb/454 g) medium-sized ripe black plums

1 cup (240 ml) boiling water

2 orange jasmine or jasmine tea bags

2 tablespoons (0.8 oz/25 g) granulated sugar

4 tablespoons (2 oz/57 g) unsalted butter, cut into tablespoons

½ cup (3.8 oz/108 g) firmly packed light brown sugar

2 tablespoons (0.7 oz/20 g) finely minced crystallized ginger

CAKE

1½ cups (6.4 oz/181 g) all-purpose flour

1½ teaspoons baking powder

½ teaspoon ground ginger

¼ teaspoon salt

9 tablespoons (4.5 oz/127 g) unsalted butter, softened

SOAK THE PLUMS

1. Cut each plum in half, remove the pit, and slice into ¼-inch-thick wedges. Place the slices in a medium bowl.

2. Pour the boiling water into a cup and add the tea bags. Let the mixture infuse for 10 minutes.

3. Remove the tea bags from the water and stir in the sugar until dissolved. Pour the warm tea over the plum slices and let them stand for 20 minutes.

MAKE THE TOPPING

4. Position a rack in the center of the oven and preheat the oven to 350°F. Put the butter in a 9-inch round cake pan and place the pan over low heat. When the butter is melted, stir in the brown sugar until mostly blended (the sugar will not completely absorb the butter). Remove the pan from the heat and set aside to cool for 5 minutes.

5. Arrange a circle of the plum wedges (no need to drain them, just remove them one at a time from the tea), overlapping them slightly, around the edge of the pan, on top of the brown sugar mixture. Arrange another circle of wedges in the center, facing the opposite direction, covering the brown sugar topping completely. Sprinkle the crystallized ginger over the plums.

1 cup (7 oz/200 g) granulated sugar

2 large eggs

1½ teaspoons vanilla extract

1 cup (240 ml) whole milk

MAKE THE CAKE

6. Sift together the flour, baking powder, ginger, and salt into a medium bowl. Whisk to combine, and set aside.

7. In the bowl of an electric mixer, using the paddle attachment, beat the butter at medium-high speed until creamy, about 1 minute. Gradually add the sugar and beat at high speed until the mixture is lightened in texture and color, 2 to 3 minutes. Reduce the speed to medium and add the eggs one at a time, beating well after each addition and scraping down the sides of the bowl as needed. Beat in the vanilla extract. At low speed, add the flour mixture in three additions, alternating it with the milk in two additions and mixing just until blended.

8. Spoon the batter in large dollops over the plums, then smooth it into an even layer. Bake for 45 to 50 minutes, until the cake is golden brown and springs back when lightly touched. Set the pan on a wire rack and cool for 10 minutes.

9. Run a thin-bladed knife around the edge of the pan. Using pot holders, very carefully invert the cake onto a cake plate or platter. Serve the cake warm or at room temperature.

STORE *in the refrigerator, loosely covered, for up to 3 days.*

IF YOU ARE COLD, TEA WILL WARM YOU—IF YOU ARE TOO HEATED, IT WILL COOL YOU—IF YOU ARE DEPRESSED, IT WILL CHEER YOU— IF YOU ARE EXCITED, IT WILL CALM YOU.
—WILLIAM GLADSTONE

PEACH TATIN CAKE

I 've always loved the French dessert Tarte Tatin, in which caramelized apples are topped with a layer of pastry, baked, and then inverted. This cakey interpretation of the classic tart features a sour cream cake batter, which is poured over a layer of buttery caramel and peach slices and baked. When the cake is unmolded, the caramel coats the peaches and seeps into the cake, saturating it with a sweet, complex flavor. This cake also works well with other fruit such as nectarines or plums. Serve it warm with vanilla ice cream or whipped cream.

➤ MAKES ONE 10-INCH CAKE, SERVING 8 TO 10

CARAMEL PEACH TOPPING

1 cup (7 oz/200 g) granulated sugar

2 tablespoons (30 ml) water

5 tablespoons (2.5 oz/71 g) unsalted butter, cut into tablespoons

4 large ripe peaches (18.3 oz/520 g)

SOUR CREAM CAKE

1½ cups (6.4 oz/181 g) all-purpose flour

1½ teaspoons baking powder

¼ teaspoon baking soda

½ teaspoon ground cinnamon

½ teaspoon ground ginger

¼ teaspoon salt

1 cup (8.5 oz/242 g) sour cream

2 teaspoons vanilla extract

9 tablespoons (4.5 oz/127 g) unsalted butter, softened

PREPARE THE TOPPING

1. Position a rack in the center of the oven and preheat to 350°F. Grease the bottom and sides of a 10 x 3-inch round cake pan (don't use a springform pan, or the caramel might leak out during baking). Line the bottom of the pan with a round of parchment paper and grease the paper.

2. In a medium saucepan, combine the sugar and water, and cook over medium heat, stirring until the sugar dissolves. Stop stirring; increase the heat to high, and cook, occasionally brushing down the sides of the pan with a wet pastry brush to prevent crystallization, until the mixture turns into a golden caramel. Remove the pan from the heat and immediately whisk in the butter, one piece at a time (be careful—the mixture will bubble up furiously). Carefully pour the hot caramel into the bottom of the prepared pan.

3. Cut the peaches in half and discard the pits. Cut each peach half into 6 wedges. Arrange a circle of wedges, overlapping them slightly, around the edge of the pan, on top of the caramel. Arrange another circle of wedges in the center, facing the opposite direction, covering the caramel completely.

MAKE THE CAKE

4. Sift together the flour, baking powder, baking soda, cinnamon, ginger, and salt into a medium bowl. Whisk to combine, and set aside.

1 cup (7 oz/200 g) granulated sugar

2 large eggs

5. In a small bowl, stir together the sour cream and vanilla extract; set aside.

6. In the bowl of an electric mixer, using the paddle attachment, beat the butter at medium-high speed until creamy, about 1 minute. Gradually add the sugar and beat at high speed until the mixture is lightened in texture and color, 2 to 3 minutes. Reduce the speed to medium and add the eggs one at a time, beating well after each addition and scraping down the sides of the bowl as needed. At low speed, add the flour mixture in three additions, alternating it with the sour cream mixture in two additions and mixing just until blended.

7. Spoon the batter in large dollops over the peaches, then smooth it into an even layer. Bake for 45 to 50 minutes, until the cake is golden brown and springs back when lightly touched. Set the pan on a wire rack and cool for 10 minutes.

8. Run a thin-bladed knife around the edge of the pan. Using pot holders, very carefully invert the cake onto a cake plate or platter. Peel off the parchment paper if necessary. Serve the cake warm or at room temperature.

STORE *in an airtight container at room temperature for up to 2 days, or refrigerate for up to a week. Bring to room temperature before serving.*

THE RIPEST PEACH IS HIGHEST ON THE TREE.
—JAMES WHITCOMB RILEY

RUM-SOPPED FRUITCAKE

Why is fruitcake the object of such derision? Probably because so many of them are made with fluorescent-colored supermarket-variety candied fruit and peel. Try this version, and you'll see the difference. These dark loaves are studded with succulent chopped figs and dates, dark and golden raisins, crystallized ginger, European candied orange peel, and pecans. Then a respectable (read: outrageous) amount of dark rum is brushed on the baked cakes every day for five days before serving—so plan to make the cakes at least a week before you serve them.

➤ MAKES TWO 9 x 5-INCH LOAF CAKES, EACH SERVING 10

FRUITCAKES

1¾ cups (10 oz/283 g) dried Black Mission figs, cut into ½-inch pieces

1¼ cups (6.3 oz/180 g) dark raisins

1¼ cups (6.3 oz/180 g) golden raisins

¾ cup (4 oz/113 g) diced top-quality candied orange peel*

¾ cup (3.5 oz/100 g) pitted dates, cut into ½-inch pieces

½ cup (2.8 oz/80 g) chopped (¼-inch pieces) crystallized ginger

1¼ cups (300 ml) dark rum

3¼ cups (13.8 oz/393 g) all-purpose flour

1¼ teaspoons baking powder

¼ teaspoon baking soda

½ teaspoon salt

1 teaspoon ground cinnamon

¾ teaspoon freshly grated nutmeg

¾ teaspoon ground ginger

1. The day before you plan to make the fruitcakes, combine all the dried fruit in a large bowl. In a small saucepan, bring the rum to a simmer. Pour it over the fruit and toss with a large spoon to combine well. Cover the bowl with plastic wrap and let the fruit macerate for at least 12 hours, or until most of the alcohol has been absorbed.

2. Position a rack in the center of the oven and preheat the oven to 300°F. Grease the bottom and sides of two 9 x 5-inch loaf pans. Dust the pans with flour.

3. Sift together the flour, baking powder, baking soda, salt, cinnamon, nutmeg, ginger, cloves, and allspice into a medium bowl. Whisk to combine well, and set aside.

4. In the bowl of an electric mixer, using the paddle attachment, beat the butter at medium-high speed until light, about 1 minute. Gradually add the brown sugar and beat at high speed until well blended and light, about 3 minutes. At medium speed, add the eggs one at a time, beating well after each addition and scraping down the sides of the bowl as necessary (the mixture will not be smooth). Reduce the speed to low and add the orange zest, vanilla extract, and milk, mixing until blended (the mixture will look curdled). Add the flour mixture in three additions, alternating it with the molasses in two additions and mixing just until blended.

¾ teaspoon ground cloves

¼ teaspoon ground allspice

1½ cups (3 sticks/12 oz/340 g) unsalted butter, softened

2 cups (16.8 oz/478 g) firmly packed dark brown sugar

7 large eggs

2 teaspoons finely grated orange zest

1 tablespoon vanilla extract

½ cup (120 ml) whole milk

½ cup (120 ml) unsulphured (mild) molasses

2½ cups (8.8 oz/250 g) pecan halves

RUM SOAK

1¼ cups (300 ml) dark rum, divided

*Note: Good-quality European candied orange peel is available from The Baker's Catalogue (see Sources, page 367).

5. Remove the bowl from the mixer stand and, using a rubber spatula, fold in the macerated fruit, along with any rum in the bowl, and the pecans. Scrape the batter into the prepared pans, dividing it evenly, and smooth the tops.

6. Bake the cakes 1 hour. Tent a piece of foil over the top of each cake to prevent it from overbrowning, and bake the cakes for another 20 to 30 minutes, until a toothpick inserted into the center comes out clean.

7. Place the pans on a wire rack and brush each of the warm cakes with about 2 tablespoons of the dark rum. Cool the cakes in the pans for about 30 minutes.

8. Unmold the cakes onto the racks and let cool completely.

9. Wash the cake pans and line them with plastic wrap. Return the cakes to the pans and cover them with plastic wrap. Brush the top of each cake with 2 tablespoons of rum every day for 5 days before serving.

STORE *at room temperature, well wrapped in plastic, for up to a month.*

WHILE AN EON, AS SOMEONE HAS OBSERVED, MAY BE TWO PEOPLE AND A HAM, A FRUITCAKE IS FOREVER.
—RUSSELL BAKER

STRAWBERRY SHORTCAKE

There are many ways to make this quintessentially American cake, but this is my favorite: sweet sponge cake layers filled with softly whipped cream and juicy sugared strawberry slices. Simple yet perfect (assuming you've got ripe, flavorful strawberries). Once assembled, the cake will hold for several hours in the refrigerator, but it should be served the same day.

➤ MAKES ONE 9-INCH CAKE, SERVING 10

STRAWBERRY FILLING

Two 12-ounce cartons fresh strawberries (this is the total amount of strawberries you will need), washed and hulled

2 tablespoons (0.9 oz/25 g) granulated sugar

STRAWBERRY SYRUP

⅓ cup (2.3 oz/66 g) granulated sugar

⅓ cup (80 ml) water

½ cup sliced reserved strawberries (from above)

WHIPPED CREAM FILLING AND FROSTING

½ cup (2 oz/57 g) confectioners' sugar

2½ teaspoons cornstarch

3 cups (720 ml) heavy cream, divided

1 teaspoon vanilla extract

1 teaspoon finely grated orange zest

1 tablespoon (15 ml) Grand Marnier or Cointreau

MAKE THE FILLING

1. Choose 8 of the nicest-looking strawberries and reserve them for the top of the cake. Slice the remaining strawberries ⅛ inch thick. Measure out ½ cup of the sliced strawberries and reserve them for the syrup.

2. In a medium bowl, toss the remaining sliced strawberries with the sugar. Cover the bowl and set the strawberries aside to macerate for 2 hours, or until they have released their juices.

MAKE THE SYRUP

3. In a small saucepan, combine the sugar and water and bring to a boil over medium-high heat, stirring to dissolve the sugar. Remove the pan from the heat.

4. Place the ½ cup sliced strawberries in the bowl of a food processor or a blender, add the sugar syrup, and process until smooth. Let the syrup cool completely.

MAKE THE FILLING AND FROSTING

5. In a small saucepan, whisk together the confectioners' sugar, cornstarch, and ½ cup of the heavy cream until smooth. Place the pan over medium-high heat and, whisking constantly, bring to a boil. Allow to boil for about 15 seconds. Remove the pan from the heat and let cool completely.

6. In the bowl of an electric mixer, using the whisk attachment, beat the remaining 2½ cups heavy cream with the vanilla extract,

Classic Génoise (page 74), baked in a 9-inch springform pan

orange zest, and Grand Marnier at medium-high speed until the cream just begins to thicken and the whisk leaves a trail in the cream. Add the cooled cornstarch mixture and beat until the cream forms stiff peaks.

ASSEMBLE THE CAKE

7. Using a long serrated knife, slice the génoise horizontally into 2 layers. Place one of the layers cut side up on a cardboard cake round or serving plate. Brush with half of the strawberry syrup. Spoon the macerated strawberries, with all their juices, on top of the layer. Spread 2 cups of the whipped cream over the berries in an even layer. Top with the other cake layer, cut side up. Brush the layer with the remaining syrup. Frost the top and sides of the cake with the remaining whipped cream.

8. Garnish the top of the cake with the reserved whole strawberries. Serve the cake immediately or refrigerate until ready to serve.

STORE: *This cake is best served the day it's made.*

WHITE CHOCOLATE RASPBERRY ALMOND CAKE

The flavors of white chocolate, raspberry, and almond team up to create some magic in this grand cake. Make this in the summer when you can find perfectly ripe and sweet local raspberries. Note that the ganache needs to chill for at least six hours before whipping, so plan accordingly. Like most cakes made with fresh berries, this is best served the same day it's made.

➤ MAKES ONE 9-INCH CAKE, SERVING 12

RASPBERRY FILLING

One 6-ounce (170-g) container fresh raspberries

¼ cup (2.7 oz/77 g) seedless raspberry preserves

Almond Génoise (page 76)

1 cup Basic Soaking Syrup (page 332), flavored with kirsch

Double batch of Whipped White Chocolate Ganache (page 318)

¾ cup (2.2 oz/64 g) blanched sliced almonds, lightly toasted (see page 36)

GARNISH

One 6-ounce (170-g) container fresh raspberries

Confectioners' sugar for dusting

MAKE THE FILLING

1. Place the raspberries in a medium bowl. Place the preserves in a small saucepan or a microwave-safe cup and heat over low heat on the stovetop or on high power in the microwave until just melted. Scrape the melted preserves over the raspberries and toss with a rubber spatula to coat them.

ASSEMBLE THE CAKE

2. Place one of the cake layers on a cardboard cake round or cake plate. Brush the top generously with some of the syrup. Spoon the filling mixture evenly over the cake. Scrape about 1 cup of the whipped ganache over the raspberries and, using a small offset metal spatula, spread it into an even layer.

3. Brush the top of the remaining cake layer generously with syrup. Place it upside down on top of the filling. Brush the top generously with more syrup. Set aside about ¾ cup of the whipped ganache to garnish the top of the cake. Frost the sides and top of the cake with the remaining ganache. Pat toasted almonds onto the sides of the cake.

GARNISH THE CAKE

4. Arrange the raspberries in concentric circles on top of the cake, starting in the center and moving out toward the edge. Scrape the reserved whipped ganache into a pastry bag fitted with a medium star tip (such as Ateco #5), and pipe 8 rosettes around the top edge of the cake.

5. Right before serving, lightly dust the raspberries with confectioners' sugar.

STORE: *This cake is best served the day it's made.*

BLACK FOREST CAKE

Hailing from the Black Forest region of Germany, this cake is found in every Konditorei from Berlin to Munich. Though the classic is made with a chocolate sponge cake, I make my Americanized version with four layers of a moist, deep chocolate sour cream cake sandwiched with kirsch-flavored whipped cream and tart cherries for a totally over-the-top, mile-high showstopper. One bite, and you can't help but exclaim, "Wunderbar!"

➤ MAKES ONE 9-INCH CAKE, SERVING 12

CHERRY SOAKING SYRUP

⅓ cup (80 ml) water

¼ cup (1.8 oz/50 g) granulated sugar

3 tablespoons (45 ml) kirsch

CHERRY WHIPPED CREAM

2¾ cups (660 ml) heavy cream

¼ cup (1 oz/29 g) confectioners' sugar

2 tablespoons (30 ml) kirsch

1 teaspoon vanilla extract

Sour Cream Chocolate Cake Layers (page 124)

CHERRY LAYER

2 cups (11.4 oz/324 g) fresh sour cherries, pitted, or one 15-ounce (425-g) can sour cherries, drained

GARNISH

2 cups grated chocolate (see page 55)

MAKE THE SOAKING SYRUP

1. In a small saucepan, combine the water and sugar and bring to a boil over medium-high heat, stirring occasionally to dissolve the sugar. Remove the pan from the heat and stir in the kirsch. Set aside at room temperature.

MAKE THE WHIPPED CREAM

2. In the bowl of an electric mixer, using the whisk attachment, beat the cream with the confectioners' sugar, kirsch, and vanilla extract at high speed until medium firm peaks begin to form. The whipped cream should be used as soon as possible; cover and refrigerate while you trim and slice the layers.

ASSEMBLE THE CAKE

3. Using a long serrated knife, trim off the domed top of each cake layer so that it is perfectly level (save the trimmings for snacking). Cut each cake horizontally in half, to make 4 layers. Place one of the layers cut side up on a cardboard cake round or serving plate and brush it generously with some of the soaking syrup. Spread 1 cup of the whipped cream over the cake. Scatter one-third of the cherries over the cream. Top with another cake layer and repeat the soaking and layering two more times. Top with the last cake layer, smooth side up, and soak it with the remaining syrup.

4. Set aside about ½ cup of the whipped cream for garnish. Frost the top and sides of the cake with the remaining cream (the sides don't have to look perfect, as you will cover them with grated chocolate). Pat the grated chocolate onto the sides of the cake.

8 fresh sour cherries with stems (optional)

Scrape the reserved cream into a pastry bag fitted with a medium star tip (such as Ateco #6), and pipe 8 rosettes around the edge of the top of the cake. Top each rosette with a fresh cherry, if desired. Serve the cake, or refrigerate for up to 3 hours.

STORE: *This cake is best served the day it's made; store leftovers in the refrigerator.*

10

FLOURLESS

CAKES

F lourless cakes and tortes are made with little or no flour, giving them a dense texture and intense flavor. Some are made with finely ground nuts, which provide structure as well as flavor. In the absence of flour, flourless cakes depend largely on eggs for their structure. There are three general techniques for making flourless cakes. For the first, whole eggs are whipped and combined with the other ingredients. As the eggs cook in the oven's heat, they thicken and set, making for a dense-textured cake. The lack of flour leaves the eggs vulnerable to the heat, which is why some flourless cakes are cooked in a water bath (also known as a bain-marie); it protects the cake from direct heat and yields a cake with an interior that is creamy throughout. A second method involves heating and whipping whole eggs until they triple in volume. Then the oven heat expands the egg proteins, making for a lighter cake. The third technique involves making a meringue base and produces a cake with a texture similar to angel food cake. Since meringues are so delicate, this is the most fragile type of flourless cake.

Although the eggs provide some structure, flourless cakes are delicate, which is why they are often baked in springform pans. This allows you to remove the sides of the pan while leaving the cake on the base, thus reducing the risk of damaging your cake. In any case, the cakes' delicacy requires that they be cooled completely before unmolding. One last note: since they lack structure from flour, flourless cakes tend to sink a bit in the center as they cool (OK, some actually *fall*). Don't be alarmed, this is natural and unavoidable, due to the lack of flour. And it results in a nice depression to pile whipped cream into.

INDIVIDUAL WARM CHOCOLATE CAKES

The warm molten chocolate cake exploded (literally) onto the dessert scene in the early 1990s. Today it remains a very popular item on dessert menus at elegant restaurants. Timing is key in making these cakes. Once they're baked, they should stand for a minute but then must be immediately unmolded, garnished, and served, *tout de suite.* Vanilla ice cream is an ideal accompaniment—the frisson of the hot chocolate with the cold ice cream is downright sensual.

➤ MAKES 6 INDIVIDUAL CAKES
➤ SPECIAL EQUIPMENT: SIX 6-OUNCE DISPOSABLE ALUMINUM CUPS OR CERAMIC RAMEKINS

WARM CHOCOLATE CAKES

Granulated sugar for dusting cups

9 ounces (255 g) bittersweet chocolate, coarsely chopped

4 tablespoons (2 oz/113 g) unsalted butter, cut into tablespoons

½ cup (3.5 oz/100 g) granulated sugar, divided

4 large eggs, separated

⅛ teaspoon salt

¼ teaspoon cream of tartar

Confectioners' sugar for dusting

Cocoa powder for dusting

Vanilla ice cream for serving

MAKE THE CAKES

1. Position a rack in the center of the oven and preheat the oven to 375°F. Generously butter the insides of six 6-ounce disposable aluminum cups or ceramic ramekins. Dust the cups with granulated sugar and tap out the excess. Arrange the cups on a baking sheet and set aside.

2. Put the chocolate and butter in a medium stainless steel bowl and place the bowl over a pot of barely simmering water. Heat, stirring frequently, until the chocolate is completely melted and the mixture is smooth. Remove the bowl from the pot and whisk in ¼ cup of the sugar. Whisk in the egg yolks.

3. In the bowl of an electric mixer, using the whisk attachment, beat the egg whites with the salt at medium speed until foamy. Add the cream of tartar and beat at medium-high speed until the whites just begin to form soft peaks. Add the remaining ¼ cup sugar 1 tablespoon at a time, then beat at high speed until stiff peaks form. Gently fold the egg whites into the chocolate mixture one-third at a time. Divide the batter among the prepared cups.

4. Bake the cakes, on the baking sheet, for 15 to 20 minutes, until they are cracked on top (the centers should still be moist—a toothpick won't come out clean). Let the cakes stand for 1 minute before unmolding.

THERE COMES A TIME
IN EVERY WOMAN'S
LIFE WHEN THE ONLY
THING THAT HELPS IS
A GLASS OF
CHAMPAGNE.

—BETTE DAVIS, IN *OLD ACQUAINTANCE*

5. Run a paring knife around the edge of each cake to loosen it from the cup, and invert onto a serving plate. Sift a light dusting of confectioners' sugar on top, then an even lighter dusting of cocoa powder. Serve each cake with a scoop of vanilla ice cream alongside.

STORE: *These cakes must be served shortly after they are made.*

CHOCOLATE ALMOND TORTE

Because it's baked gently in a water bath, this intense chocolate torte has a beautiful soft texture that almost melts in your mouth. Freshly ground lightly toasted almonds make the cake unusually moist and give it the subtle fragrance of nuts. The torte is lovely served with sweetened whipped cream and fresh raspberries, which offset the flavor of the chocolate, but if you're a chocolate purist, by all means serve it unadorned.

► MAKES ONE 9-INCH CAKE, SERVING 10

CHOCOLATE ALMOND TORTE

13 ounces (368 g) bittersweet chocolate, coarsely chopped

1 cup plus 5 tablespoons (10.5 oz/300 g) unsalted butter, cut into tablespoons

2 tablespoons (30 ml) brandy

⅔ cup (2.8 oz/80 g) slivered almonds, lightly toasted (see page 37)

1 cup (7 oz/200 g) granulated sugar, divided

¼ teaspoon salt

4 large eggs

GARNISH

Classic Whipped Cream (page 339)

Fresh raspberries

1. Position a rack in the center of the oven and preheat the oven to 350°F. Grease the bottom and sides of a 9 x 3-inch springform pan. Line the bottom of the pan with a round of parchment paper and grease the paper. Cut an 18-inch square of heavy-duty aluminum foil and wrap the foil around the outside of the pan.

2. Put the bittersweet chocolate and butter in a medium stainless steel bowl and place over a pot of barely simmering water. Heat, stirring frequently, until the chocolate and butter are completely melted. Remove the bowl from the pot and set the mixture aside to cool until tepid, then stir in the brandy.

3. Put the almonds and ¼ cup of the sugar in the bowl of a food processor and process until the almonds are finely ground. Add the salt and pulse until combined.

4. In the bowl of an electric mixer, using the whisk attachment, beat the eggs at medium speed until blended. Gradually adding the remaining ¾ cup sugar, increase the speed to high and beat until light and pale, about 4 minutes. Reduce the speed to low and add the tepid chocolate and the ground almond mixture, mixing until almost completely blended. Remove the bowl from the mixer stand and finish blending by hand with a rubber spatula.

5. Scrape the batter into the prepared pan. Place the pan in a roasting pan or large baking pan. Place the roasting pan in the oven and pour enough hot water into the pan to come almost halfway up the

sides of the springform pan. Bake the cake for 40 to 45 minutes, until a toothpick inserted in the center of the cake comes out clean, or with a few moist crumbs clinging to it. Set the pan on a wire rack and carefully loosen the foil. Let the cake cool in the pan for 30 minutes.

6. Run a knife around the sides of the pan to loosen the cake. Remove the side of the pan and carefully invert the cake onto a cardboard cake round or cake plate. Remove the bottom of the pan and the parchment round. Refrigerate the cake for at least 2 hours before serving.

7. To serve, cut the cake with a thin-bladed sharp knife, wiping the knife clean between each cut. Garnish each slice with a dollop of whipped cream and a few fresh raspberries.

STORE *in the refrigerator, loosely covered, for up to a week.*

CHOCOLATE INTENSITY

Here it is: death-by-chocolate-cake. But what a sweet way to go! This is a magical cake—unadulterated chocolate bliss. The texture is similar to that of a very creamy truffle, but even fudgier. It is critical that you use a top-quality chocolate for this recipe, such as one of the two suggested below.

➤ MAKES ONE 9-INCH CAKE, SERVING 8 TO 10

TRUFFLE CAKE

8 ounces (227 g) Scharffen Berger or Valrhona 62% cocoa bittersweet chocolate, finely chopped

1½ cups (3 sticks/12 oz/340 g) unsalted butter, cut into tablespoons

1 cup (7 oz/200 g) granulated sugar

½ cup (120 ml) brewed coffee

6 large eggs

1 teaspoon vanilla extract

⅛ teaspoon salt

1⅓ cups Bittersweet Chocolate Glaze (page 306)

MAKE THE CAKE

1. Position a rack in the center of the oven and preheat the oven to 350°F. Grease the bottom and sides of a 9-inch round cake pan. Line the bottom of the pan with a round of parchment paper and butter the paper.

2. Place the chopped chocolate in a large bowl and set aside.

3. Place the butter, sugar, and coffee in a medium saucepan and cook over medium-high heat, stirring occasionally, until the butter is melted and the mixture begins to boil. Immediately pour the hot mixture over the chopped chocolate. Let stand for 1 minute, then gently whisk until the chocolate is completely melted and the mixture is smooth.

4. In a medium bowl, whisk the eggs vigorously until the yolks and whites are completely blended. Whisk in the vanilla extract and salt. Whisk the egg mixture into the chocolate mixture until blended.

5. Pour the batter into the prepared pan. Place the pan in a roasting pan or large baking pan. Put in the oven and pour enough hot water into the pan to come halfway up the sides of the cake pan. Bake the cake in the water bath for 35 to 45 minutes, until the center is shiny but set (it should jiggle slightly). Transfer the cake pan to a wire rack and let the cake cool for 20 minutes.

6. Run a thin-bladed paring knife around the edge of the pan to loosen the cake. Place a cardboard cake round on top of the pan and invert the cake onto it. Remove the pan and carefully peel off the parchment paper. Refrigerate the cake for at least 2 hours before glazing.

GLAZE THE CAKE

7. Place the chilled cake, still on the cake round, on a wire rack set over a baking sheet. Slowly pour the hot glaze onto the center of the cake. Using a small metal offset spatula, smooth the glaze over the top and sides of the cake, letting the excess glaze drip onto the baking sheet.

8. Scrape the extra glaze from the baking sheet and put it into a small sealable plastic bag. Seal the bag and cut a tiny hole in one of the bottom corners. Gently squeeze the bag over the top of the cake, drizzling the glaze in a zigzag pattern. Refrigerate the cake for at least 1 hour before serving.

STORE *in the refrigerator, loosely covered, for up to 5 days.*

SUNKEN CHOCOLATE TORTE

This flourless torte sinks in the center as it cools, forming an indentation that is ideal for containing a sweet mountain of Kahlúa-enhanced whipped cream. Chocolate shavings make a pretty garnish, but if you're pressed for time, a light sprinkle of cocoa powder is another nice touch.

➤ MAKES ONE 9-INCH CAKE, SERVING 8

SUNKEN CHOCOLATE CAKE

9 ounces (255 g) bittersweet chocolate, coarsely chopped

½ cup (1 stick/4 oz/113 g) unsalted butter, cut into tablespoons

6 large eggs, separated, at room temperature

¼ teaspoon salt

¼ teaspoon cream of tartar

⅔ cup (4.6 oz/132 g) granulated sugar

3 tablespoons (0.8 oz/22 g) cornstarch

1 teaspoon vanilla extract

KAHLÚA WHIPPED CREAM TOPPING

1½ cups (360 ml) heavy cream

¼ cup (1 oz/29 g) confectioners' sugar

2 tablespoons (30 ml) Kahlúa

¾ teaspoon vanilla extract

MAKE THE CAKE

1. Position a rack in the center of the oven and preheat the oven to 350°F. Grease the bottom and sides of a 9 x 3-inch springform pan.

2. Melt the chocolate with the butter in the top of a double boiler over barely simmering water, stirring occasionally, until completely smooth. Remove the chocolate from the heat and set aside to cool until tepid.

3. In the bowl of an electric mixer, using the whisk attachment, beat the egg whites with the salt at medium speed until foamy. Add the cream of tartar and beat at medium-high speed until the whites just begin to form soft peaks. While continuing to beat, add the sugar 1 tablespoon at a time, then beat at high speed until stiff peaks form.

4. Remove the bowl from the mixer stand and sift the cornstarch over the beaten egg whites. Gently fold in the cornstarch. Whisk in the egg yolks one at a time. Whisk in the vanilla extract. Gently fold in the chocolate, one-third at a time.

5. Scrape the batter into the prepared pan and smooth the top. Bake the cake for 35 to 40 minutes, until a toothpick inserted into the center comes out with a few moist crumbs clinging to it. Cool the cake completely in the pan on a wire rack. The center of the cake will sink as the cake cools—this is normal.

MAKE THE TOPPING

6. In the bowl of an electric mixer, using the whisk attachment, beat the cream at high speed until the whisk begins to leave trails in the cream. Add the confectioners' sugar, Kahlúa, and vanilla extract and beat until the cream just begins to form stiff peaks.

FINISH THE CAKE

7. Remove the side of the springform pan and transfer the cake to a serving plate. Scrape the whipped cream topping over the top of the cake, mounding it in the center. Garnish the cream with grated chocolate.

STORE, *without the topping, in the refrigerator, loosely covered, for up to 5 days; with the topping, refrigerate for up to 3 hours.*

CHOCOLATE ALMOND-COCONUT CAKE

This exceptional recipe comes from talented pastry chef David DiFrancesco of The Pitcher Inn in Warren, Vermont. Reminiscent of an Almond Joy candy bar, the flourless chocolate-almond cake is topped with a chewy layer of coconut and then coated with a smooth bittersweet glaze. It's an exquisite combination that is bound to please kids and adults alike.

➤ MAKES ONE 9-INCH CAKE, SERVING 10

CHOCOLATE ALMOND CAKE

2 tablespoons (0.5 oz/15 g) all-purpose flour

½ cup plus 2 tablespoons (2 oz/57 g) Dutch-processed cocoa powder

12 ounces (1 cup plus 3 table-spoons/341 g) canned almond paste

1¼ cups (8.8 oz/250 g) granulated sugar

4 large eggs

1 cup (2 sticks/8 oz/227 g) unsalted butter, softened

1 large egg yolk

COCONUT LAYER

2⅔ cups (7.5 oz/213 g) unsweetened grated coconut (available at health food stores)

½ cup (120 ml) light corn syrup

MAKE THE CAKE

1. Position a rack in the center of the oven and preheat the oven to 350°F. Grease the bottom and sides of a 9 x 3-inch springform pan. Line the bottom of the pan with a round of parchment paper and grease the paper.

2. Sift together the flour and cocoa powder into a medium bowl. Whisk to combine, and set aside.

3. Break the almond paste into 1-inch chunks and place it in the bowl of an electric mixer. Add the sugar and 1 of the eggs and, using the paddle attachment, beat the mixture on low speed until smooth, about 1 minute. Add the softened butter and beat on medium speed until light, about 3 minutes. Add the remaining 3 eggs one at a time, beating well after each addition and scraping down the sides of the bowl as necessary. Beat in the egg yolk. At low speed, add the cocoa mixture, mixing just until blended.

4. Remove the bowl from the mixer stand and stir a few times with a rubber spatula to ensure that the batter is evenly blended. Scrape the batter into the prepared pan and smooth it into an even layer.

5. Bake the cake for 40 to 50 minutes, until the top is firm and a toothpick inserted into the center comes out with a few moist crumbs clinging to it. Cool the cake in the pan on a wire rack for 20 minutes.

1⅓ cups Bittersweet Chocolate Glaze (page 306)

Classic Whipped Cream (page 339) or Coconut Whipped Cream (page 344) for serving

6. Remove the side of the springform pan. Place a 9-inch cardboard cake round on top of the cake and invert. Remove the bottom of the pan and the parchment paper. Cool the cake completely on the wire rack.

MAKE THE COCONUT LAYER

7. Place the coconut in the bowl of a food processor and pulse until finely chopped. Add the corn syrup and pulse until the coconut is evenly moistened.

ASSEMBLE AND GLAZE THE CAKE

8. Spread the coconut mixture over the cake in an even layer. Set the cake on the wire rack, over a sheet of wax paper. Pour the warm glaze over the top of the cake and use a small offset metal spatula to smooth it evenly over the top and sides. Refrigerate the cake until the glaze is set, about 20 minutes.

9. Place the cake on a serving platter. Cut into wedges and serve with the whipped cream.

STORE *in the refrigerator, loosely covered, for up to 5 days.*

FLOURLESS CHOCOLATE RASPBERRY ROLL

This flourless chocolate sponge cake is filled with a kirsch-flavored whipped cream and fresh raspberries and then rolled up jelly-roll style. While the sophisticated dark chocolate glaze and white chocolate drizzle give the cake a sleek look, it's also quite delicious unglazed—just dust the top with sifted confectioners' sugar. One caveat: this cake should be served the day it is made.

▶ MAKES ONE 9-INCH ROLL, SERVING 8
▶ SPECIAL EQUIPMENT: ONE 10½ X 15½-INCH JELLY-ROLL PAN

FLOURLESS CHOCOLATE CAKE

6 ounces (170 g) bittersweet chocolate, coarsely chopped

¼ cup (60 ml) water

5 large eggs, separated, at room temperature, plus 1 large egg

½ cup (3.5 oz/100 g) granulated sugar, divided

1 tablespoon (15 ml) vanilla extract

¼ teaspoon salt

Confectioners' sugar for dusting

RASPBERRY WHIPPED CREAM FILLING

1 cup heavy cream

2 tablespoons (0.5 oz/14 g) confectioners' sugar

1 tablespoon (15 ml) kirsch or brandy

1 teaspoon vanilla extract

One 6-ounce (170-g) container fresh raspberries

MAKE THE CAKE

1. Position a rack in the center of the oven and preheat the oven to 350°F. Line the bottom of a 10½ x 15½-inch jelly-roll pan with aluminum foil. Grease the foil and the sides of the pan. Dust the pan with flour.

2. Melt the bittersweet chocolate with the water in the top of a double boiler over barely simmering water, stirring occasionally. Remove the chocolate from the heat and set aside to cool until tepid.

3. In the bowl of an electric mixer, using the whisk attachment, beat the egg yolks and whole egg together at medium speed until blended. Gradually add ¼ cup of the sugar, the vanilla extract, and salt and beat at high speed until the mixture is pale and forms a thick ribbon when the whisk is lifted, about 4 minutes. Gently fold the yolk mixture into the chocolate mixture, and set aside.

4. In a clean mixer bowl, using the clean whisk attachment, beat the egg whites at medium-high speed until they begin to turn opaque. Gradually add the remaining ¼ cup sugar and beat at high speed until the whites form stiff peaks. Gently fold one-third of the whites into the chocolate mixture. Fold in the remaining whites. Scrape the batter into the prepared pan and smooth it into an even layer.

1⅓ cups Bittersweet Chocolate Glaze (page 306)

WHITE CHOCOLATE DRIZZLE

2 ounces (57 g) high-quality white chocolate, finely chopped

5. Bake the cake for 12 to 15 minutes, until a tester inserted into the center comes out clean. Cool the cake in the pan on a wire rack for 10 minutes.

6. Run a thin-bladed knife around the edges of the cake to loosen it from the sides of the pan. Lightly dust a kitchen towel with sifted confectioners' sugar. Invert the cake onto a large cutting board and remove the pan. Gently peel off the foil. Lay the kitchen towel, sugar side down, on the cake, place a wire rack on the towel, and invert the cake again so that it is right side up. Starting with a long side, roll the cake up, with the towel, into a loose cylinder. Let cool completely.

MAKE THE FILLING AND ASSEMBLE THE CAKE

7. In the bowl of an electric mixer, using the whisk attachment, beat the heavy cream with the confectioners' sugar, kirsch or brandy, and vanilla extract at high speed until stiff peaks just begin to form.

8. Set aside 8 of the nicest raspberries for garnish. Stir the remaining raspberries into the whipped cream.

9. Gently unroll the cooled cake. Spread the whipped cream filling over the cake, leaving a ½-inch border on all sides. Carefully reroll the cake, using the kitchen towel to nudge it along. Using a serrated knife, trim off the crusty ends of the cake. Carefully transfer the roll to a wire rack, seam side down, and refrigerate while you prepare the glaze.

GLAZE AND GARNISH THE CAKE

10. Place the wire rack with the cake on it on a baking sheet. Pour the glaze over the cake, covering it completely. Return the cake to the refrigerator for 10 minutes to set the glaze.

11. Melt the white chocolate in the top of a double boiler over barely simmering water, stirring frequently. Scrape the melted chocolate into a small sealable plastic bag and seal the bag. Using scissors, snip a tiny hole in one of the bottom corners of the bag.

Drizzle the white chocolate over the top of the cake in a diagonal zigzag pattern. Garnish the top of the cake with the reserved raspberries. Serve the cake immediately, or refrigerate.

STORE *loosely covered in the refrigerator for up to 8 hours.*

CHOCOLATE VALENTINE CAKE

The secret ingredient in this pretty heart-shaped cake is whipped cream, which replaces butter as the fat and gives it an airy texture. The cake is baked in a water bath, insulating it from direct heat, and making it as creamy around the edges as it is in the center. After baking, the cake is coated in a dark chocolate glaze and then drizzled with white chocolate tinted pastel pink, making it the ultimate chocolate Valentine's dessert. If you're not in the mood for love, just for chocolate, the cake can also be made in a standard 9-inch round cake pan and drizzled with plain white chocolate.

➤ MAKES ONE 9-INCH CAKE, SERVING 10
➤ SPECIAL EQUIPMENT: 9-INCH HEART-SHAPED PAN

FLOURLESS CHOCOLATE CAKE

10 ounces (283 g) bittersweet chocolate, coarsely chopped

⅓ cup (80 ml) water

5 large eggs

½ cup (3.5 oz/100 g) granulated sugar

¼ teaspoon salt

⅔ cup (160 ml) heavy cream

RASPBERRY LAYER

¼ cup (2.7 oz/77 g) seedless raspberry jam (not preserves)

⅔ cup Bittersweet Chocolate Glaze (page 306)

WHITE CHOCOLATE DRIZZLE

1 ounce (28 g) high-quality white chocolate, finely chopped

Pink paste food coloring

MAKE THE CAKE

1. Position a rack in the center of the oven and preheat the oven to 350°F. Place a 9-inch heart-shaped pan on a piece of parchment paper and trace around it with a pencil. Cut out the heart shape from the parchment paper. Grease the bottom and sides of the pan. Line the bottom of the pan with the parchment heart, with the pencil lines down. Grease the paper.

2. Put the chocolate and water in a medium stainless steel bowl and place the bowl over a pot of barely simmering water. Heat, stirring frequently, until the chocolate is completely melted and the mixture is smooth. Remove the bowl from the pot and set the chocolate aside to cool until tepid.

3. In the bowl of an electric mixer, whisk together the eggs, sugar, and salt by hand. Set the bowl over the same saucepan of simmering water, making sure that the bottom of the bowl does not touch the water, and heat the mixture, whisking constantly, until the eggs are warm. Transfer the bowl to the mixer stand and, using the whisk attachment, beat on high speed until the mixture has tripled in volume, about 3 minutes.

4. In a clean mixer bowl, using the clean whisk attachment, beat the heavy cream at high speed until firm peaks just begin to form.

5. Using a rubber spatula, gently fold the cooled chocolate into the egg mixture. Fold in the whipped cream.

6. Scrape the batter into the prepared pan and place the pan in a roasting pan or larger baking pan. Place the roasting pan in the oven and pour enough very hot water into the pan so that it comes halfway up the sides of the cake pan. Bake the cake for 45 to 52 minutes, until a toothpick inserted into the center comes out clean. Transfer the pan to a wire rack and let the cake cool in the pan for 25 minutes.

7. Run a paring knife around the edge of the pan to loosen the cake, and carefully invert the cake onto the wire rack. Cool completely, then refrigerate the cake for 2 hours (if your wire rack doesn't fit in the refrigerator, very carefully—the cake is quite delicate at this point—slide the cake onto a cardboard cake round).

GLAZE THE CAKE

8. Place the cake on a cake round if it is not already on one. Set the cake on a wire rack over a baking sheet. Using a small offset metal spatula, spread the raspberry jam evenly over the top and sides of the cake. Pour the warm glaze on top of the cake and, using the clean spatula, spread it evenly over the top and sides, covering it completely. Refrigerate the cake for at least 30 minutes.

FINISH THE CAKE

9. Put the white chocolate in a small stainless steel bowl and place the bowl over a pot of barely simmering water. Heat, stirring frequently, until the chocolate is completely melted. Remove the chocolate from the heat.

10. Put a tiny dab of pink paste food coloring on the tip of a toothpick and add it to the white chocolate. Whisk the chocolate to blend in the color. The chocolate should be a pretty pastel pink color—don't add too much food coloring. Scrape the chocolate into a small parchment paper cone or into a small sealable plastic bag. If using the bag, seal it and snip a tiny hole in one of the bottom corners. Remove the cake from the refrigerator and drizzle the chocolate in a diagonal zigzag pattern over the top.

11. Refrigerate the cake for at least 20 minutes to set the chocolate.

12. Let the cake stand at room temperature for 30 minutes before serving.

STORE *in the refrigerator, loosely covered, for up to 5 days.*

11

CHEESECAKES

RICOTTA TORTE • CLASSIC NEW YORK CHEESECAKE • RICH CHOCOLATE CHEESECAKE • CHERRY-TOPPED CHEESECAKE CUPS • CREAMY PUMPKIN CHEESECAKE WITH GINGER-PECAN CRUST • LEMON SOUFFLÉ CHEESECAKE WITH BLUEBERRY TOPPING • HAZELNUT VANILLA CHEESECAKE • APPLE CHEESECAKE BRÛLÉE • WHITE CHOCOLATE PEACH CHEESECAKE • GOAT CHEESE CHEESECAKE WITH FIG TOPPING • RASPBERRY-TOPPED LEMON CHEESECAKE • MARBLED MASCARPONE CHEESECAKE • BROWNIE LATTE CHEESECAKE

M ore of a dense, rich custard than a cake, cheesecake occupies a lofty status in the dessert world. Cheesecakes, in one form or another, are ubiquitous on dessert menus across the country. They first became popular in America in the late nineteenth century, after a couple of dairy farmers from upstate New York developed a rich, cream-based cheese inspired by French Neufchâtel. Recipes for a cake that showcased its richness soon appeared, and an American dessert classic was born. Less popular but equally deserving are cheesecakes made with ricotta or cottage cheese, which produces a less dense version of the standard cream cheese cake.

My usual preference is to bake cheesecakes in a water bath, which insulates the delicate custard-like filling from direct heat and allows the center and edges of the cake to bake at the same rate. The technique produces a cake with an ultra-creamy texture and eliminates the problem of cracking on top of the cake. To ensure that water from the bath does not seep into the foil and make the crust soggy, it is crucial that you wrap the pan properly before baking. Use heavy-duty aluminum foil, which comes in extra-wide rolls and can be wrapped around the springform pan without any seams.

I've also included a few cheesecakes that are baked without a water bath, including Classic New York Cheesecake (page 218) and Ricotta Torte (page 217). The Classic New York Cheesecake is baked first at a surprisingly high temperature for a short time, to brown the surface, then at a very low temperature for a long period of time, for an ultra-creamy interior. The Ricotta Torte is baked like a conventional cake, at moderate heat for a relatively short time. Because the texture of ricotta cheese is so much lighter than cream cheese, the resulting cake is remarkably light and airy.

Whichever cheesecake you choose, its texture and flavor will usually benefit from thorough chilling. Follow the recommendations for refrigeration in each recipe and then allow time for the cake to stand at room temperature before serving. This will soften its texture and bring out the subtle flavor nuances.

RICOTTA TORTE

This Italian-style cheesecake has a rustic look and an ultra-light texture. It is best served slightly warm with a dollop of whipped cream. For the creamiest texture and richest flavor, seek out fresh whole-milk ricotta from an Italian market.

➤ MAKES ONE 9-INCH CAKE, SERVING 10

⅔ cup (2.8 oz/80 g) amaretti cookie or almond biscotti crumbs, divided

2 cups (1 lb/454 g) whole-milk ricotta cheese (preferably fresh)

¼ cup (2.1 oz/60 g) sour cream

6 large eggs, separated, at room temperature

¾ cup (5.3 oz/150 g) granulated sugar, divided

2 tablespoons (0.5 oz/15 g) all-purpose flour

1 teaspoon vanilla extract

1 tablespoon (15 ml) amaretto or ¼ teaspoon almond extract

1 teaspoon finely grated orange zest

⅛ teaspoon salt

¼ teaspoon cream of tartar

1. Position a rack in the center of the oven and preheat the oven to 350°F. Grease the bottom and sides of a 9 x 3-inch springform pan. Sprinkle the bottom of the pan with ⅓ cup of the cookie crumbs.

2. In the bowl of a food processor, combine the ricotta cheese and sour cream and process until smooth. Add the egg yolks and ½ cup of the sugar and process until well blended. Add the flour, vanilla extract, amaretto or almond extract, orange zest, and salt and process until blended. Transfer the mixture to a large bowl.

3. In the bowl of an electric mixer, using the whisk attachment, beat the egg whites and cream of tartar at medium-high speed until soft peaks begin to form. Gradually add the remaining ¼ cup sugar and beat at high speed until the whites form stiff, shiny peaks. Gently fold one-third of the whites into the ricotta mixture. Fold in the remaining whites in two more additions.

4. Scrape the batter into the prepared pan and smooth the top. Sprinkle the remaining ⅓ cup cookie crumbs over the top.

5. Place the pan on a baking sheet and bake the cake for 35 to 45 minutes, until the top is browned and cracked and the center jiggles but is not liquid. Transfer the pan to a wire rack and cool for 30 minutes.

6. Run a thin knife around the edge of the pan to loosen the cake. Remove the side of the pan and cool cake until just slightly warm.

7. To serve, slice the cake using a thin-bladed sharp knife.

STORE *in the refrigerator, covered, for up to 3 days.*

CLASSIC NEW YORK CHEESECAKE

The densest, richest, and tallest of cheesecakes, New York Cheesecake is much like the city for which it's named. This cheesecake has more cream cheese than most, and it is not baked in a water bath; instead, it is baked in an unorthodox way—first at a very high temperature for 10 minutes, then at a very low temperature for 55 minutes. The high temperature ensures a golden brown top and a nice rise, while the low temperature results in a creamy interior. Because the cake isn't insulated by water, though, the top is more vulnerable to cracking. Try not to open the oven door while it's baking, as drafts encourage cracks to form, and follow the instructions for gradual cooling. But even if you do get a few cracks on top, this will not detract from the taste of this superlative cheesecake.

➤ MAKES ONE 9-INCH CAKE, SERVING 16 TO 20

GRAHAM CRACKER CRUST

1¼ cups (5 oz/142 g) graham cracker crumbs

3 tablespoons (1.3 oz/37 g) granulated sugar

4 tablespoons (2 oz/57 g) unsalted butter, melted

FILLING

2½ pounds (1.13 kg) cream cheese, softened

1⅔ cups (11.7 oz/332 g) granulated sugar

2 tablespoons (0.5 oz/15 g) cornstarch

5 large eggs

2 large egg yolks

½ cup (120 ml) heavy cream

1 teaspoon finely grated lemon zest

1 teaspoon vanilla extract

MAKE THE CRUST

1. Position a rack in the center of the oven and preheat the oven to 350°F. Grease the bottom and sides of a 9 x 3-inch springform pan.

2. In a medium bowl, combine the graham cracker crumbs, sugar, and melted butter. Pat the mixture into the bottom of the prepared pan. Bake the crust for 8 minutes, or until lightly browned.

3. Set the pan on a wire rack and cool the crust completely. Increase the oven temperature to 450°F.

MAKE THE FILLING

4. In the bowl of an electric mixer, using the paddle attachment, beat the cream cheese at low speed until creamy and lump-free, about 2 minutes, scraping down the sides of the bowl as necessary. Gradually add the sugar and beat until blended. Add the cornstarch and mix until blended. Add the eggs and yolks one at a time, mixing well after each addition and scraping down the sides of the bowl as necessary. Add the heavy cream, lemon zest, and vanilla extract and mix until blended. Remove the bowl from the mixer stand and scrape the bottom of the bowl with a rubber spatula to ensure that the batter is smooth.

5. Scrape the batter into the prepared pan (it will almost fill the pan). Bake the cake for 10 minutes. Without opening the oven door, reduce the temperature to 200°F, and bake the cake for another 55 minutes, or until it has risen and is golden brown around the edges. Turn the oven off, prop the oven door open using a wooden spoon, and let the cake cool in the oven for 1 hour (this gradual cooling will help to prevent the top of the cake from cracking).

6. Transfer the cake to a wire rack and cool for 15 minutes. Run a thin knife between the cake and the side of the pan to loosen the cake, and let cool completely.

7. Refrigerate the cheesecake for at least 4 hours before serving.

8. To serve, remove side of pan and slice the cake with a thin-bladed sharp knife, wiping the knife clean between each cut.

STORE *in the refrigerator, loosely covered, for up to 5 days.*

RICH CHOCOLATE CHEESECAKE

Shamelessly rich and indulgent, this cake is a chocolate-lover's dream come true. The combination of bittersweet chocolate and cocoa powder yields a cheesecake with a real chocolate kick, and a shot of Kahlúa heightens its intensity. A key factor in the success of this recipe is to make sure that the cream cheese, eggs, and heavy cream are not cold (cool is OK), as that would cause the melted chocolate to harden up in the batter.

➤ MAKES ONE 9-INCH CAKE, SERVING 12

CHOCOLATE CRUMB CRUST

1½ cups (6.3 oz/180 g) Nabisco's Famous Chocolate Wafer crumbs

4 tablespoons (2 oz/57 g) unsalted butter, melted

CHOCOLATE FILLING

12 ounces (340 g) bittersweet chocolate, coarsely chopped

1½ pounds (680 g) cream cheese, softened

1 cup (7 oz/200 g) granulated sugar, divided

3 tablespoons (0.5 oz/15 g) natural (not Dutch-processed) cocoa powder

4 large eggs, at room temperature

¾ cup (180 ml) heavy cream (cool but not cold)

2 teaspoons vanilla extract

2 tablespoons (30 ml) Kahlúa or Cognac

MAKE THE CRUST

1. Position a rack in the center of the oven and preheat the oven to 350°F. Grease the bottom and sides of a 9 x 3-inch springform pan. Cut an 18-inch square of heavy-duty aluminum foil and wrap the foil around the outside of the pan.

2. In a medium bowl, combine the chocolate wafer crumbs and melted butter. Pat the mixture into the bottom of the prepared pan. Bake the crust for 8 minutes, until set.

3. Set the pan on a wire rack and cool the crust completely. Leave the oven on.

MAKE THE FILLING

4. Melt the chocolate in the top of a double boiler over barely simmering water, stirring occasionally. Remove the pan from the heat, leaving the chocolate over the hot water.

5. In the bowl of an electric mixer, using the paddle attachment, beat the cream cheese at medium-low speed until creamy and lump-free, about 2 minutes, scraping down the sides of the bowl as necessary. Gradually add ¼ cup of the sugar and beat until blended. Add the cocoa powder and mix until blended. Remove the bowl from the mixer stand.

6. In a clean mixer bowl, using the whisk attachment, beat the eggs at medium speed until blended, about 1 minute. Gradually

THE ONLY WAY TO
KEEP YOUR HEALTH IS
TO EAT WHAT YOU
DON'T WANT, DRINK
WHAT YOU DON'T
LIKE, AND DO WHAT
YOU'D RATHER NOT.
—MARK TWAIN

add the remaining ¾ cup sugar and beat at high speed until tripled in volume, about 2 minutes. Remove the bowl and whisk from the mixer stand and replace them with the bowl containing the cream cheese mixture and the paddle attachment. Mixing at low speed, gradually add the egg mixture to the cream cheese mixture, scraping down the sides of the bowl as necessary to ensure that the mixture is even-textured. Mix in the melted chocolate. Add the heavy cream, vanilla extract, and Kahlúa or Cognac and mix until blended. Remove the bowl from the mixer stand and stir the filling several times to ensure that it is evenly blended.

7. Scrape the filling over the baked crust in the pan. Place the pan in a roasting pan or large baking pan. Place the roasting pan in the oven and pour enough hot water into the pan to come 1 inch up the sides of the springform pan. Bake the cheesecake in the water bath for 65 to 75 minutes, until the center of the cake is set but slightly wobbly (the cake will set completely as it cools).

8. Remove the cake pan from the water bath. Place the pan on a wire rack and carefully loosen the foil. Immediately run the tip of a paring knife around the sides of the pan, to prevent the top from cracking. Let the cake cool completely.

9. Refrigerate the cheesecake for at least 4 hours before serving.

10. To serve, slice the cake with a thin-bladed sharp knife, wiping the knife clean between each cut.

STORE *in the refrigerator, loosely covered, for up to 5 days.*

CHERRY-TOPPED CHEESECAKE CUPS

I nspired by the classic cherry-topped diner-style cheesecake, these cheesecake cupcakes sink slightly in the center during cooling, forming a natural cupped shape that holds a bright Morello cherry topping. The flavors of the sweet cheese and the sour cherries combine beautifully, and the cupcake form allows you to enjoy these on the go.

➤ MAKES 12 CUPCAKES

GRAHAM CRACKER CRUSTS

1 cup (4.2 oz/120 g) graham cracker crumbs

1 tablespoon (0.4 oz/12 g) granulated sugar

4 tablespoons (2 oz/57 g) unsalted butter, melted

CHEESECAKE FILLING

12 ounces (340 g) cream cheese, softened

¾ cup (5.3 oz/150 g) granulated sugar

1 teaspoon vanilla extract

½ teaspoon finely grated lemon zest

⅛ teaspoon salt

2 large eggs

1 large egg yolk

½ cup (4.2 oz/121 g) sour cream

MAKE THE CRUSTS

1. Position a rack in the center of the oven and preheat the oven to 325°F. Line 12 standard muffin cups with paper liners.

2. In a medium bowl, stir together the graham cracker crumbs and sugar until blended. Stir in the melted butter. Divide the mixture among the muffin cups and, using your fingers, pat it into an even layer in the bottom of each cup.

3. Bake the crusts for 5 to 7 minutes, until very lightly browned and fragrant. Cool the crusts on a wire rack while you make the filling.

MAKE THE FILLING

4. In the bowl of an electric mixer, using the paddle attachment, beat the cream cheese at low speed until creamy and smooth, about 2 minutes. Gradually add the sugar and beat until well blended, about 1 minute. Blend in the vanilla extract, lemon zest, and salt. Add the eggs and yolk one at a time, scraping down the sides of the bowl as necessary and mixing until well blended. Add the sour cream and mix until combined. Remove the bowl from the mixer stand and stir the filling a few times by hand to make sure it is smooth and well blended.

5. Ladle the filling into the muffin cups, filling them to the top. Bake the cheesecake cups for 20 to 25 minutes, until the tops begin to crack and the centers are set. Set the pan on a wire rack and cool

One 24-ounce jar Morello cherries in light syrup (see Sources, page 366)

2 tablespoons (0.8 oz/25 g) granulated sugar

1 teaspoon freshly squeezed lemon juice

1½ teaspoons cornstarch

1 tablespoon (15 ml) cold water

½ teaspoon vanilla extract

completely (the cheesecake cups will sink slightly in the center as they cool).

MAKE THE TOPPING

6. Drain the cherries, reserving the syrup. Measure out 1¼ cups cherries and 1 cup syrup (the remaining cherries and syrup can be stored in the jar in the refrigerator for another use). Place the syrup in a small saucepan, add the sugar and lemon juice, and bring to a boil over medium-high heat. Boil the syrup until it is reduced to ¾ cup, 2 to 3 minutes. Remove the pan from the heat.

7. In a small cup, stir together the cornstarch and cold water until smooth. Whisk this mixture into the syrup and return it to medium-high heat. Heat, whisking constantly, until it comes to a boil. Boil, stirring, until thickened, about 1 minute. Remove the pan from the heat and stir in the vanilla extract and the reserved cherries. Let the topping cool for about 20 minutes.

8. Spoon several cherries and some of the syrup over each cheesecake cup. Remove the cups from the pan and refrigerate for at least 1 hour before serving.

STORE *in the refrigerator, in a covered container, for up to 3 days.*

CREAMY PUMPKIN CHEESECAKE WITH GINGER-PECAN CRUST

With a ginger-and-pecan-flavored pastry crust and a spiced pumpkin-cheese filling, this cake is a wonderful alternative to the pumpkin pie served at every Thanksgiving dinner. The recipe for sugared pumpkin seeds will yield more than you'll need as a garnish for the cake, but the seeds are wonderful as a snack on their own. Or put the extra seeds in an elegant dish and serve them alongside the cake.

➤ MAKES ONE 9-INCH CAKE, SERVING 12 TO 16

GINGER-PECAN CRUST

1 cup (4.3 oz/121 g) all-purpose flour

¼ cup (1.9 oz/54 g) firmly packed light brown sugar

⅛ teaspoon salt

⅓ cup (1.2 oz/33 g) pecans

¼ cup (1.4 oz/40 g) chopped crystallized ginger

½ cup (1 stick/4 oz/113 g) cold unsalted butter, cut into ½-inch cubes

1 tablespoon (15 ml) cold water

PUMPKIN CHEESECAKE FILLING

1 cup (240 ml) pumpkin puree

½ cup (120 ml) heavy cream

2 teaspoons vanilla extract

1 teaspoon ground cinnamon

½ teaspoon ground ginger

¼ teaspoon freshly grated nutmeg

MAKE THE CRUST

1. Position a rack in the center of the oven and preheat the oven to 350°F. Lightly grease the bottom and sides of a 9 x 3-inch spring-form pan. Cut an 18-inch square of heavy-duty aluminum foil and wrap the foil around the outside of the pan.

2. Place the flour, sugar, salt, pecans, and ginger in the bowl of a food processor and process until the pecans are finely ground. Add the butter and process until the mixture forms coarse crumbs. Add the water and process until the dough starts to come together. Press the dough into an even layer over the bottom of the prepared pan.

3. Bake the crust for 25 to 30 minutes, until it is just beginning to brown. Place the pan on a wire rack and cool completely. Reduce the oven temperature to 325°F.

MAKE THE FILLING

4. In a medium bowl, whisk together the pumpkin puree, heavy cream, vanilla extract, cinnamon, ginger, nutmeg, and salt. Set aside.

5. In the bowl of an electric mixer, using the paddle attachment, beat the cream cheese at medium-low speed until creamy, about 2 minutes, scraping down the sides of the bowl as necessary. Gradually add the sugars and beat until blended. Add the pumpkin mixture and mix until blended. Add the cornstarch and mix just until combined. Add the eggs one at a time, mixing well after each addition

¼ teaspoon salt

1¼ pounds (567 g) cream cheese, softened

½ cup (3.5 oz/100 g) granulated sugar

½ cup (3.8 oz/108 g) firmly packed light brown sugar

1 tablespoon (0.3 oz/7 g) cornstarch

4 large eggs

SUGARED PUMPKIN SEEDS

½ cup (2.5 oz/70 g) hulled raw pumpkin seeds

1 large egg white

Pinch of salt

2 tablespoons (0.9 oz/25 g) granulated sugar

⅛ teaspoon ground cinnamon

GARNISH

Classic Whipped Cream (page 339)

and scraping down the sides of the bowl as necessary.

6. Scrape the batter into the cooled crust. Place the wrapped pan in a roasting pan or large baking pan. Pour enough hot water into the roasting pan to come 1 inch up the sides of the springform pan. Bake the cheesecake in the water bath for 70 to 80 minutes, until the center of the cake is set but slightly wobbly (the cake will set completely as it cools).

7. Remove the cake pan from the water bath, place the pan on a wire rack, and carefully loosen the foil. Immediately run the tip of a paring knife around the sides of the pan, to prevent the top from cracking. Let the cake cool completely.

8. Refrigerate the cheesecake for at least 4 hours before serving.

MAKE THE PUMPKIN SEEDS

9. Position a rack in the center of the oven and preheat the oven to 325°F. Lightly grease a baking sheet.

10. Place the pumpkin seeds in a small bowl. In another small bowl, whisk the egg white just until frothy. Add just enough of the egg white to the pumpkin seeds to coat them. Add the salt, sugar, and cinnamon, and toss well to coat the seeds.

11. Spread the seeds in a single layer on the prepared baking sheet. Bake, tossing them occasionally with a metal spatula, for 15 to 20 minutes, until they begin to dry and color. Place the pan on a wire rack and cool completely.

12. With your fingers, separate any clumps of seeds. (The seeds can be stored in an airtight container for up to a week.)

13. To serve, remove the side of the pan and slice the cake with a thin-bladed sharp knife, wiping the knife clean between each cut. Garnish each slice with a dollop of whipped cream and a sprinkling of sugared pumpkin seeds.

STORE *in the refrigerator, loosely covered, for up to 5 days.*

Lemon Soufflé Cheesecake with Blueberry Topping

This delicate cake is a far cry from the dense cheesecakes found in diners and coffee shops. It is as light as a feather, with a soufflé-like texture and an ultra-lemony flavor. A juicy fresh blueberry compote is spooned over each slice before serving for a fresh late-summer flavor.

➤ MAKES ONE 9-INCH CAKE, SERVING 10 TO 12

GRAHAM CRACKER CRUST

1¼ cups (5.3 oz/150 g) graham cracker crumbs

2 tablespoons (0.88 oz/25 g) granulated sugar

4 tablespoons (2 oz/57 g) unsalted butter, melted

LEMON SOUFFLÉ FILLING

2 pounds (907 g) cream cheese, softened

1⅓ cups (9.4 oz/266 g) granulated sugar, divided

4 large eggs, separated

1 tablespoon (0.2 oz/6 g) finely grated lemon zest

¼ cup (60 ml) freshly squeezed lemon juice

1 teaspoon vanilla extract

½ cup (4.2 oz/121 g) sour cream

MAKE THE CRUST

1. Position a rack in the center of the oven and preheat the oven to 350°F. Lightly grease the bottom and sides of a 9 x 3-inch springform pan. Cut an 18-inch square of heavy-duty aluminum foil and wrap the foil around the outside of the pan.

2. In a medium bowl, combine the graham cracker crumbs, sugar, and melted butter. Pat the mixture evenly into the bottom of the prepared pan. Bake the crust for 8 minutes, or until lightly browned.

3. Set the pan on a wire rack and cool the crust completely. Reduce the oven temperature to 325°F.

MAKE THE FILLING

4. In the bowl of an electric mixer, using the paddle attachment, beat the cream cheese at medium-low speed until creamy, about 2 minutes. Gradually add 1 cup of the sugar and beat until blended. Add the egg yolks one at a time, mixing well after each addition and scraping down the sides of the bowl as necessary. Add the lemon zest, lemon juice, and vanilla extract and mix until blended. Add the sour cream and mix until combined, scraping down the sides of the bowl as necessary.

5. In a clean mixer bowl, using the whisk attachment, beat the egg whites at medium speed until they begin to turn opaque. Very gradually add the remaining ⅓ cup sugar, then increase the speed to high and beat until soft peaks form. Using a rubber spatula, gen-

3 cups (14 oz/397 g) fresh blueberries, divided

⅓ cup (2.3 oz/66 g) granulated
sugar

1 teaspoon freshly squeezed
lemon juice

tly fold one-third of the whites into the cream cheese mixture. Fold in the remaining whites in two more additions. Scrape the batter into the cooled crust and smooth the top into an even layer.

6. Place the pan in a roasting pan or large baking pan. Pour enough hot water into the roasting pan to come 1 inch up the sides of the springform pan. Bake the cheesecake in the water bath for 50 to 55 minutes, until just set.

7. Turn the oven off and prop its door ajar with a wooden spoon. Leave the cake in the oven for 1 hour to set completely.

8. Remove the cake from the water bath and set it on a wire rack to cool completely.

9. Refrigerate the cheesecake for at least 4 hours before serving.

MAKE THE TOPPING

10. In a small saucepan, combine 1 cup of the blueberries with the sugar. Cook over medium-low heat, stirring frequently, until the berries pop and release their juices, about 7 minutes. Strain the mixture through a fine-mesh sieve into a bowl, pressing down on the berries to release as much liquid as possible. Discard the berries in the sieve and let the blueberry juice cool.

11. Stir the remaining 2 cups berries and the lemon juice into the juices.

12. To serve, remove the sides of the pan, slice the cake with a thin-bladed sharp knife, wiping the knife clean between each cut. Serve each slice topped with a generous amount of blueberry topping.

STORE *in the refrigerator, loosely covered, for up to 2 days.*

Hazelnut Vanilla Cheesecake

The nutty fragrance of hazelnut praline paste blends sublimely with the floral notes of pure vanilla extract in this exceptional cheesecake. The crust is made from a pastry dough enhanced with ground toasted hazelnuts, and heavy cream adds a mellow richness to the filling. Make your own praline paste (page 333), or buy it at a Whole Foods or gourmet market or through mail-order (see Sources, page 366).

➤ MAKES ONE 9-INCH CAKE, SERVING 12 TO 14

HAZELNUT CRUST

1 cup (4.3 oz/121 g) all-purpose flour

¾ cup (3.7 oz/106 g) toasted, skinned hazelnuts (see page 37)

½ cup (2 oz/57 g) confectioners' sugar

¼ teaspoon salt

¼ teaspoon baking soda

½ cup (1 stick/4 oz/113 g) unsalted butter, cut into ½-inch chunks, softened

HAZELNUT VANILLA FILLING

1½ pounds (680 g) cream cheese, softened

1 cup (7 oz/200 g) granulated sugar

½ cup (5.4 oz/154 g) praline paste, homemade (page 333) or store-bought (see Sources, page 366)

¾ cup (180 ml) heavy cream

2 teaspoons vanilla extract

4 large eggs

MAKE THE CRUST

1. Position a rack in the center of the oven and preheat the oven to 350°F. Lightly grease the bottom and sides of a 9 x 3-inch spring-form pan. Cut an 18-inch square of heavy-duty aluminum foil and wrap the foil around the outside of the pan.

2. Place the flour, hazelnuts, confectioners' sugar, salt, and baking soda in the bowl of a food processor and process until the hazelnuts are finely ground. Add the butter pieces and process until the dough begins to come together. Press the dough into an even layer in the bottom of the prepared pan. Bake the crust for 25 to 30 minutes, until it is just beginning to brown.

3. Place the pan on a wire rack and cool completely. Reduce the oven temperature to 325°F.

MAKE THE FILLING

4. In the bowl of an electric mixer, using the paddle attachment, beat the cream cheese at medium-low speed until creamy and lump-free, about 2 minutes, scraping down the sides of the bowl as necessary. Gradually add the sugar and beat until blended. Add the praline paste and mix at low speed until well blended and no lumps remain. Add the heavy cream and vanilla extract and mix just until combined. Add the eggs one at a time, mixing well after each addition and scraping down the sides of the bowl as necessary.

5. Scrape the batter into the cooled crust. Place the pan in a roasting pan or large baking pan. Pour enough hot water into the roasting pan to come 1 inch up the sides of the springform pan. Bake the cheesecake in the water bath for 60 to 70 minutes, until the center of the cake is set but slightly wobbly (the cake will set completely as it cools).

6. Remove the cake pan from the water and immediately run the tip of a paring knife around the sides of the pan, to prevent the top from cracking. Transfer the pan to a wire rack and cool the cake completely.

7. Refrigerate the cheesecake for at least 4 hours before serving.

8. To serve, slice the cake with a thin-bladed sharp knife, wiping the knife clean between each cut.

STORE *in the refrigerator, loosely covered, for up to 5 days.*

Apple Cheesecake Brûlée

The glistening, mahogany-colored surface of this sleek cake is the same caramelized sugar glaze that tops a crème brûlée. But here it's cheesecake, not custard, that's concealed—and not a plain one, either. This cake is an ode to autumn—a fragrantly spiced cheese filling on top of tart, buttery apple slices, all encased in a cinnamon-flavored graham cracker crust. Note that you'll need a household butane or propane torch (available in gourmet kitchen supply shops or hardware stores) to make the burnt sugar topping. If you don't have one, skip the caramelized topping—this cake is still great without it.

➤ MAKES ONE 9-INCH CAKE, SERVING 12
➤ SPECIAL EQUIPMENT: HOUSEHOLD BUTANE OR PROPANE TORCH

APPLE LAYER

2 medium Granny Smith apples

1 tablespoon (15 ml) freshly squeezed lemon juice

2 tablespoons (1 oz/28 g) unsalted butter

2 tablespoons (0.9 oz/25 g) granulated sugar

3 tablespoons (45 ml) heavy cream

CINNAMON GRAHAM CRACKER CRUST

1¼ cups (5.3 oz/150 g) cinnamon graham cracker crumbs

3 tablespoons (1.3 oz/37 g) granulated sugar

4 tablespoons (2 oz/57 g) unsalted butter, melted

CREAM CHEESE FILLING

1½ pounds (680 g) cream cheese, softened

1. Position a rack in the center of the oven and preheat the oven to 350°F. Grease the bottom and sides of a 9 x 3-inch springform pan. Cut an 18-inch square of heavy-duty aluminum foil and wrap the foil around the outside of the pan.

MAKE THE APPLE LAYER

2. Peel and core the apples and slice them in half. Cut them into ¼-inch slices and place them in a bowl with the lemon juice, tossing the slices so that they are evenly coated.

3. Melt the butter in a large skillet over medium-high heat. When the butter is bubbling, add the apples and sauté for 2 minutes. Sprinkle the sugar over the apples and continue to cook, stirring the apples frequently, until they are nicely browned, about 5 minutes. Add the cream and continue to cook until the apples are tender, about 10 minutes. Remove the skillet from the heat and set the apples aside to cool.

MAKE THE CRUST

4. In a medium bowl, combine the cracker crumbs, sugar, and melted butter. Pat the mixture evenly into the bottom of the prepared pan. Bake the crust for 8 minutes.

5. Set the pan on a wire rack and cool the crust completely. Reduce the oven temperature to 325°F.

1½ cups (10.5 oz/300 g) granulated sugar

2 teaspoons vanilla extract

Pinch of salt

¼ teaspoon ground cinnamon

¼ teaspoon ground ginger

½ cup (4.2 oz/121 g) sour cream, at room temperature

1 tablespoon (0.3 oz/7 g) cornstarch

4 large eggs, at room temperature

BRÛLÉE TOPPING

1½ tablespoons (0.7 oz/19 g) granulated sugar

6. When the apples are cool, arrange a tight circle of slices, without overlapping them, around the edge of the pan, on top of the crust. Arrange another circle of slices in the center, covering the crust completely. (If you have any apple slices left over, save them for garnish.)

MAKE THE FILLING

7. In the bowl of an electric mixer, using the paddle attachment, beat the cream cheese at medium-low speed until creamy and smooth, about 2 minutes. Gradually add the sugar and beat until blended. Add the vanilla extract, salt, cinnamon, ginger, sour cream, and cornstarch and mix until well blended. At low speed, add the eggs one at a time, mixing well after each addition and scraping down the sides of the bowl with a rubber spatula as needed.

8. Scrape the batter over the apple layer. Place the pan in a roasting pan or large baking pan. Pour enough hot water into the roasting pan to come about 1 inch up the side of the springform pan. Bake the cake in the water bath for 70 to 80 minutes, until the center is set but slightly wobbly (the cake will continue to set up as it cools). Remove the pan from the water bath and set it on a wire rack to cool completely.

9. Refrigerate the cheesecake for at least 4 hours before caramelizing the top.

MAKE THE TOPPING

10. Run a thin-bladed knife between the edge of the pan and the cake to loosen it. Remove the side of the pan. Sprinkle the sugar over the top of the cake, covering it with a very thin, even layer. Caramelize the sugar using a butane or propane torch, holding it about 2 inches from the surface of the cake and slowly moving it over the top until the sugar melts and turns golden brown (the sugar will not brown evenly; be patient—this process can take a while, depending on what kind of torch you use).

11. Serve the cake immediately, or refrigerate for up to an hour before serving. Slice the cake with a thin-bladed knife, dipping the knife in hot water and drying it before each cut.

STORE *without the caramelized sugar topping, in the refrigerator, loosely covered, for up to 5 days; with the topping, refrigerate for up to 1 hour.*

preceding page: BANANA CAKE WITH CARAMEL ESPRESSO FROSTING (PAGES 156–157) *left:* YOGURT MOUSSE CAKE WITH HONEYED RASPBERRIES AND MINT SYRUP (PAGES 259–261) *below:* APPLE CAKE WITH MAPLE FROSTING (PAGE 175) *bottom:* FIG AND MARSALA WINE CAKE (PAGES 182–183) *right:* CREAMY PUMPKIN CHEESECAKE WITH GINGER-PECAN CRUST (PAGES 224–225)

left: Chocolate Guinness Cake (pages 130–131) *below:* Individual Glazed Chocolate Buttermilk Cakes (pages 142–143) *bottom:* Sticky Toffee Pudding Cake (pages 136–137) *right:* White Chocolate Strawberry Meringue Cake (pages 292–293)

left: Rich Marble Pound Cake
with Chocolate Glaze (pages
102–103) *below:* Pumpkin Walnut
Cake (page 132) *bottom:* Lemon
Mousse Cake with Fresh
Raspberries (pages 264–266) *right:*
Tiramisu Cake (pages 250–251)

left: Bittersweet Chocolate Mousse Cake (pages 246–247) *below:* Chocolate Walnut Torte with Cognac Cream (pages 161–163) *bottom:* Tres Leches Cake (pages 134–135)

WHITE CHOCOLATE PEACH CHEESECAKE

Adding white chocolate to cheesecake may seem like gilding the lily, but in this case, it makes a good thing even better. The result is a cake that is creamier and a little less tangy than a standard cheesecake. For the peach topping, seek out perfectly ripe white peaches. If you can't find them, use ripe nectarines or raspberries or blueberries.

➤ Makes one 9-inch cheesecake, serving 12

PASTRY CRUST

¾ cup (3.2 oz/91 g) all-purpose flour

¼ cup (1.1 oz/31 g) whole wheat flour

2 tablespoons (0.88 oz/25 g) granulated sugar

2 tablespoons (0.9 oz/27 g) firmly packed dark brown sugar

⅛ teaspoon salt

⅛ teaspoon ground ginger

⅛ teaspoon ground cinnamon

½ cup (1 stick/4 oz/113 g) unsalted butter, cut into ½-inch cubes and chilled

1 tablespoon (15 ml) cold water

WHITE CHOCOLATE CHEESECAKE FILLING

7 ounces (200 g) high-quality white chocolate, finely chopped

1½ pounds (680 g) cream cheese, softened

½ cup (3.5 oz/100 g) granulated sugar

MAKE THE CRUST

1. Position a rack in the center of the oven and preheat the oven to 350°F. Lightly grease the bottom and sides of a 9 x 3-inch springform pan. Cut an 18-inch square of heavy-duty aluminum foil and wrap the foil around the outside of the pan.

2. Place the flours, sugars, salt, ginger, and cinnamon in the bowl of a food processor and process until blended. Add the butter and process until the mixture forms coarse crumbs. Add the water and process until the dough starts to come together. Press the dough into an even layer over the bottom of the prepared pan.

3. Bake the crust for 25 to 30 minutes, until it is just beginning to brown. Place the pan on a wire rack to cool completely. Reduce the oven temperature to 325°F.

MAKE THE FILLING

4. Place the white chocolate in a stainless steel bowl and set the bowl over a medium saucepan filled one-third of the way with barely simmering water. Heat the chocolate, stirring frequently, until it is completely melted and smooth. Remove the bowl from the saucepan and let the chocolate cool until tepid.

1½ teaspoons vanilla extract

1 teaspoon finely grated lemon zest

4 large eggs

½ cup (4.2 oz/121 g) sour cream

2 medium-sized ripe peaches

⅓ cup (3.6 oz/103 g) apricot preserves

1 tablespoon (15 ml) water

5. In the bowl of an electric mixer, using the paddle attachment, beat the cream cheese at medium-low speed until creamy, about 2 minutes, scraping down the sides of the bowl as necessary. Gradually add the sugar and beat until blended. Mix in the vanilla extract and lemon zest. Add the eggs one at a time, mixing well after each addition and scraping down the sides of the bowl as necessary. Add the sour cream and mix until blended. Add the tepid white chocolate and mix until blended.

6. Scrape the batter into the cooled crust. Place the pan in a roasting pan or large baking pan. Pour enough hot water into the roasting pan to come 1 inch up the sides of the springform pan. Bake the cheesecake in the water bath for 65 to 75 minutes, until the top of the cake is set but slightly wobbly (the cake will set completely as it cools).

7. Remove the cake pan from the water bath, transfer to a wire rack, and carefully loosen the foil. Immediately run the tip of a paring knife around the sides of the pan, to prevent the top from cracking. Let the cake cool completely.

8. Refrigerate the cheesecake for at least 4 hours before making the topping.

MAKE THE TOPPING

9. Cut the peaches in half and discard the pits. Slice the peach halves about ⅛ inch thick. Arrange a circle of the peach slices, overlapping them slightly, around the edge of the chilled cheesecake. Arrange another circle of wedges in the center, facing the opposite direction, covering the cheesecake completely.

10. Pass the apricot preserves through a fine-mesh strainer into a small saucepan. Stir in the water and bring to a boil over medium heat, stirring constantly. Remove the pan from the heat and, using a pastry brush, brush the tops of the peaches with the hot glaze.

11. Refrigerate the cake for at least 1 hour before serving.

12. To serve, slice the cheesecake with a sharp thin-bladed knife, dipping the blade in hot water and wiping it dry after each slice.

STORE *without the topping, in the refrigerator, covered, for up to 5 days; with the topping, refrigerate, loosely covered, for up to 8 hours.*

GOAT CHEESE CHEESECAKE WITH FIG TOPPING

The idea of making goat cheese the star ingredient of a cake might scare off some conventionally minded bakers, but the truth is that when it is used along with American-style cream cheese, it yields an unbelievably creamy cheesecake with a very mild but intriguing flavor. A topping of honey-drizzled fresh figs adds a sweet, musky finish, and a sprinkle of toasted almonds contributes crunch. Make sure to use a mild, soft goat cheese for this recipe, such as Montrachet, not a hard aged one.

➤ MAKES ONE 9-INCH CAKE, SERVING 10 TO 12

HONEY GRAHAM CRUST

½ cup (1.5 oz/42 g) sliced blanched almonds

1 cup (4.2 oz/120 g) honey graham cracker crumbs

3 tablespoons (1.3 oz/37 g) granulated sugar

4 tablespoons (2 oz/57 g) unsalted butter, melted

GOAT CHEESE FILLING

1 pound (454 g) cream cheese, softened

8 ounces (227 g) soft goat cheese

¾ cup (5.3 oz/150 g) granulated sugar

2 tablespoons (30 ml) honey

4 large eggs

2 teaspoons finely grated lemon zest

1½ teaspoons vanilla extract

1 cup (8.5 oz/242 g) sour cream

MAKE THE CRUST

1. Position a rack in the center of the oven and preheat the oven to 350°F. Grease the bottom and sides of a 9 x 3-inch springform pan. Cut an 18-inch square of heavy-duty aluminum foil and wrap the foil around the outside of the pan.

2. Place the almonds in the bowl of a food processor and process until finely ground. Transfer to a medium bowl, add the graham cracker crumbs and sugar, and stir until well blended. Add the melted butter and stir until blended. Pat the mixture into the bottom of the prepared pan. Bake the crust for 8 minutes, or until lightly browned.

3. Set the pan on a wire rack and cool the crust completely. Reduce the oven temperature to 300°F.

MAKE THE FILLING

4. In the bowl of an electric mixer, using the paddle attachment, beat the cream cheese and goat cheese at medium-low speed until creamy, about 1½ minutes. Gradually add the sugar and mix at medium speed until blended. Mix in the honey. Add the eggs one at a time, beating well after each addition and scraping down the sides of the bowl with a rubber spatula as necessary. Add the lemon zest, vanilla extract, and sour cream and mix until combined. Remove the bowl from the mixer stand and stir the batter a few times with the rubber spatula to make sure it is evenly blended.

1 pint (480 ml) fresh figs, cut lengthwise into quarters

2 tablespoons (30 ml) honey

¼ cup (0.8 oz/21 g) sliced blanched almonds, lightly toasted (see page 36)

5. Scrape the batter over the cooled crust and smooth the top. Place the pan in a roasting pan or large baking pan. Pour enough water into the roasting pan to come about 1 inch up the sides of the cake pan. Bake the cake in the water bath for 60 to 70 minutes, until the cake is just set in the center but slightly wobbly (the cake will set up as it cools).

6. Remove the pan from the water bath and place it on a wire rack. Run a paring knife between the cake and the side of the pan, to prevent the cake from cracking. Cool the cake completely.

7. Refrigerate the cheesecake for at least 4 hours before making the fig topping.

MAKE THE TOPPING

8. Remove the side of the springform pan. Arrange the figs cut side up and close together on top of the cake, covering it completely. Heat the honey until warm (in a small container in the microwave for 5 to 10 seconds or in a small saucepan on the stove) and drizzle it over the figs. Sprinkle the figs with the toasted almonds. Serve the cake immediately, or refrigerate for up to 4 hours.

9. To serve, slice the cake with a thin-bladed sharp knife, wiping the knife clean between each cut.

STORE *in the refrigerator, loosely covered, for up to 2 days.*

RASPBERRY-TOPPED LEMON CHEESECAKE

Though this cake is made with rich ingredients, it's got a light texture and a fresh lemon flavor. And because it doesn't require baking, it's the ideal choice for a summer dinner party dessert. If you like, you can skip the raspberry topping and serve it with Gingered Berry Compote (page 35), a refreshing accompaniment to the lemon-scented cheesecake.

➤ MAKES ONE 9-INCH CAKE, SERVING 10 TO 12

HONEY GRAHAM CRACKER CRUST

1¼ cups (5 oz/142 g) honey graham cracker crumbs

3 tablespoons (1.3 oz/37 g) granulated sugar

4 tablespoons (2 oz/57 g) unsalted butter, melted

CHEESECAKE FILLING

1 cup (240 ml) whole milk, divided

2½ teaspoons powdered gelatin

1 cup (7 oz/200 g) granulated sugar

12 ounces (340 g) cream cheese

1 cup (240 ml) heavy cream

1 cup (8.5 oz/242 g) sour cream

1 tablespoon plus 1 teaspoon (0.3 oz/8 g) finely grated lemon zest

1 teaspoon vanilla extract

MAKE THE CRUST

1. Position a rack in the center of the oven and preheat the oven to 350°F. Grease the bottom and sides of a 9 x 3-inch springform pan.

2. In a medium bowl, combine the graham cracker crumbs, sugar, and melted butter. Pat the mixture evenly into the bottom of the prepared pan. Bake the crust for 8 minutes, until lightly browned. Set the pan on a wire rack and cool the crust completely.

MAKE THE FILLING

3. Place ½ cup of the milk in a small container. Sprinkle the gelatin over the milk and set aside to soften.

4. Place the remaining ½ cup milk, the sugar, and cream cheese in a medium saucepan and cook over medium-low heat, whisking constantly, until the cream cheese melts and the mixture is smooth, about 3 minutes. Add the gelatin mixture and whisk until the gelatin is dissolved. Pour the mixture through a fine-mesh sieve into a medium bowl, and cool to room temperature.

5. In the bowl of an electric mixer, using the whisk attachment, beat the cream, sour cream, lemon zest, and vanilla extract at high speed until the mixture just begins to form soft peaks. At low speed, beat in the cooled cream cheese mixture. Increase the speed to medium and mix until the filling is well blended and smooth.

⅓ cup (3.7 oz/103 g) seedless raspberry jam (not preserves)

Three 6-ounce (510-g) containers fresh raspberries

GARNISH

Confectioners' sugar for dusting

6. Scrape the filling into the prepared pan, and refrigerate for at least 4 hours, until set.

MAKE THE RASPBERRY TOPPING

7. Remove the cheesecake from the refrigerator. Run a sharp thin-bladed knife under hot water and wipe it dry, then run the knife between the cake and the side of the pan to loosen the cake (run the knife under the water again a few times, wiping it dry, to keep it hot). Carefully remove the side of the springform pan. Return the cheesecake to the refrigerator while you prepare the topping.

8. In a small saucepan, bring the raspberry jam to a simmer over low heat. Cook, stirring constantly, for about 1 minute, until smooth and thickened. Remove the pan from the heat and cool to room temperature.

9. Using a pastry brush, gently brush the jam over the top of the cake, covering it completely. Starting in the center, arrange the raspberries in concentric circles over the jam, covering the top of the cake. Refrigerate for at least 1 hour before serving.

10. Thirty minutes before serving, remove the cheesecake from the refrigerator. To serve, slice the cheesecake with a sharp thin-bladed knife, dipping the blade in hot water and wiping it dry after each slice. Dust the top of each slice lightly with sifted confectioners' sugar.

STORE, *without the topping, in the refrigerator, covered, for up to 5 days; with the topping, refrigerate, loosely covered, for up to 8 hours.*

RASPBERRIES ARE BEST NOT WASHED. AFTER ALL, ONE MUST HAVE FAITH IN SOMETHING.
—ANN BATCHELDER

Marbled Mascarpone Cheesecake

Mascarpone is an indulgently rich cream cheese from the Lombardy region of Italy. It has a smooth, silky texture and a mildly tangy flavor, which makes it an ideal cheesecake enhancer. Here it's paired with American-style cream cheese in a luscious black-and-white marbled cake with a delicate chocolate biscotti crust. Benissimo.

➤ Makes one 9-inch cake, serving 12

BISCOTTI CRUST

⅓ cup (1.4 oz/40 g) chocolate biscotti crumbs (crushed in a food processor)

MARBLED MASCARPONE FILLING

7 ounces (200 g) bittersweet chocolate, coarsely chopped

⅓ cup (80 ml) water

1½ pounds (680 g) cream cheese, softened

1½ cups (10.5 oz/300 g) granulated sugar

5 large eggs, at room temperature

1 cup (8.5 oz/240 g) mascarpone cheese, at room temperature

2 teaspoons vanilla extract

MAKE THE CRUST

1. Position a rack in the center of the oven and preheat the oven to 325°F. Butter the bottom and sides of a 9 x 3-inch springform pan. Dust the pan with the biscotti crumbs, covering the bottom and sides. Cut an 18-inch square of heavy-duty aluminum foil and wrap the foil around the outside of the pan.

MAKE THE FILLING

2. In the top of a double boiler, melt the chocolate with the water over barely simmering water, stirring occasionally. Remove the chocolate from the heat and set aside to cool.

3. In the bowl of an electric mixer, using the paddle attachment, beat the cream cheese at medium-low speed until creamy and smooth, about 2 minutes. Gradually add the sugar and beat until blended. At low speed, add the eggs one at a time, mixing well after each addition and scraping down the sides of the bowl with a rubber spatula as needed.

4. Spoon the mascarpone cheese into a medium bowl and stir it with a wooden spoon until smooth. Stir in the vanilla extract. Stir about 1 cup of the cream cheese mixture into the mascarpone until well blended and smooth. Mixing at low speed, gradually add this mixture to the remaining batter in the bowl. Remove the bowl from the mixer stand and stir the batter with a spatula a few times to make sure it is evenly blended.

5. Stir 1½ cups of the batter into the melted chocolate. Scrape the remaining white batter into the prepared pan. Lightly spoon the chocolate batter on top of the white batter so that it is almost completely covered. Using a large spoon, pull the white batter up from the bottom of the pan (without disturbing the crumbs) to create a marbled effect; do this about ten times around the edges of the pan and in the center, so that the whole cake is marbleized (but don't overdo it, or the two batters will end up blended instead of marbleized).

6. Place the pan into a roasting pan or a large baking pan. Pour enough hot water into the larger pan to come about 1 inch up the sides of the springform pan. Bake the cake in the water bath for 70 to 75 minutes, until the center is set but slightly wobbly (the cake will continue to set up as it cools). Remove the pan from the water bath and set the pan on a wire rack to cool completely.

7. Refrigerate the cheesecake for at least 4 hours before serving.

8. To serve, slice the cake with a thin-bladed sharp knife, wiping the knife clean between each cut.

STORE *in the refrigerator, loosely covered, for up to 5 days.*

BROWNIE LATTE CHEESECAKE

C heesecake brownies have long been a hit on the bake sale circuit, and with good reason: creamy cheesecake filling and fudgy brownies are an inspired taste combination. Here's a spin on that classic, updated for the Gen-X quasi-bohemian coffee house set. First you bake a brownie layer, which forms the chocolate base. Then you pour a Kahlúa-and-espresso-flavored cheesecake filling on top and bake that. The whole thing is topped off by whipped cream and chocolate-covered espresso beans, for a killer dessert that is bound to cause a stampede at your next bake sale.

➤ MAKES ONE 9-INCH CAKE, SERVING 12 TO 16

BROWNIE BASE

4 ounces (113 g) bittersweet chocolate, coarsely chopped

½ cup (1 stick/4 oz/113 g) unsalted butter, cut into table-spoons

1 tablespoon (0.1 oz/3 g) instant espresso powder

1 teaspoon vanilla extract

¼ teaspoon salt

1 cup (7 oz/200 g) granulated sugar

2 large eggs

½ cup (2.1 oz/60 g) all-purpose flour

LATTE CHEESECAKE FILLING

1½ pounds (680 g) cream cheese, softened

1½ cups (10.5 oz/300 g) granu-lated sugar

1 tablespoon (15 ml) vanilla extract

2 teaspoons espresso powder, dis-solved in 1 tablespoon hot water

MAKE THE BROWNIE BASE

1. Position a rack in the center of the oven and preheat the oven to 325°F. Lightly grease the bottom and sides of a 9 x 3-inch spring-form pan. Cut an 18-inch square of heavy-duty aluminum foil and wrap the foil around the outside of the pan.

2. In the top of a double boiler, melt the chocolate with the butter over barely simmering water, stirring occasionally. Transfer the mixture to a medium bowl and stir in the espresso powder, vanilla extract, and salt. Whisk in the sugar until combined. Whisk in the eggs one at a time, until blended. Stir in the flour until no traces remain.

3. Scrape the batter into the prepared pan and smooth it into an even layer. Bake the brownie for 25 to 30 minutes, until a tooth-pick inserted into the center comes out with a few moist crumbs clinging to it. Place the pan on a wire rack and let cool while you make the filling. Leave the oven on.

MAKE THE FILLING

4. In the bowl of an electric mixer, using the paddle attachment, beat the cream cheese at medium-low speed until creamy and smooth, about 2 minutes. Gradually add the sugar and beat until blended. Add the vanilla extract, espresso mixture, Kahlúa, salt, sour cream, and cornstarch and mix until well blended. At low speed, add the eggs one at a time, mixing well after each addition

2 tablespoons (30 ml) Kahlúa

Pinch of salt

½ cup (4.2 oz/121 g) sour cream

1 tablespoon (0.3 oz/7 g) cornstarch

4 large eggs

GARNISH

Classic Whipped Cream (page 339)

Chocolate-covered espresso beans

and scraping down the sides of the bowl with a rubber spatula as needed.

5. Scrape the batter onto the brownie base. Place the pan in a roasting pan or large baking pan. Pour enough hot water into the roasting pan to come about 1 inch up the sides of the springform pan. Bake the cake in the water bath for 70 to 80 minutes, until the center is set but slightly wobbly (the cake will continue to set up as it cools). Remove the pan from the water bath and cool the cake completely in the pan on a wire rack.

6. Refrigerate the cheesecake for at least 4 hours before serving.

7. To serve, slice the cake with a thin-bladed sharp knife, wiping the knife clean between each cut. Garnish each slice with a dollop of whipped cream and a few chocolate-covered espresso beans.

STORE *in the refrigerator, loosely covered, for up to 5 days.*

12

MOUSSE AND
ICE CREAM
CAKES

BITTERSWEET CHOCOLATE MOUSSE CAKE • WHITE CHOCOLATE ESPRESSO ICEBOX CAKE • TIRAMISU CAKE • BANANA WALNUT CHIFFON CAKE WITH MAPLE MOUSSE • CHOCOLATE COCONUT MOUSSE CAKE • CHOCOLATE MOUSSE LAYER CAKE • YOGURT MOUSSE CAKE WITH HONEYED RASPBERRIES AND MINT SYRUP • CHOCOLATE PEANUT BUTTER MOUSSE CAKE • LEMON MOUSSE CAKE WITH FRESH RASPBERRIES • ORANGES AND CREAM CAKE • MILK CHOCOLATE–ESPRESSO MOUSSE CAKE • LIME CHIFFON CAKE WITH GINGER MOUSSE • SOUSED BANANA ICE CREAM CRUNCH CAKE • CHOCOLATE COOKIES AND CREAM ICE CREAM CAKE • RASPBERRY MOUSSE CAKE • WHITE CHOCOLATE EGGNOG MOUSSE CAKE • TOASTED ALMOND CHOCOLATE BAKED ALASKA

A mousse is an airy mixture (*mousse* means "froth" or "foam" in French) made with either beaten egg whites or whipped cream. Mousse cakes can be as simple as a baked crust with a mousse filling, or they can be composed of multiple cake layers separated by mousse. In a nonchocolate mousse, the addition of a little gelatin is usually necessary. I'm not a big fan of gelatin, though—used in too great a quantity, it makes mousses rubbery—so I try to use the smallest amount necessary to support the mousse filling in a cake. Know that there is a fine line between the correct amount of gelatin and not quite enough gelatin here, and measure with care.

Ice cream cakes are real crowd pleasers, and one of the simplest types of cakes to make. They can be as basic as a layer of ice cream smoothed into a cookie crust, or they can be made from layers of cake (and sometimes sauce) filled and topped with ice cream. Soften the ice cream before scooping it into the pan—this makes smoothing it into an even layer much easier. Dipping your spatula in hot water (wipe it dry before using) also makes things go a little more smoothly. If you're making an ice cream cake a few days ahead, wrap it well, first with plastic wrap, then with aluminum foil, so that it doesn't absorb any unpleasant odors or taste of freezer burn.

BITTERSWEET CHOCOLATE MOUSSE CAKE

I like to make this ultra-simple mousse cake for dinner parties, especially when I'm pressed for time. The cake doesn't take long to put together, and it can chill while I prep the rest of the meal. Since chocolate is the star ingredient here, use the best you can find—it will make all the difference.

➤ MAKES ONE 9½-INCH CAKE, SERVING 10 TO 12

CHOCOLATE COOKIE CRUST

1½ cups (6.3 oz/180 g) Nabisco Famous Chocolate Wafer crumbs

4 tablespoons (2 oz/57 g) unsalted butter, melted

BITTERSWEET CHOCOLATE MOUSSE FILLING

1 pound (454 g) bittersweet chocolate, coarsely chopped

¾ cup (160 ml) whole milk

⅔ cup (4.6 oz/132 g) granulated sugar

1 teaspoon instant espresso powder

Pinch of salt

1½ teaspoons vanilla extract

2½ cups (600 ml) heavy cream

GARNISH

Classic Whipped Cream (page 339)

2 tablespoons (0.5 oz/15 g) Nabisco Famous Chocolate Wafer crumbs

MAKE THE CRUST

1. Butter the bottom of a 9 x 3-inch springform pan. In a medium bowl, stir together the cookie crumbs with the melted butter until combined. Pat the crumb mixture onto the bottom of the pan in an even layer. Refrigerate the crust while you make the mousse.

MAKE THE MOUSSE

2. Place the chocolate in the bowl of a food processor and process just until finely ground. (Leave the chocolate in the processor.)

3. In a small saucepan, combine the milk, sugar, espresso powder, and salt and cook over medium heat, stirring frequently, until the sugar dissolves and the milk comes to a boil. With the food processor running, pour the hot milk mixture through the feed tube and process until the chocolate is completely melted. Scrape down the sides of the bowl, add the vanilla extract, and process until blended. Scrape the mixture into a large bowl and let cool.

4. In the bowl of an electric mixer, using the whisk attachment, beat the heavy cream at high speed until soft peaks form. Using a rubber spatula, gently fold one-third of the whipped cream into the chocolate mixture. Fold in the remaining cream until completely blended.

5. Scrape the mousse onto the crust and spread it into an even layer. Refrigerate the cake for at least 3 hours.

UNMOLD THE CAKE

6. Run a sharp thin-bladed knife under hot water and wipe dry, then run the knife between the cake and the side of the pan to release the cake; reheat the knife as necessary. Remove the side of the springform pan. If necessary, run a small metal spatula around the side of the cake to smooth any rough patches.

7. To serve, slice the cake with a hot knife, wiping it clean between each cut. Serve each slice topped with a dollop of whipped cream and a sprinkle of wafer crumbs.

STORE *in the refrigerator, loosely covered, for up to 3 days.*

WHITE CHOCOLATE ESPRESSO ICEBOX CAKE

This cake was inspired by the old-fashioned icebox cake recipe that is printed on the back of the package of Nabisco Famous Chocolate Wafers, with a sophisticated white chocolate and espresso mousse taking the place of the whipped cream sandwiching the dark wafers. Since it can be frozen for up to two weeks, this cake is an ideal make-ahead dessert for a dinner party or other gathering. For a delightful bit of excess, serve each slice in a pool of Warm Chocolate Sauce (page 352).

➤ MAKES ONE 8½ x 4½-INCH CAKE, SERVING 8

WHITE CHOCOLATE ESPRESSO
MOUSSE

¼ cup (60 ml) water

1½ teaspoons powdered gelatin

2¼ cups (540 ml) heavy cream,
divided

⅓ cup (0.9 oz/26 g) espresso
beans

9 ounces (255 g) high-quality
white chocolate, finely chopped

2 teaspoons vanilla extract

1 tablespoon (15 ml) Frangelico
(hazelnut liqueur; optional)

27 Nabisco Famous Chocolate
Wafers

1. Line an 8½ x 4½-inch loaf pan with plastic wrap, letting it extend a few inches over each short end.

MAKE THE MOUSSE

2. Pour the water into a small heatproof cup. Sprinkle the gelatin over the water and let it soften for 5 minutes.

3. In a small saucepan, combine ½ cup of the heavy cream with the espresso beans and bring the cream to a boil over medium-high heat. Remove the pan from the heat and let the mixture infuse for 15 minutes.

4. Meanwhile, put the cup with the gelatin in it in a small skillet or saucepan. Pour in enough water to come halfway up the side of the cup. Heat the water while stirring the gelatin until the gelatin granules have completely dissolved. Turn off the heat, but leave the cup of gelatin in the hot water.

5. Place the white chocolate in a large bowl. Strain the espresso cream and discard the espresso beans. Return the cream to the saucepan and bring it to a gentle boil. Pour the hot cream and the hot gelatin mixture over the white chocolate. Let the mixture stand for about 30 seconds to melt the chocolate, then whisk until the chocolate is completely melted and smooth. Whisk in the vanilla extract and Frangelico, if using. Set aside to cool to tepid, about 15 minutes.

6. In the bowl of an electric mixer, using the whisk attachment, beat the remaining 1¾ cups heavy cream to soft peaks. Gently whisk about one-third of the cream into the cooled white chocolate mixture. Using a rubber spatula, gently fold in the remaining whipped cream in two additions.

ASSEMBLE THE CAKE

7. Scrape about 1½ cups of the mousse into the lined pan and smooth it into an even layer. Using a small metal spatula, spread a chocolate wafer with about 1 tablespoon of the mousse. Stand the wafer upright in the mousse about ¼ inch from a short end of the pan, with the coated side of the wafer pressing lightly against a long side of the pan. Spread another wafer with the same amount of mousse and position it so that it forms a sandwich with the first wafer, with the mousse on the second wafer pressing lightly against the first wafer. Repeat with 7 more wafers to make a row of 9 wafers across the width of the pan. Fill the gap between the last chocolate wafer and the side of the pan with mousse. Make two more rows of sandwiched wafers to fill the pan. Scrape the remaining mousse on top of the wafers, letting it fill all the gaps between the wafers and the sides of the pan, and spread the mousse into an even layer with a metal spatula. Cover it with plastic wrap, pressing it gently against the mousse. Freeze the cake for at least 4 hours, or until firm.

UNMOLD THE CAKE

8. Shortly before serving, peel off the plastic wrap from the top of the cake and invert it onto a cake plate or platter. Peel off the other piece of plastic wrap. Trim off any uneven edges from the base of the cake.

9. To serve, use a sharp knife to cut the cake into ¾-inch slices. Place on individual plates and let the slices stand at room temperature for 10 minutes to thaw before serving.

STORE *in the freezer, well covered, for up to 2 weeks.*

TIRAMISU CAKE

iramisu means "pick me up" in Italian, and with all the espresso soaking the cake layers in this classic dessert, it's easy to see why it was so named. Here's a cake version of the standard Italian sweet, made to be sliced into wedges instead of scooped out of a baking dish. Like most multiple-component cakes, it takes a bit of time to make and assemble, but the results are guaranteed to give you and your guests a lift.

➤ MAKES ONE 9-INCH CAKE, SERVING 10

ESPRESSO SYRUP

1 cup (240 ml) hot espresso or strong coffee

¼ cup (1.7 oz/50 g) granulated sugar

½ teaspoon vanilla extract

MASCARPONE CREAM

6 large egg yolks

¾ cup (5.3 oz/150 g) granulated sugar

1 tablespoon (15 ml) water

1 pound (454 g) mascarpone cheese

3 tablespoons (45 ml) dark rum

1½ teaspoons powdered gelatin

¾ cup (180 ml) heavy cream

1 teaspoon vanilla extract

Classic Génoise (page 74), baked in two 9-inch round pans

MAKE THE SYRUP

1. In a small bowl or liquid measuring cup, combine the espresso and sugar, stirring until the sugar is dissolved. Stir in the vanilla extract, and set the syrup aside.

MAKE THE MASCARPONE CREAM

2. In a medium stainless steel bowl, whisk together the egg yolks, sugar, and water. Place the bowl over a pot of simmering water (the bottom of the bowl should not touch the water) and whisk constantly until the mixture thickens and is hot to the touch, about 7 minutes. Immediately scrape the mixture into a bowl. Cover and refrigerate until completely cool, about 15 minutes.

3. In the bowl of an electric mixer, using the paddle attachment, beat the mascarpone cheese at medium speed until creamy, about 30 seconds. Gradually beat in the cooled egg yolk mixture and mix until blended.

4. Place the rum in a small heatproof cup. Sprinkle the gelatin on top and let the mixture stand for 5 minutes.

5. Set the cup of gelatin in a pan of simmering water and stir occasionally until the gelatin is dissolved and the mixture is clear. Whisk the warm gelatin mixture into the mascarpone until blended.

6. In the bowl of an electric mixer, using the whisk attachment, beat the heavy cream with the vanilla extract at high speed until it forms soft peaks. Gently fold the whipped cream into the mascarpone mixture.

ASSEMBLE THE CAKE

7. Using a serrated knife, trim the sides of each cake layer all the way around so that the yellow crumb is exposed and each cake measures about 8¼ inches in diameter. Place one of the layers (either side up) on a plate and brush it generously with ¼ cup of the espresso syrup, saturating it. Invert the layer and center it in the bottom of a 9 x 3-inch springform pan. Brush the top of the layer with another ¼ cup syrup. Pour half of the mascarpone cream on top and smooth it into an even layer; let the cream seep into the gap between the cake and the side of the pan. Brush the remaining cake layer generously with ¼ cup of the syrup, then invert the layer and place it on top of the mascarpone cream layer. Brush the top of the cake with the remaining syrup. Top with the remaining mascarpone cream, again letting the cream seep into the gap between the cake and the side of the pan and smoothing it into an even layer. Refrigerate the cake for at least 4 hours, until set.

UNMOLD THE CAKE

8. Run a sharp thin-bladed knife under hot water and wipe dry, then run the knife between the cake and the side of the pan to release the cake; reheat the knife as necessary. Remove the side of the pan. Pat the grated chocolate onto the sides of the cake. Dust the top of the cake with cocoa powder. Refrigerate the cake if not serving immediately. Thirty minutes before serving, remove the cake from the refrigerator.

9. To serve, slice the cake with a hot knife, wiping it clean between each cut.

STORE *in the refrigerator, loosely covered, for up to 3 days.*

THE HOSTESS MUST BE LIKE THE DUCK—CALM AND UNRUFFLED ON THE SURFACE, AND PADDLING LIKE HELL UNDERNEATH.
—ANONYMOUS

BANANA WALNUT CHIFFON CAKE WITH MAPLE MOUSSE

I've always liked the idea of pairing banana and maple, both naturally sweet, ripe flavors, and this cake, enhanced with a coffee syrup and crunchy walnuts, was a triumph the first time I made it. The maple flavor of the mousse comes mostly from maple syrup; the maple flavoring boosts the flavor a little, but it is optional. For an even more robust maple character, use Grade B syrup, which has a more assertive flavor than the delicate Grade A syrup (both are available from The Baker's Catalogue; see Sources, page 365). To maximize the banana flavor, be sure to use very ripe bananas.

➤ MAKES ONE 9-INCH CAKE, SERVING 10

COFFEE SYRUP

⅔ cup (160 ml) hot coffee

2 tablespoons (0.8 oz/25 g) granulated sugar

½ teaspoon vanilla extract

MAPLE MOUSSE

¼ cup (60 ml) water

1½ teaspoons powdered gelatin

¾ cup (180 ml) maple syrup (Grade A or B)

6 large egg yolks

1 teaspoon vanilla extract

¼ teaspoon maple flavoring (optional)

1½ cups (360 ml) heavy cream

Banana Walnut Chiffon Cake (page 67)

MAKE THE SYRUP

1. Pour the coffee into a cup and stir in the sugar until it is dissolved. Stir in the vanilla extract.

MAKE THE MOUSSE

2. Pour the water into a medium saucepan and sprinkle the gelatin over it. Let the gelatin soften for 5 minutes.

3. Whisk the maple syrup and egg yolks into the gelatin mixture. Place the pan over medium heat and cook, whisking constantly, until the mixture thickens and reaches 180°F on an instant-read thermometer. Pour the mixture through a fine-mesh sieve into a medium bowl. Stir in the vanilla extract and maple flavoring, if using.

4. Set the bowl in a large bowl filled about one-third of the way with ice water (be careful that the water doesn't splash into the maple mixture). Stir the mixture frequently until it is completely cool, about 10 minutes.

5. In the bowl of an electric mixer, using the whisk attachment, whip the heavy cream at medium-high speed until it forms firm peaks. Fold in the maple mixture. (The mousse should be used immediately.)

ASSEMBLE THE CAKE

6. Using a long serrated knife, cut the banana cake horizontally into 2 layers. Using the serrated knife, trim the sides of each cake layer all the way around so that the yellow crumb is exposed and each layer measures about 8¼ inches in diameter. Place a layer cut side up in the bottom of a 9 x 3-inch springform pan, centering it in the pan. Generously brush the cake with half of the coffee syrup. Scrape 2⅓ cups of the mousse onto the cake and, using a small offset metal spatula, spread it into an even layer, letting the mousse fill the gap between the cake and the side of the pan. Center the remaining cake layer, cut side up, on top. Brush the cake with the remaining coffee syrup. Scrape the remaining mousse on top and spread it into an even layer as before. Refrigerate the cake for at least 3 hours, until set.

UNMOLD THE CAKE

7. Run a sharp thin-bladed knife under hot water and wipe dry. Run the knife between the cake and the side of the springform pan to loosen the cake; reheat the knife as necessary. Remove the side of the pan. Use a small metal spatula to smooth the mousse on the sides of the cake if necessary. Refrigerate the cake if not serving immediately.

8. To serve, garnish the top of the cake with dollops of whipped cream and sugared walnuts, if you like. Cut the cake using a thin-bladed knife.

STORE *in the refrigerator, loosely covered, for up to 3 days.*

Chocolate Coconut Mousse Cake

Deep, dark chocolate cake layers and a creamy rum-spiked coconut mousse combine to fashion a sophisticated cake with down-home flavor. This cake is bound to conjure up a few childhood memories, particularly if you loved Mounds bars as much as I did (and do). For dinner parties or special occasions, serve this with Warm Chocolate Sauce (page 352) or Caramel Sauce (page 348).

➤ MAKES ONE 9-INCH CAKE, SERVING 10

COCONUT MOUSSE

2⅓ cups (320 ml) whole milk, or as necessary

1 cup (2.8 oz/80 g) sweetened flaked coconut

2¼ cups (540 ml) heavy cream, divided

1 tablespoon powdered gelatin

6 large egg yolks

⅓ cup (2.3 oz/67 g) granulated sugar

1 tablespoon (15 ml) dark rum

1 teaspoon vanilla extract

Devilishly Moist Chocolate Cake (page 121)

GARNISH

2 cups (5.6 oz/160 g) sweetened flaked coconut, divided

MAKE THE MOUSSE

1. In a medium saucepan, heat the milk and coconut over medium heat until it comes to a gentle boil. Remove the pan from the heat and set aside to steep for 1 hour.

2. Strain the milk into a large glass measure or a bowl, pressing down on the coconut with a spoon to extract as much liquid as possible. Measure the milk; you should have 2 cups. If you have less, add a little milk to make up the difference.

3. Place ½ cup of the heavy cream in a small cup and sprinkle the gelatin on top. Set aside to soften for 5 minutes.

4. Return the strained milk to the saucepan and reheat to a gentle boil. Remove the pan from the heat. Meanwhile, in a medium bowl, whisk together the egg yolks and sugar until well blended. Whisk in about ½ cup of the hot milk. Return the mixture to the saucepan and cook over medium heat, stirring constantly with a wooden spoon, until it thickens and reaches 175°F on an instant-read thermometer; a path should remain in the sauce when you run your finger across the back of the spoon. Remove the pan from the heat and add the gelatin mixture, stirring until the gelatin is dissolved.

5. Pour the hot mixture into a medium bowl and set the bowl in a large bowl filled about one-third of the way with ice water (be careful that the water doesn't splash into the coconut mixture). Stir the coconut mixture frequently until it is chilled, about 15 minutes. Stir in the rum and vanilla extract.

6. In the bowl of an electric mixer, using the whisk attachment, beat the remaining 1¾ cups heavy cream at high speed until soft mounds begin to form and the whisk leaves a trail in the cream. Reduce the speed to low, pour in the coconut mixture, and mix at low speed until blended. Remove the bowl from the mixer stand and stir the mousse with a rubber spatula a few times to blend completely. Refrigerate the mousse until it just begins to set, about 20 minutes.

ASSEMBLE THE CAKE

7. Using a long serrated knife, cut the cake horizontally into 3 layers. Reserve the bottom layer for the top of the cake. Place one of the other layers in the bottom of a 9 x 3-inch springform pan. Stir the chilled mousse, then scrape 2 cups of it onto the cake. Using a small offset metal spatula, spread it into an even layer, going all the way to the edges of the cake. Top with another cake layer. Top with another 2 cups of coconut mousse and spread it into an even layer. Top with the reserved layer, cut side down, and spread the remaining coconut mousse over it, making it as smooth and even as possible.

8. Sprinkle 1 cup of the coconut over the top of the cake. Chill for at least 4 hours.

UNMOLD THE CAKE

9. Run a sharp thin-bladed knife under hot water and wipe dry. Run the knife between the cake and the side of the pan to loosen the cake; reheat the knife as necessary. Remove the side of the pan. Using a small offset metal spatula, smooth the mousse onto the sides of the cake. Pat the remaining 1 cup of coconut around the sides of the cake. Refrigerate the cake if not serving immediately.

10. Thirty minutes before serving, remove the cake from the refrigerator. Slice the cake with a hot knife, wiping it clean between each cut.

STORE *in the refrigerator, covered, for up to 2 days.*

CHOCOLATE MOUSSE LAYER CAKE

🍫 🍫 🍫

Chocolate mousse is such a simple dessert, yet it remains one of the most satisfying, both in flavor and texture. Here I pair a simple bittersweet chocolate version, sans egg whites or yolks, with an intense chocolate layer cake (a scaled-down version of the Sour Cream Chocolate Cake Layers on page 124) and top it all off with a luxurious chocolate glaze. Plain or Coconut Whipped Cream is an ethereal accompaniment.

➤ MAKES ONE 9-INCH CAKE, SERVING 12 TO 16

SOUR CREAM CHOCOLATE CAKE

1¾ cups (7.5 oz/212 g) all-purpose flour

1⅔ cups (11.7 oz/332 g) granulated sugar

⅓ cup (1 oz/28 g) natural (not Dutch processed) cocoa powder

1 teaspoon baking soda

¼ teaspoon salt

2 large eggs

½ cup (4.3 oz/121 g) sour cream

2 teaspoons vanilla extract

½ cup (1 stick/4 oz/113 g) unsalted butter, melted and cooled

⅓ cup (80 ml) safflower or corn oil

¾ cup (180 ml) ice-cold water

MAKE THE CAKE

1. Position a rack in the center of the oven and preheat the oven to 350°F. Grease the bottom and sides of a 9 x 3-inch springform pan. Line the bottom of the pan with a round of parchment paper, and grease the paper. Dust the paper and the sides of the pan with flour and tap out the excess.

2. Sift together the flour, sugar, cocoa powder, baking powder, baking soda, and salt into a medium bowl. Whisk to combine, and set aside.

3. In another medium bowl, whisk together the eggs until blended. Whisk in the sour cream and vanilla extract until blended. Set aside.

4. In the bowl of an electric mixer, using the paddle attachment, mix the melted butter and oil together at low speed. Add the cold water and mix to blend. Add the dry ingredients all at once and mix at medium-low speed for 1 minute. Add the egg mixture and mix for another minute, scraping down the sides of the bowl with a rubber spatula as necessary. Scrape the batter into the prepared pan.

5. Bake the cake for 45 to 50 minutes, until a toothpick inserted into the center comes out clean. Set the pan on a wire rack and cool the cake for 20 minutes.

9 ounces (255 g) bittersweet chocolate, coarsely chopped

½ cup (120 ml) whole milk

¼ cup (1.8 oz/50 g) granulated sugar

1 teaspoon instant espresso powder

Pinch of salt

2 teaspoons vanilla extract

1 cup (240 ml) heavy cream

1⅓ cups Bittersweet Chocolate Glaze (page 306)

Classic Whipped Cream (page 339) or Coconut Whipped Cream (page 344)

6. Invert the cake onto the rack. Reinvert the cake and cool completely.

MAKE THE FILLING

7. Place the chocolate in the bowl of a food processor and process until finely ground. (Leave the chocolate in the processor.)

8. In a small saucepan, combine the milk, sugar, espresso powder, and salt and bring to a boil over medium heat, stirring until the sugar dissolves. With the food processor running, pour the hot milk through the feed tube, and process until the chocolate is completely melted. Scrape down the sides of the bowl, add the vanilla extract, and process until blended. Scrape the mixture into a large bowl and let cool for 10 minutes.

9. In the bowl of an electric mixer, using the whisk attachment, beat the heavy cream at high speed until soft peaks form. Using a rubber spatula, gently fold one-third of the whipped cream into the chocolate mixture. Fold in the remaining cream until completely blended. (The mousse should be used immediately.)

ASSEMBLE THE CAKE

10. Using a long serrated knife, trim off the domed top of the cake so that the cake is perfectly level; reserve the trimmings. Cut the cake horizontally into 2 layers.

11. Place one of the cake layers in the bottom of a 9 x 3-inch springform pan. Scrape half of the chocolate mousse over the cake layer and spread it into an even layer. Top with the other layer. Scrape over the remaining mousse and spread it into an even layer.

12. Cover the top of the pan with plastic wrap or foil and freeze the cake for at least 3 hours, until firm.

GLAZE AND GARNISH THE CAKE

13. Place the reserved cake trimmings in the bowl of a food processor and process to fine crumbs. Set aside.

14. Remove the cake from the freezer. Run a sharp thin-bladed knife under hot water and wipe it dry. Run the knife between the cake and the side of the pan to release the cake; reheat the knife as necessary. Remove the side of the pan. Using a small offset metal spatula, smooth the mousse on the sides of the cake.

15. Place the cake on a wire rack and set the rack over a baking sheet. Pour the warm glaze over the top of the cake and use the offset metal spatula to smooth it evenly over the top and sides. Pat the cake crumbs over the sides of the cake (and the top, if you like). Refrigerate the cake for at least 1 hour (to thaw) before serving.

16. About 30 minutes before serving, remove the cake from the refrigerator. Cut the cake into wedges and serve with the whipped cream.

STORE *in the refrigerator, loosely covered, for up to 3 days.*

Yogurt Mousse Cake with Honeyed Raspberries and Mint Syrup

C ombining the bright flavors of yogurt, Earl Grey tea, raspberry, honey, and mint, this unusual mousse cake is as light as air and makes a refreshing ending to any meal. Try substituting your own favorite tea for the Earl Grey.

➤ MAKES ONE 9-INCH CAKE, SERVING 8

EARL GREY SYRUP

½ cup (3.5 oz/100 g) granulated sugar

½ cup (120 ml) water

1 Earl Grey tea bag

1 teaspoon freshly squeezed lemon juice

YOGURT MOUSSE

2 cups (17 oz/484 g) plain organic whole milk yogurt

1 teaspoon finely grated lemon zest

½ teaspoon vanilla extract

1½ cups plus ⅓ cup (440 ml) heavy cream, divided

2 teaspoons unflavored powdered gelatin

¾ cup (3 oz/86 g) confectioners' sugar

Classic Génoise (page 74), baked in two 9-inch pans

MAKE THE CLASSIC GÉNOISE

1. Make the Classic Génoise according to the directions on page 74 and cool completely.

MAKE THE EARL GREY SYRUP

2. In a small saucepan, combine the sugar and water and place over medium-high heat. Heat, stirring constantly, until the mixture comes to a boil and the sugar is completely dissolved. Remove the pan from the heat and add the tea bag. Let steep for 15 minutes, stirring occasionally.

3. Remove the tea bag, pressing down on it to extract any liquid. Stir in the lemon juice. Transfer the syrup to a small container, cover, and set aside.

MAKE THE YOGURT MOUSSE

4. Set a sieve lined with two layers of cheesecloth over a bowl and scrape the yogurt into the sieve. Let the yogurt drain at room temperature for 45 minutes.

5. Spoon the drained yogurt (you should have just over 1 cup) into a medium bowl and whisk until smooth. Whisk in the lemon zest and vanilla extract.

2 tablespoons (1.5 oz/42 g) honey

One 6-ounce (170-g) container fresh raspberries

Mint Syrup (page 349)

6. Put ⅓ cup of the heavy cream in a small, heatproof cup. Sprinkle the gelatin over the cream and let it soften for a few minutes. Fill a small saucepan one-third of the way with water and bring to a simmer over medium heat.

7. Meanwhile, put the remaining 1½ cups cream in the bowl of an electric mixer. Using the whisk attachment, beat at high speed until the cream begins to form soft mounds. Gradually add the confectioners' sugar and beat until stiff peaks form.

8. Place the cup containing the cream and gelatin mixture into the pan of simmering water. Stir until the gelatin dissolves completely. Pour the gelatin through a sieve into the yogurt. Whisk until blended. Gently fold the yogurt mixture into the whipped cream.

ASSEMBLE THE CAKE

9. Using a long, serrated knife, cut each layer of the Classic Génoise horizontally into 2 layers, forming a total of four layers (you will need only three layers for this recipe; reserve the remaining layer for snacking). Place one of the layers, cut side up, on a cardboard cake round or cake plate. Brush the layer generously with Earl Grey syrup, using about one-third of the syrup. Using a small, metal offset spatula, spread about 1½ cups of yogurt mousse over the cake layer. Top with another cake layer, cut side up. Brush the cake with another third of the syrup. Top with another 1½ cups of yogurt mousse, spreading it over the cake evenly. Top with another cake layer, cut side up. Brush the cake with the remaining syrup. Scrape the reamining mousse on top of the cake and spread it over the top and sides of the cake. Refrigerate the cake while you make the honeyed raspberries and Mint Syrup.

MAKE THE HONEYED RASPBERRIES

10. Warm the honey in a microwave oven (for about 10 seconds at high power) or in a small saucepan over low heat. Put the berries in a medium bowl and pour over the warm honey. Using a rubber spatula, toss the raspberries with the honey until they are evenly coated. Arrange the berries (they will start to clump as they cool) in the center of the cake, piling them up.

MAKE THE MINT SYRUP

11. Make the Mint Syrup as directed on page 349.

SERVE THE CAKE

12. Cut the cake into wedges and serve with Mint Syrup drizzled over the cake and on the plate.

STORE *in the refrigerator, loosely covered, for up to 3 days.*

Chocolate Peanut Butter Mousse Cake

These are classic American childhood flavors, combined in a very grown-up way. The cake features a crispy chocolate wafer crust topped with layers of peanut butter and chocolate mousse, then finished with a chocolate glaze and a sprinkling of crunchy peanuts. Nothing especially complicated here, but the cake does take some time to assemble. If you prefer, skip the glaze and top the cake with sweetened whipped cream and chopped peanuts.

➤ Makes one 9-inch cake, serving 10

CHOCOLATE WAFER CRUST

1½ cups (6.3 oz/180 g) Nabisco Famous Chocolate Wafer cookie crumbs

4 tablespoons (2 oz/57 g) unsalted butter, melted

PEANUT BUTTER MOUSSE

5 ounces (142 g) cream cheese, softened

2 tablespoons (1 oz/28 g) unsalted butter, softened

1¼ cups (5 oz/144 g) confectioners' sugar

¾ cup (7 oz/200 g) creamy peanut butter

¼ teaspoon salt

2½ cups (600 ml) heavy cream

CHOCOLATE MOUSSE

5 ounces (142 g) bittersweet chocolate, coarsely chopped

3.5 ounces (100 g) milk chocolate, coarsely chopped

MAKE THE CRUST

1. Lightly grease the bottom of a 9 x 3-inch springform pan. In a medium bowl, stir together the cookie crumbs with the melted butter until combined. Pat the crumb mixture onto the bottom of the pan in an even layer. Refrigerate the crust while you make the peanut butter mousse.

MAKE THE PEANUT BUTTER MOUSSE

2. In the bowl of an electric mixer, using the paddle attachment, beat the cream cheese and butter at medium-low speed until creamy, about 1 minute. Add the confectioners' sugar and mix until well blended. Add the peanut butter and salt and mix until blended, scraping down the sides of the bowl as necessary. Remove the bowl from the mixer stand and set aside.

3. In a clean mixer bowl, using the whisk attachment, beat the heavy cream at high speed until soft peaks form. Gently fold 1 cup of the whipped cream into the peanut butter mixture until almost blended. Fold in another 1½ cups of the whipped cream until completely blended.

4. Scrape the mousse into the prepared pan and spread it into an even layer. Refrigerate while you make the chocolate mousse. Cover the remaining whipped cream and refrigerate until ready to use.

⅓ cup (80 ml) whole milk

⅓ cup (2.4 oz/67 g) granulated sugar

1 teaspoon vanilla extract

⅔ cup Bittersweet Chocolate Glaze (page 306)

GARNISH

Chopped unsalted peanuts or Sugared Peanuts (page 337)

MAKE THE CHOCOLATE MOUSSE

5. Place the chocolates in the bowl of a food processor and process until finely ground. (Leave the chocolate in the food processor.)

6. In a small saucepan, combine the milk and sugar and bring to a boil over medium heat, stirring frequently until the sugar dissolves. With the food processor running, pour the hot milk through the feed tube, and process until the chocolate is completely melted. Scrape down the sides of the bowl, add the vanilla extract, and process until blended. Scrape the mixture into a large bowl.

7. Using a rubber spatula, gently fold one-third of the reserved whipped cream into the mousse. Fold in the remaining cream until completely blended. Scrape the mousse onto the peanut butter mousse layer. Loosely cover the cake and freeze for at least 1 hour, until firm.

GLAZE THE CAKE

8. Run a sharp thin-bladed knife under hot water and wipe dry, then run the knife between the cake and the side of the pan to release the cake; reheat the knife as necessary. Remove the side of the pan. Pour the glaze over the top of the cake, trying not to let it drip down the sides, and, using a small metal spatula, spread the glaze evenly over the top of the cake. Sprinkle the top of the cake with the peanuts.

9. Refrigerate the cake for at least 1 hour before serving.

10. About 30 minutes before serving, remove the cake from the refrigerator. To serve, slice the cake with a hot knife, wiping it clean between each cut.

STORE *in the refrigerator, loosely covered, for up to 3 days.*

LEMON MOUSSE CAKE WITH FRESH RASPBERRIES

I adore lemon mousse and couldn't resist the opportunity to conjure up a cake with it as the star element. This creamy, rich mousse has just the right degree of sharpness, and I've combined it with a simple lemon chiffon cake, spicy ginger syrup, and fresh raspberries. Garnished with whipped cream and fresh raspberries, the cake is as pretty as it is irresistible.

➤ MAKES ONE 9-INCH CAKE, SERVING 10 TO 12

LEMON CHIFFON CAKE

1 cup (4 oz/114 g) cake flour

¾ cup (5.3 oz/150 g) granulated sugar, divided

1 teaspoon baking powder

¼ teaspoon salt

4 large eggs, separated, at room temperature

⅓ cup (80 ml) safflower or other neutral vegetable oil

1 teaspoon finely grated lemon zest

2 tablespoons (30 ml) strained freshly squeezed lemon juice

2 tablespoons (30 ml) whole milk

½ teaspoon vanilla extract

¼ teaspoon cream of tartar

GINGER SYRUP

⅔ cup (160 ml) water

½ cup (3.5 oz/100 g) granulated sugar

½-inch piece fresh ginger, peeled and thinly sliced

MAKE THE CAKE

1. Position a rack in the center of the oven and preheat the oven to 325°F. Grease the bottom of a 9 x 3-inch springform pan. Dust the bottom of the pan with flour.

2. Sift together the flour, ½ cup of the sugar, the baking powder, and salt into a medium bowl. Whisk to combine, and set aside.

3. In the bowl of an electric mixer, using the paddle attachment, beat the egg yolks, vegetable oil, lemon zest, lemon juice, milk, and vanilla extract at medium speed until blended, about 1 minute. Reduce the speed to low and add the flour mixture one-quarter at a time, mixing just until blended.

4. In a clean mixer bowl, using the whisk attachment, beat the egg whites and cream of tartar at medium speed until soft peaks form. Gradually beat in the remaining ¼ cup sugar, then increase the speed to high and beat until the whites are stiff but not dry. Using a rubber spatula, briskly fold about one-quarter of the whites into the cake batter. Gently fold in the remaining whites. Scrape the batter into the prepared pan and smooth the top.

5. Bake the cake for 22 to 28 minutes, until it is golden brown on top and a toothpick inserted into the center comes out clean. Cool the cake in the pan on a wire rack for 10 minutes.

2 tablespoons (30 ml) water

1 teaspoon powdered gelatin

8 large egg yolks

1¼ cups (8.8 oz/250 g) granulated sugar

⅔ cup (160 ml) strained freshly
squeezed lemon juice

⅛ teaspoon salt

10 tablespoons (1¼ sticks/
5 oz/142 g) unsalted butter, cut
into tablespoons

1 cup plus 2 tablespoons
(270 ml) heavy cream

One 6-ounce (170-g) container
fresh raspberries

GARNISH

Classic Whipped Cream (page
339)

6. Invert the cake onto the rack and let cool completely upside
down.

MAKE THE SYRUP

7. In a small saucepan, combine the water and sugar and bring to a
boil over medium-high heat, stirring occasionally to dissolve the
sugar. Remove the pan from the heat and add the ginger slices. Set
aside at room temperature.

MAKE THE MOUSSE

8. Place the water in a small heatproof cup. Sprinkle the gelatin
over the water and let soften for 5 minutes.

9. Set the cup of gelatin in a pan of simmering water for a few
minutes, stirring occasionally until the gelatin is dissolved and the
mixture is clear. Remove from the heat but leave the cup of gelatin
in the hot water.

10. Set a fine-mesh sieve over a medium bowl; set aside. In a
medium heavy nonreactive saucepan, whisk together the egg yolks
and sugar until blended. Stir in the lemon juice, salt, and butter
and cook over medium heat, whisking constantly, until the mixture
thickens, 7 to 10 minutes (do not let the mixture boil, or it will
curdle). The mixture should leave a path on the back of a wooden
spoon when you draw your finger across it. Remove the pan from
the heat and stir in the warm gelatin mixture. Immediately strain
the mixture through the sieve, pressing it through with a rubber
spatula. Set aside while you whip the cream.

11. In the bowl of an electric mixer, using the whisk attachment,
beat the heavy cream at high speed until medium-firm peaks form.
Place the whipped cream in the refrigerator.

12. Set the bowl containing the lemon mixture in a large bowl
filled about one-third of the way with ice water (be careful that the
water doesn't splash into the lemon mixture). Stir the lemon mixture frequently until it is slightly cooler than room temperature,
about 10 minutes.

13. Fold a large spoonful of the whipped cream into the lemon mixture to lighten it. Gently fold in the remaining cream.

ASSEMBLE THE CAKE

14. If necessary, run a paring knife around the side of the pan to release the cake. Invert the cake, then turn it right side up. Using a long serrated knife, cut the cake horizontally into 2 layers. Place the top layer cut side up in the bottom of a 9 x 3-inch springform pan. Set aside.

15. Remove the ginger slices from the syrup and discard. In a small bowl, combine ⅔ cup of the raspberries with 1 tablespoon of the syrup; set aside. Using a pastry brush, saturate the top of the cake layer in the pan with about half of the remaining syrup. Scrape about 2¼ cups of the lemon mousse onto the cake. Using a small offset metal spatula, spread it into an even layer. Sprinkle the syrup-coated raspberries (without any excess syrup) over the mousse, distributing them evenly. Top with the other cake layer, cut side up. Brush the cake with the remaining ginger syrup. Scrape the remaining lemon mousse on top and spread it into an even layer, filling in the gap between the cake and the side of the pan.

16. Refrigerate the cake until the mousse is set, at least 3 hours.

17. Run a thin-bladed knife between the cake and the side of the pan, and remove the side of the pan. Garnish the top of the cake with sweetened whipped cream, either piped or dolloped, and the reserved raspberries. Slice the cake using a thin-bladed sharp knife.

STORE *in the refrigerator, loosely covered, for up to 3 days.*

ORANGES AND CREAM CAKE

T ake a bite of this cake and you'll undoubtedly think of a Creamsicle, albeit one made with freshly squeezed orange juice and pure vanilla extract. It's wonderful in the winter, when oranges are plentiful, but it's also a refreshing dessert for a hot summer night when you don't have any change, or the ice cream truck is miles away.

➤ MAKES ONE 9-INCH CAKE, SERVING 10

ORANGE GÉNOISE

1 cup (3.5 oz/100 g) sifted cake flour

⅛ teaspoon salt

4 large eggs

½ cup (3.5 oz/100 g) granulated sugar

1 teaspoon finely grated orange zest

1 teaspoon vanilla extract

4 tablespoons (2 oz/57 g) unsalted butter, melted and cooled

ORANGE SYRUP

¼ cup (1.8 oz/50 g) granulated sugar

¼ cup (60 ml) water

¼ cup (60 ml) freshly squeezed orange juice

2 tablespoons (30 ml) Grand Marnier or Cointreau (optional)

MAKE THE GÉNOISE

1. Position a rack in the center of the oven and preheat the oven to 350°F. Grease the bottom and sides of a 9-inch round cake pan. Dust the pan with flour.

2. Sift together the cake flour and salt into a medium bowl. Whisk to combine, and set aside.

3. In the bowl of an electric mixer, whisk together the eggs and sugar by hand. Set the bowl over a saucepan of simmering water (make sure that the bottom of the bowl does not touch the water) and heat, whisking constantly, until the eggs are warm. Transfer the bowl to the electric mixer stand and, using the whisk attachment, beat on high speed until the mixture has tripled in volume, about 8 minutes. Reduce the speed to low and beat in the orange zest and vanilla extract.

4. Sift one-third of the flour mixture over the batter and gently fold it in with a rubber spatula. Sift in the remaining flour mixture in two more additions, again folding in gently. Put the melted butter in a small bowl, scoop about ¾ cup of the cake batter into the bowl, and stir until blended. Fold this mixture into the remaining cake batter. Scrape the batter into the prepared pan.

5. Bake the cake for 18 to 22 minutes, until the top springs back when lightly touched and a tester inserted into the center comes out clean. Cool the cake in the pan on a wire rack for 15 minutes.

¼ cup (60 ml) water

2 teaspoons powdered gelatin

1½ tablespoons (0.3 oz/9 g) finely grated orange zest

¾ cup (180 ml) freshly squeezed orange juice

⅓ cup (80 ml) freshly squeezed lemon juice

¾ cup (5.3 oz/150 g) granulated sugar

6 large egg yolks

2 tablespoons (30 ml) Grand Marnier or Cointreau (optional)

1 teaspoon vanilla extract

1½ cups (360 ml) heavy cream

GARNISH

Classic Whipped Cream (page 339)

Candied Orange Zest (page 354)

6. Invert the cake onto the wire rack and cool completely.

MAKE THE SYRUP

7. In a small saucepan, combine the sugar and water and bring to a boil, stirring to dissolve the sugar. Remove the pan from the heat and stir in the orange juice and liqueur, if using. Set aside to cool.

MAKE THE MOUSSE

8. Pour the water into a medium saucepan and sprinkle the gelatin over it. Let the gelatin soften for 5 minutes.

9. Whisk the orange zest, orange juice, lemon juice, sugar, and egg yolks into the gelatin. Place the pan over medium heat and cook, whisking constantly, until the mixture thickens and reaches 180°F on an instant-read thermometer. Pour the mixture through a fine-mesh sieve into a medium bowl. Stir in the orange liqueur, if using, and vanilla extract.

10. Set the bowl containing the orange mixture in a large bowl filled about one-third of the way with ice water (be careful that the water doesn't splash into the orange mixture). Stir the orange mixture frequently until it is completely cool, about 10 minutes.

11. In the bowl of an electric mixer, using the whisk attachment, whip the heavy cream at medium-high speed to firm peaks. Fold in the orange mixture. (The mousse should be used immediately.)

ASSEMBLE THE CAKE

12. Using a long serrated knife, cut the génoise horizontally into 2 layers. Place a cake layer cut side up in the bottom of a 9 x 3-inch pan, centering it in the pan. Generously brush the cake with half of the orange syrup. Scrape half of the mousse onto the cake and, using a small offset metal spatula, spread it into an even layer, letting the mousse fill the gap between the cake and the side of the pan. Center the remaining cake layer, cut side up, on top. Brush with the remaining orange syrup. Scrape the remaining mousse on top and spread it into an even layer as before.

13. Refrigerate the cake for at least 3 hours, until set.

UNMOLD THE CAKE

14. Run a thin-bladed sharp knife under hot water and wipe dry. Run the knife between the cake and the side of the springform pan to loosen the cake; reheat the knife as necessary. Remove the side of the pan. Use a small metal spatula to smooth the mousse on the sides of the cake if necessary. Refrigerate the cake if not serving immediately.

15. To serve, garnish the top of the cake with the whipped cream (either piped or dolloped) and candied orange zest. Slice the cake using a thin-bladed knife sharp.

STORE *in the refrigerator, loosely covered, for up to 3 days.*

MILK CHOCOLATE–ESPRESSO MOUSSE CAKE

Crunchy espresso meringue, creamy milk chocolate mousse, billowy Kahlúa-spiked cream—this cake is like a mocha latte with all the extras. Because it can be assembled up to two days ahead and then garnished à la minute with the Kahlúa Cream, I like to make this for dinner parties when I have plenty of other things to prepare. If you want an alcohol-free version of the cake, substitute cold espresso for the Kahlúa in the topping. Use Swiss milk chocolate for the mousse, the best you can get.

➤ MAKES ONE 9-INCH CAKE, SERVING 10

MILK CHOCOLATE MOUSSE

9 ounces (255 g) high-quality milk chocolate, coarsely chopped

3 ounces (85 g) bittersweet chocolate, coarsely chopped

½ cup (120 ml) whole milk

1 tablespoon (15 ml) vanilla extract

1½ cups (360 ml) heavy cream

Espresso Meringue Rounds (page 286)

KAHLÚA CREAM

1½ cups (360 ml) heavy cream

¼ cup (1 oz/29 g) confectioners' sugar

¼ cup (60 ml) Kahlúa

MAKE THE MOUSSE

1. Place both chocolates in the bowl of a food processor and pulse until the chocolate is finely chopped. (Leave the chocolate in the processor.)

2. In a small saucepan, heat the milk over medium-high heat until just under a boil. With the processor running, pour the hot milk through the feed tube, and process until the chocolate is completely melted and the mixture is smooth. Add the vanilla extract and process until combined. Scrape the chocolate mixture into a large bowl.

3. In the bowl of an electric mixer, using the whisk attachment, beat the heavy cream at high speed until firm peaks just start to form. Using a rubber spatula, gently fold one-third of the whipped cream into the chocolate mixture. Fold in the remaining cream in two more additions.

ASSEMBLE THE CAKE

4. Place one of the meringue rounds, right side up, in the bottom of a 9 x 3-inch springform pan. Scrape 3 cups of the mousse over the meringue and, using a small offset metal spatula, spread it into an even layer, filling the gap between the meringue and the sides of the pan. Place the other meringue round on top of the mousse. Scrape the remaining mousse on top and spread it into an even layer, filling the gap between the meringue and the sides of the pan.

5. Cover the pan with plastic wrap (don't let it touch the mousse) and freeze the cake for at least 2 hours, until firm.

Unmold the cake

6. About 1½ hours before serving, remove the cake from the freezer and uncover it. Dip a thin-bladed knife in hot water and wipe it dry. Run the knife around the side of the pan to loosen the cake; reheat the knife as needed. Remove the side of the pan. Place the cake in the refrigerator to thaw.

Make the Kahlúa cream

7. In the bowl of an electric mixer, using the whisk attachment, beat the heavy cream, confectioners' sugar, and Kahlúa at high speed until firm peaks form.

Garnish the cake

8. Scrape the whipped cream over the top of the cake and, using a small metal spatula, spread it into dramatic swirls and mounds (it will seem like a lot of cream). Serve immediately, or refrigerate until ready to serve.

9. To serve, slice the cake into wedges using a thin-bladed knife dipped in hot water and wiped dry between each cut.

STORE, *without the topping, in the refrigerator, loosely covered, for up to 2 days; with the topping, refrigerate for up to 3 hours.*

LIME CHIFFON CAKE WITH GINGER MOUSSE

Lime, like lemon, works wonderfully with fresh ginger in sweet as well as savory dishes. Here I've imbibed a moist lime chiffon cake with a sprightly lime syrup and layered it with a celestial ginger mousse for a fresh-tasting knockout of a mousse cake. A garnish of whipped cream and glistening crystallized ginger makes the cake a showstopping dinner party dessert, guaranteed to draw raves.

➤ MAKES ONE 9-INCH CAKE, SERVING 10

LIME SYRUP

3 tablespoons (45 ml) water

2 tablespoons (30 ml) strained freshly squeezed lime juice

⅓ cup (2.3 oz/66 g) granulated sugar

GINGER MOUSSE

2 cups (480 ml) heavy cream, divided

1 tablespoon plus 2 teaspoons (0.8 oz/25 g) finely grated fresh ginger

3 tablespoons (45 ml) water

1½ teaspoons powdered gelatin

6 large egg yolks

⅔ cup (4.6 oz/132 g) granulated sugar

Lime Chiffon Cake (page 67)

MAKE THE SYRUP

1. In a small saucepan, combine the water, lime juice, and sugar and bring to a boil over medium-high heat, stirring occasionally to dissolve the sugar. Remove the pan from the heat and set aside.

MAKE THE MOUSSE

2. In a small saucepan, combine ½ cup of the heavy cream with the grated ginger and bring to a boil over medium-high heat. Remove the pan from the heat and let the mixture infuse for 15 minutes.

3. Strain the cream into a small container, pressing down on the ginger to extract as much liquid as possible; discard the ginger. Return the cream to the saucepan and set aside.

4. Put the water into a small heatproof cup and sprinkle over the gelatin. Set aside to soften for 5 minutes.

5. In a medium bowl, whisk together the egg yolks and sugar until blended. Place the ginger-infused cream over medium-high heat and bring just to a boil. Gradually whisk the hot cream into the yolk mixture. Place the bowl with the yolk mixture over a pot of simmering water (the water should not touch the bottom of the bowl) and heat, whisking constantly, until the mixture registers 160°F on an instant-read thermometer. Remove the bowl from the water and set aside.

6. Set the cup of gelatin in the pot of simmering water for a few minutes (make sure the water does not seep into the cup), stirring occasionally until the gelatin is dissolved and the mixture is clear. Pour the gelatin into the ginger mixture and whisk to combine. Set the bowl in a large bowl filled about one-third of the way with ice water (be careful that the water doesn't splash into the ginger mixture). Stir the ginger mixture frequently until it is slightly cooler than room temperature, about 5 minutes, then remove the bowl from the ice bath and set aside.

7. In the bowl of an electric mixer, using the whisk attachment, beat the remaining 1½ cups heavy cream at high speed until medium-firm peaks form. Using a rubber spatula, gently fold about one-third of the whipped cream into the ginger base to lighten it. Gently fold in the remaining whipped cream.

ASSEMBLE THE CAKE

8. Using a long serrated knife, cut the cake horizontally into 2 layers. Place the top layer cut side up in the bottom of a 9 x 3-inch springform pan. Using a pastry brush, generously brush the cake with about half of the lime syrup. Scrape about 2½ cups of the ginger mousse onto the cake, filling in the gap between the cake and the sides of the pan. Using a small offset metal spatula, spread it into an even layer. Top with the other cake layer, cut side up. Brush with the remaining lime syrup. Scrape the remaining mousse on top and spread it into an even layer, filling in the gap between the cake and the side of the pan.

9. Refrigerate the cake until the mousse is set, at least 3 hours.

10. Run a thin-bladed knife between the cake and the side of the pan, and remove the side of the pan. Garnish the top of the cake with the whipped cream (either piped or dolloped) and crystallized ginger. Slice the cake using a thin-bladed sharp knife.

STORE *in the refrigerator, loosely covered, for up to 3 days.*

SOUSED BANANA ICE CREAM CRUNCH CAKE

his recipe was given to me by Melanie Dubberley, a top New York food stylist and good friend. The flavors in the cake—sesame, ginger, and banana—are faintly reminiscent of the wonderful fried banana packets served as dessert in some Thai and Chinese restaurants. But you don't have to have Asian food to enjoy this cake, it's a great ending to just about any meal.

➤ MAKES ONE 8-INCH SQUARE CAKE, SERVING 6

SESAME CRUNCHIES

⅓ cup (1.3 oz/38 g) graham cracker crumbs

⅓ cup (1.2 oz/33 g) pecans

⅓ cup (2.3 oz/67 g) lightly packed light brown sugar

1 tablespoon plus 1 teaspoon (0.3 oz/8 g) white sesame seeds

¼ teaspoon ground ginger

4 tablespoons (2 oz/57 g) unsalted butter, melted

SOUSED BANANA FILLING

1 tablespoon (0.4 oz/12 g) granulated sugar

3 tablespoons (45 ml) dark rum, divided

1 medium banana (choose a banana with a green tip)

1 tablespoon (0.5 oz/14 g) unsalted butter

1 teaspoon finely grated fresh ginger

⅓ cup (1.3 oz/38 g) chopped pecans

MAKE THE SESAME CRUNCHIES

1. Position a rack in the center of the oven and preheat the oven to 400°F. Line a baking sheet with parchment paper.

2. Combine the graham cracker crumbs and pecans in the bowl of a food processor and process until the pecans are finely ground. Transfer the mixture to a large bowl, add the brown sugar, sesame seeds, and ginger, and mix until well blended. Add the melted butter and mix until blended. Scrape the mixture onto the prepared baking sheet and, using a small metal offset spatula, spread it into a rectangle that measures roughly 6 x 8 inches.

3. Bake for 10 to 12 minutes, until the mixture is golden brown and bubbling (it will spread). Place the sheet on a wire rack and cool completely.

4. Break the rectangle into pieces and place them in a food processor. Process until the mixture forms crumbs that are the size of tiny peas mixed with coarse meal. Set aside.

MAKE THE FILLING

5. In a small cup, stir the sugar into 1 tablespoon of the rum; set aside.

6. Peel the banana and slice lengthwise in half, then slice crosswise into ½-inch pieces. Set aside.

6 tablespoons (4.3 oz/123 g) store-bought butterscotch or caramel sauce

Banana Ice Cream (page 356) or Quick Banana Ice Cream (page 358), frozen until firm

7. In a small saucepan, melt the butter over medium heat. Add the ginger and pecans and cook over medium-high heat until the pecans are golden and the ginger is fragrant, about 2 minutes. Add the sugar and rum mixture and cook, stirring, until the sugar is dissolved. Add the bananas and butterscotch or caramel sauce. Toss gently to coat the bananas. Remove the pan from the heat and stir in the remaining 2 tablespoons rum. Let cool, then transfer to a freezer-safe container, cover loosely, and freeze until ready to use.

ASSEMBLE THE CAKE

8. If the ice cream is hard, let it soften at room temperature for about 15 minutes. Line the bottom of an 8-inch square baking pan with a piece of parchment or wax paper that measures 8 x 16 inches, letting the ends extend over two opposite sides of the pan. Dot the paper on the bottom of the pan with a few dabs of butter or shortening. Place a second sheet of paper the same size crosswise over the first sheet, letting the ends extend over the other two sides of the pan. Reserve about 2 tablespoons of the crunchies for garnish. Sprinkle half of the remaining crunchies over the bottom of the pan. Spread half of the ice cream over the crunchies, smoothing it into an even layer. Cover loosely with the ends of the paper and place in the freezer for at least 45 minutes (return the remaining ice cream to the freezer).

9. Spread the banana filling over the ice cream and sprinkle with the remaining crunchies. Loosely cover with the paper ends and freeze the cake for another 45 minutes.

10. Spread the remaining ice cream over the filling and crunchies and smooth it into an even layer. Sprinkle the reserved crunchies over the top. Cover with plastic wrap and freeze for at least 4 hours before serving.

11. To serve the cake, let it stand at room temperature for 5 minutes. Using the overhanging ends of the parchment paper, gently lift the cake out of the pan. Using a large knife, cut the cake into 6 squares. Serve immediately.

STORE *in the freezer, well wrapped, for up to 1 week.*

CHOCOLATE COOKIES AND CREAM ICE CREAM CAKE

Years ago, when I was a cooking school student in Paris, an American friend arrived in class after a trip home with a highly coveted package of Oreo cookies. Much to the chagrin and puzzlement of our instructor, Chef Claude, we excitedly whipped up a batch of cookies-and-cream ice cream and indulged in that purely American luxury. Twenty years later, vanilla ice cream chock-full of crushed Oreo cookies has not lost its considerable appeal for me, and this dessert, moist chocolate cake sandwiched with ganache and ice cream and drizzled with warm ganache, showcases it in a way that might impress even Chef Claude.

➤ MAKES ONE 9-INCH CAKE, SERVING 10

BITTERSWEET GANACHE

8 ounces (227 g) bittersweet chocolate, coarsely chopped

1 cup (240 ml) heavy cream

Cookies and Cream Ice Cream (page 359), or use 2 pints store-bought cookies and cream ice cream, slightly softened

Devilishly Moist Chocolate Cake (page 121)

MAKE THE GANACHE

1. Place the chocolate in the bowl of a food processor and process until finely ground. (Leave the chocolate in the processor.)

2. In a small saucepan, bring the milk to a gentle boil over medium heat. With the food processor running, pour the hot milk through the feed tube, and process until the chocolate is completely melted. Scrape down the sides of the bowl and process until smooth. Scrape the ganache into a bowl and cover the surface with plastic wrap. Let stand until ready to use. (The ganache can be made up to 1 month in advance and stored in an airtight container in the refrigerator; bring to room temperature before using.)

ASSEMBLE THE CAKE

3. Using a long serrated knife, cut the cake horizontally into 3 layers. Set aside the least attractive layer. Place one of the remaining cake layers in the bottom of a 9 x 3-inch springform pan. Pour ½ cup of the ganache over the cake and, using a small offset metal spatula, spread it into an even layer. Freeze the cake for 15 minutes, or until the ganache is set.

4. Spoon 2 cups (1 pint) of the ice cream on top of the ganache. Using the offset spatula, spread it into a smooth layer. Top the ice cream with another cake layer. Spread the cake with another ½ cup ganache. Freeze the cake for 15 minutes, or until the ganache is set.

5. While the cake is freezing, break off about one-quarter of the remaining cake layer (save the rest for snacking) and place it in the bowl of a food processor. Process until fine crumbs are formed.

6. When the cake has been in the freezer for 15 minutes, spoon the remaining pint of ice cream on top and spread it into an even layer. Sprinkle the cake crumbs on top of the ice cream. Freeze the cake for at least 1 hour, until firm.

7. To serve, let the cake stand at room temperature for 5 to 10 minutes, then run a knife around the inside of the pan and remove the side.

8. Meanwhile, place the remaining ganache in a small microwavable pitcher and microwave on medium power for about 1 minute, until fluid (or place the pitcher in a skillet of simmering water until warm). Slice the cake and drizzle with the warm ganache.

STORE *in the freezer, well wrapped, for up to 1 month.*

RASPBERRY MOUSSE CAKE

A classic cake that never seems to lose its appeal. Because it's made with flash-frozen (also known as IQF) raspberries, you can enjoy it year-round, without seasonal constraint. The cake can be made in stages—the chiffon cake and orange syrup a few days ahead—and assembled, without the frosting, a day or two before serving. The whipped cream frosting should be lavished on no more than three hours before serving. Fresh raspberries make a pretty garnish but are optional.

➤ MAKES ONE 9-INCH CAKE, SERVING 12

RASPBERRY MOUSSE

One 12-ounce (340 g) package frozen unsweetened raspberries

1 cup (7 oz/200 g) granulated sugar

1½ tablespoons (22 ml) freshly squeezed lemon juice

¼ cup (60 ml) cold water

1½ teaspoons powdered gelatin

1½ cups (360 ml) heavy cream

ORANGE SYRUP

½ cup (3.5 oz/100 g) granulated sugar

½ cup (120 ml) water

2 tablespoons (30 ml) Grand Marnier or Cointreau

Classic Chiffon Cake (page 66)

RASPBERRY JAM LAYER

½ cup (5.4 oz/154 g) seedless raspberry jam (not preserves), divided

MAKE THE MOUSSE

1. In a medium saucepan, combine the frozen raspberries, sugar, and lemon juice and cook over medium heat, stirring frequently, until the raspberries release their liquid and the mixture comes to a simmer. Remove the pan from the heat and strain the raspberry mixture through a fine-mesh sieve into a large bowl, pressing down on the solids to extract as much liquid as possible. Set aside to cool.

2. Pour the water into a small cup and sprinkle the gelatin on top. Set aside to soften for 5 minutes.

3. Fill a small saucepan one-third of the way with water and bring to a simmer over medium heat. Set the cup of water and gelatin in the pan, turn the heat off, and stir until the gelatin dissolves completely. Whisk the gelatin mixture into the raspberry mixture.

4. In the bowl of an electric mixer, using the whisk attachment, beat the cream at high speed until firm peaks just begin to form. Gently fold about one-third of the whipped cream into the cooled raspberry mixture. Fold in the remaining whipped cream. Cover the bowl with plastic wrap and refrigerate the mousse for 1 hour, or until chilled but not set.

MAKE THE SYRUP

5. Combine the sugar and water in a small saucepan and bring to a boil over medium heat, stirring to dissolve the sugar. Remove the

WHIPPED CREAM FROSTING

1 cup (240 ml) heavy cream

2 tablespoons (0.5 oz/15 g) confectioners' sugar

½ teaspoon vanilla extract

OPTIONAL GARNISH

8 fresh raspberries

pan from the heat and let the syrup cool to room temperature, then stir in the orange liqueur.

ASSEMBLE THE CAKE

6. Using a long serrated knife, slice the chiffon cake horizontally in half to form 2 layers. Place one of the layers cut side up in the bottom of a 9 x 3-inch springform pan. Brush the cake with half of the orange syrup, letting it soak into the cake. Spoon ¼ cup of the raspberry jam onto the cake and, using a small offset metal spatula, spread it in an even layer. Spoon 2 cups of the mousse over the cake and spread it into an even layer all the way to the edges of the pan. Place the other cake layer cut side up on top of the mousse. Brush the cake with the remaining syrup, then spread it with the remaining ¼ cup raspberry jam. Scrape the remaining mousse on top of the cake and spread it into an even layer, letting it fill the gap between the cake and the edge of the pan. Refrigerate the cake for at least 4 hours, until the mousse is firm.

MAKE THE FROSTING

7. In the bowl of an electric mixer, using the whisk attachment, beat the heavy cream, confectioners' sugar, and vanilla extract at high speed until firm peaks form. Refrigerate while you unmold the cake.

FROST AND GARNISH THE CAKE

8. Dip a paring knife in hot water and wipe it dry. Run the knife around the edge of the pan, to loosen the cake. Remove the side of the pan.

9. Set aside ½ cup of the whipped cream to garnish the top of the cake. Spread the remaining whipped cream over the top and sides of the cake in a thin, even layer. Scrape the reserved cream into a pastry bag fitted with a medium open star tip (such as Ateco #6). Pipe 8 rosettes around the top edge of the cake. Top each rosette with a fresh raspberry, if you like. Serve the cake immediately, or refrigerate for up to 3 hours before serving.

STORE, *without the topping, in the refrigerator, loosely covered, for up to 2 days; with the topping, refrigerate for up to 3 hours.*

WHITE CHOCOLATE EGGNOG MOUSSE CAKE

Occasionally, during the frenzied period of recipe development that accompanies the writing of a cookbook, I'll drop a finished tart or cake off at my local tennis club for the staff and members to enjoy. After depositing this cake at the club one day, I received a barrage of phone calls and notes from folks declaring it to be the best cake they had ever tasted. Hyperbole, perhaps, but I would certainly rank this as one of *my* favorite mousse cakes. Made with layers of light spice cake and a creamy, rummy white-chocolate-and-nutmeg-flavored mousse, the flavor is dead-on eggnog. It's ideal for a Christmas or holiday party, and it can be made ahead—just top it with the sweetened whipped cream and a sprinkle of freshly grated nutmeg right before serving.

➤ MAKES ONE 9-INCH CAKE, SERVING 12

RUM SYRUP

½ cup (3.5 oz/100 g) granulated sugar

½ cup (120 ml) water

3 tablespoons (45 ml) dark rum

WHITE CHOCOLATE EGGNOG MOUSSE

3.5 ounces (100 g) high-quality white chocolate, chopped

¼ cup (60 ml) dark rum, divided

1½ teaspoons powdered gelatin

6 large egg yolks

⅔ cup (4.6 oz/132 g) granulated sugar

2 teaspoons vanilla extract

½ teaspoon freshly grated nutmeg

1½ cups (360 ml) heavy cream

MAKE THE SYRUP

1. Combine the sugar and water in a small saucepan and bring to a boil over medium heat, stirring to dissolve the sugar. Remove the pan from the heat and let the syrup cool to room temperature, then stir in the rum.

MAKE THE MOUSSE

2. Place the chocolate in a medium bowl and set the bowl over a pan filled one-third of the way with barely simmering water. Melt the chocolate, stirring frequently, until smooth. Remove the chocolate from the heat and let cool until tepid.

3. Pour 3 tablespoons of the rum into a small heatproof cup and sprinkle the gelatin on top. Set aside to soften for 5 minutes.

4. In a medium bowl, whisk together the egg yolks, sugar, and the remaining tablespoon of rum. Set the bowl over a pot filled one-third of the way with simmering water and heat, whisking constantly, until the yolks are hot and register 160°F on an instant-read thermometer. Remove the bowl from the pot of water and whisk in the vanilla extract and nutmeg. Set aside.

Spiced Chiffon Cake (page 67)

WHIPPED CREAM TOPPING

1 cup (240 ml) heavy cream

2 tablespoons (0.5 oz/14 g) confectioners' sugar

½ teaspoon vanilla extract

GARNISH

Freshly grated nutmeg

5. Set the cup of rum and gelatin in the pot of simmering water, turn the heat off, and stir until the gelatin dissolves completely. Whisk the rum mixture into the yolk mixture, then whisk the yolk mixture into the white chocolate. Set aside to cool to tepid.

6. In the bowl of an electric mixer, using the whisk attachment, beat the heavy cream at high speed until firm peaks just begin to form. Gently fold about one-third of the whipped cream into the cooled yolk mixture. Fold in the remaining whipped cream.

ASSEMBLE THE CAKE

7. Using a long serrated knife, slice the chiffon cake horizontally in half into 2 layers. Place one of the layers cut side up in the bottom of a 9 x 3-inch springform pan. Brush the cake with half of the rum syrup, letting it soak into the cake. Spoon 2 cups of the mousse over the cake and spread it evenly all the way to the edges of the pan. Place the other cake layer cut side up on top of the mousse. Brush the cake with the remaining syrup. Scrape the remaining mousse on top of the cake and spread it into an even layer, letting it fill the gap between the cake and the edge of the pan. Refrigerate the cake for at least 3 hours.

GARNISH THE CAKE

8. Dip a paring knife in hot water and wipe it dry. Run the knife around the edge of the pan, to loosen the cake. Remove the side of the pan.

9. In the bowl of an electric mixer, using the whisk attachment, beat the cream, sugar, and vanilla extract at high speed until firm peaks form. Scrape the whipped cream on top of the cake. Using a small metal spatula, spread it into decorative swirls. Grate a small amount of nutmeg on top. Serve the cake immediately, or refrigerate for up to 3 hours before serving.

STORE, *without the topping, in the refrigerator, loosely covered, up to 2 days; with the topping, refrigerate for up to 3 hours.*

Toasted Almond Chocolate Baked Alaska

Baked Alaska was created in 1867 by Charles Ranhofer, chef of the famous Delmonico's restaurant in New York, to celebrate the U.S. purchase of Alaska from Russia. It was originally called Alaska-Florida Cake, but was later renamed the catchier Baked Alaska. When making the Toasted Almond Crunch Ice Cream (page 360), save the egg whites to use for the meringue. A small blowtorch (the kind sold in gourmet kitchen stores) comes in handy here for browning the meringue, but you can use the oven if you don't have one. The meringue recipe makes what may seem like too much, but this amount is essential in order to insulate the ice cream from the heat of the blowtorch or oven and prevent it from melting.

➤ MAKES ONE 9-INCH CAKE, SERVING 10

Toasted Almond Crunch Ice Cream (page 360), frozen until firm, or 2 pints store-bought ice cream in the flavor of your choice

½ recipe Deeply Dark Devil's Food Cake (page 122)

ITALIAN MERINGUE

2 cups (14 oz/400 g) granulated sugar

1 cup (240 ml) water

7 large egg whites, at room temperature

¼ teaspoon cream of tartar

Confectioners' sugar for dusting

Sugared Almonds (page 337)

Warm Chocolate Sauce (page 352)

MAKE THE ICE CREAM LAYER

1. Line a 9-inch round cake pan with plastic wrap, letting it extend a few inches over the side. Spread the ice cream evenly in the pan. Cover with the plastic wrap and freeze until very firm, at least 4 hours.

ASSEMBLE THE CAKE

2. Place the cake on a foil-lined cardboard round set in the bottom of a 9 x 3-inch springform pan. Uncover the ice cream and carefully invert it onto the cake layer. Peel off the plastic wrap, and place the cake in the freezer.

SHORTLY BEFORE YOU ARE READY TO SERVE THE DESSERT, MAKE THE MERINGUE

3. In a medium saucepan, combine the sugar and water and bring to a boil over medium heat, stirring to dissolve the sugar. Stop stirring, raise the heat to high, and cook the sugar syrup until it registers 238°F on a candy thermometer. Meanwhile, begin beating the egg whites.

4. In the bowl of an electric mixer, using the whisk attachment, beat the whites and cream of tartar at medium speed until the whites form soft peaks.

5. When the syrup reaches 238°F, remove the pan from the heat and, with the mixer off, immediately pour about ¼ cup of the hot syrup over the beaten eggs. Beat at high speed until blended, about 10 seconds. Turn the mixer off and add another ¼ cup syrup. Beat at high speed for another 10 seconds. Repeat this process until all of the syrup is used. Using a rubber spatula, scrape down the sides of the bowl and beat at medium-high speed until the egg mixture is completely cool, about 10 minutes.

FROST AND BROWN THE DESSERT

6. The meringue can be browned using a household propane blowtorch (the preferred method) or the oven. If using the torch, have it ready. If using the oven, preheat it to 425°F.

7. The meringue can be piped onto the cake or spread on with a spatula. If piping it, scrape it into a large pastry bag fitted with a medium star tip (such as Ateco #6). Remove the cake from the freezer (if you are using the oven, it should be preheated at this point). If piping the meringue, first pipe vertical lines of meringue around the sides of the cake from bottom to top, covering the sides completely, then pipe shells or rosettes over the top of the cake, covering it completely. If spreading the meringue, use a small offset metal spatula to spread a thick layer around the sides of the cake, then scrape the remaining meringue on top of the cake and spread and swirl it decoratively using the back of a spoon. Dust the top of the cake with sifted confectioners' sugar.

8. If you are using the blowtorch, pass it over the meringue to brown the top and sides of the cake. If using the oven, place the cake on a baking sheet, immediately put it in the oven, and bake until the meringue is browned on top, 5 to 8 minutes.

9. Sprinkle the dessert with the almonds and serve immediately with the chocolate sauce.

STORE: *This cake should be served the day it's made.*

13

MERINGUE
CAKES

Meringue cakes are composed of layers of egg whites that are beaten with sugar and baked until hard. The egg white mixture for these cakes usually has twice the amount of sugar you would use to make a soft meringue. The texture of baked meringues varies; they can be crisp and dry throughout, or crisp on the outside and cakey inside. The French dacquoise is a meringue to which ground nuts are added; it has a slightly moist, chewy interior. The meringue layers are frequently alternated with sponge layers, particularly in European-style cakes. Because they are not rich, they pair well with buttercream.

Crisp meringue layers should be baked in a very low oven (200°F) for a long time (usually about 1 to 2 hours) so that they dry completely without browning. Don't attempt to make meringue on a humid day, as the moisture in the air may soften the meringue. Sometimes a little flour or cornstarch is folded into the beaten whites to stabilize the meringue. If you are filling and/or frosting a meringue cake with a moist mixture such as whipped cream, pastry cream, or mousse, this should be done shortly before serving in order to keep the meringue crisp.

A vacherin is a meringue shell that holds a filling, usually whipped cream or ice cream and fresh fruit. The meringue can be piped into small, individual-sized vacherins, or a large cake-sized shell, which is then sliced into portions. Either way, I like to drizzle the dessert with sauce just before serving—it's amazing how this increases the "wow factor" exponentially.

ESPRESSO MERINGUE ROUNDS

Freshly ground coffee gives these fragile disks of meringue a pretty speckled appearance and a robust coffee flavor. Though they are a key component of the Milk Chocolate Espresso–Mousse Cake (page 270), they can also be alternated with layers of génoise or sponge cake and filled with buttercream or whipped ganache.

➤ MAKES TWO 8-INCH MERINGUE ROUNDS

4 large egg whites

Pinch of salt

¼ teaspoon cream of tartar

1 cup (7 oz/200 g) granulated sugar

2 teaspoons instant espresso powder, dissolved in 2 teaspoons hot water

2 tablespoons (0.3 oz/8 g) freshly ground coffee

1. Position two racks near the center of the oven and preheat the oven to 225°F. Using a cake pan or cardboard cake round as a guide, draw an 8-inch circle on each of two pieces of parchment paper. Turn the sheets upside down and place each one on a baking sheet.

2. In the bowl of an electric mixer, using the whisk attachment, beat the egg whites at medium speed until foamy. Add the salt and cream of tartar and beat at medium-high speed until soft peaks begin to form. Gradually add the sugar, about 1 tablespoon at a time, then increase the speed to high and beat the whites until stiff peaks form. Remove the bowl from the mixer stand and, using a rubber spatula, fold in the espresso mixture and ground coffee.

3. Scrape the meringue into a large (18-inch) pastry bag fitted with a medium plain tip (such as Ateco #6). Starting at the center of one of the traced circles, pipe a spiral of meringue out to the edges, filling the circle completely. (Or, if you prefer, scoop some of the meringue into the center of the circle and spread it over the circle with a small metal spatula.) Repeat with the remaining circle. If there is meringue left over, pipe or spoon some dollops around the circles for cookies.

4. Bake the meringues for 1 hour, or until dry to the touch. Turn the oven off and leave the meringues in the oven for another hour.

5. Gently peel the meringue circles off the parchment paper.

STORE *in an airtight container in a cool, dry place for up to 2 weeks.*

PERFECT PAVLOVA

Thís classic Australian dessert was named for the Russian ballerina Anna Pavlova, who probably appeared as light as a cloud as she fluttered across the stage. It's no surprise that her honorary dessert is also as light as a puff of air, with a meringue shell holding sweet whipped cream and a fresh fruit topping, and a tangy berry sauce adding some zing to the show.

➤ MAKES ONE 9-INCH CAKE, SERVING 8

MERINGUE SHELL

5 large egg whites, at room temperature

Pinch of salt

¼ teaspoon cream of tartar

1¼ cups (8.8 oz/250 g) granulated sugar

WHIPPED CREAM FILLING

1¼ cups (300 ml) heavy cream

¼ cup (1 oz/29 g) confectioners' sugar

½ teaspoon vanilla extract

FRUIT TOPPING

2 cups (8 oz/227 g) mixed fresh berries (such as raspberries, blueberries, and quartered strawberries)

1 ripe peach or nectarine, pitted and cut into 12 wedges

Red Berry Sauce (page 350)

MAKE THE MERINGUE SHELL

1. Position a rack in the center of the oven and preheat the oven to 225°F. Using a cake pan or cardboard cake round as a guide, draw a 9-inch circle on a piece of parchment paper. Turn the paper upside down and place it on a baking sheet.

2. In the bowl of an electric mixer, using the whisk attachment, beat the egg whites at medium speed until foamy. Add the salt and cream of tartar and beat at medium-high speed until soft peaks begin to form. Gradually add the sugar, about 1 tablespoon at a time, then increase the speed to high and beat the whites until stiff peaks form.

3. Scrape the meringue into a large (18-inch) pastry bag fitted with a medium star tip (such as Ateco #6). Starting at the center of the circle, pipe a spiral of meringue out to the edges, filling the circle completely. (Or, if you prefer, scoop some of the meringue into the center of the circle and spread it over the circle with a small metal spatula.) Pipe a row of rosettes around the edge of the circle. (Or spoon dollops of meringue around the edge.) Pipe another row of rosettes on top of the first row, piping each one between two rosettes. (Or spoon on another row of dollops.)

4. Bake the meringue for 1 hour, or until it is lightly colored and dry to the touch. Turn the oven off and leave the meringue in the oven for at least 2 hours.

UP TO 2 HOURS BEFORE SERVING, MAKE THE FILLING

5. In the bowl of an electric mixer, using the whisk attachment, beat the cream with the confectioners' sugar and vanilla extract at high speed until soft peaks form. If not ready to serve, cover the filling and refrigerate.

6. Right before serving, spoon the filling into the meringue shell. Top with the berries and peach or nectarine wedges. To serve, cut the Pavlova into wedges, and serve with the berry sauce.

STORE *in the refrigerator, uncovered, for up to 8 hours.*

INDIVIDUAL MERINGUE CUPS WITH LIME CREAM AND FRESH BERRIES

With its crown of glistening sugared berries, tart lime filling, and crunchy meringue base, this dessert looks like it could have come straight from a toney Paris pâtisserie. The meringue shells can be made up to five days ahead and then filled and garnished a few hours before serving.

➤ MAKES 6 INDIVIDUAL MERINGUES

MERINGUE CUPS

4 large egg whites, at room temperature

Pinch of salt

¼ teaspoon cream of tartar

1 cup (7 oz/200 g) superfine sugar

LIME CREAM

4 large egg yolks

½ cup (3.5 oz/100 g) granulated sugar

6 tablespoons (90 ml) freshly squeezed lime juice

4 tablespoons (2 oz/57 g) unsalted butter, cut into tablespoons

1 teaspoon finely grated lime zest

¾ cup (180 ml) heavy cream

MAKE THE MERINGUES

1. Position a rack in the center of the oven and preheat the oven to 225°F. Trace six 3½-inch circles onto a sheet of parchment paper. Turn the parchment paper upside down and place it on the baking sheet.

2. In the bowl of an electric mixer, using the whisk attachment, beat the egg whites at medium speed until foamy. Add the salt and cream of tartar and beat at medium-high speed until soft peaks begin to form. Gradually add the sugar, about 1 tablespoon at a time, then increase the speed to high and beat the whites until stiff peaks form.

3. Scrape the meringue into a large (18-inch) pastry bag fitted with a medium plain tip (such as Ateco #4). Starting in the center of each circle, pipe a spiral of meringue in toward the edge, filling the circle completely. Pipe a ring of meringue around the edge of each circle. Pipe another ring of meringue on top of the first, to form cups.

4. Bake the meringues for 2 hours, or until they are very lightly colored and dry to the touch. Let them cool completely.

MAKE THE LIME CREAM

5. Set a fine-mesh sieve over a medium bowl and set aside. In a medium heavy nonreactive saucepan, whisk together the egg yolks

2 cups (8 oz/227 g) mixed fresh
raspberries, sliced strawberries,
and red currants

Confectioners' sugar for dusting

and sugar until blended. Stir in the lime juice and butter, and cook over medium heat, whisking constantly, until the mixture turns opaque and thickens enough to leave a path on the back of a wooden spoon when you draw your finger across it. Remove the pan from the heat and immediately strain the custard through the sieve, pressing it through with a rubber spatula. Stir in the lime zest. Set the mixture aside while you whip the cream. Or, if you are not ready to serve the meringues, refrigerate the mixture, covered, until ready to use.

6. Shortly before serving, in the bowl of an electric mixer, using the whisk attachment, beat the heavy cream at high speed until medium-firm peaks form. Place the bowl of whipped cream in the refrigerator.

7. If the lime mixture has not been refrigerated, set the bowl containing the lime mixture in a large bowl filled about one-third of the way with ice water (be careful that the water doesn't splash into the lime mixture). Stir the mixture frequently until it is slightly cooler than room temperature, about 10 minutes.

8. Fold a large spoonful of the whipped cream into the lime base to lighten it. Gently fold in the remaining cream.

9. Spoon the lime cream into the meringue cups, dividing it evenly. Top each meringue with mixed berries, then dust lightly with confectioners' sugar and serve.

STORE *the unfilled meringue shells in an airtight container in a cool dry place for up to 5 days; once filled, they should be served immediately.*

WHITE CHOCOLATE STRAWBERRY MERINGUE CAKE

Pristine white meringue layers form the foundation of this pretty showstopper, with an orange-scented white chocolate cream and lots of fresh sliced strawberries composing the filling and topping. Make the cake in late spring or early summer, when the strawberry season is at its peak and local berries are abundant.

➤ MAKES ONE 9-INCH CAKE, SERVING 8

MERINGUE LAYERS

5 large egg whites, at room temperature

Pinch of salt

¼ teaspoon cream of tartar

1 cup (7 oz/200 g) granulated sugar

WHITE-CHOCOLATE CREAM FILLING

7 ounces (200 g) high-quality white chocolate, finely chopped

2½ cups (600 ml) heavy cream, divided

1 teaspoon finely grated orange zest

2 pints (1 lb/454 g) fresh strawberries, washed, hulled, and cut in half

MAKE THE MERINGUE LAYERS

1. Position two racks near the center of the oven and preheat the oven to 225°F. Using a cake pan or cardboard cake round as a guide, draw a 9-inch circle on each of two pieces of parchment paper. Turn each paper upside down and place it on a baking sheet.

2. In the bowl of an electric mixer, using the whisk attachment, beat the egg whites at medium speed until foamy. Add the salt and cream of tartar and beat at medium-high speed until soft peaks begin to form. Gradually add the sugar, about 1 tablespoon at a time, then increase the speed to high and beat the whites until stiff peaks form.

3. Scrape the meringue into a large (18-inch) pastry bag fitted with a medium plain tip (such as Ateco #6). Starting at the center of one of the circles, pipe a spiral of meringue out the edges, filling the circle completely. (Or, if you prefer, scoop some of the meringue into the center of the circle and spread it over the circle with a small metal spatula.) Repeat to fill the other circle. Use the remaining meringue to pipe 1¼-inch-wide dollops onto the baking sheet; these can be eaten as cookies.

4. Bake the meringue layers for 1 hour, until lightly colored and dry to the touch. Turn the oven off and leave the meringues in the oven for at least another 2 hours, or overnight.

MAKE THE FILLING

5. Place the white chocolate and ½ cup of the heavy cream in the top of a double boiler over barely simmering water. Heat, stirring frequently, until the chocolate is melted and smooth. Remove the chocolate from the heat and let cool to room temperature.

6. In the bowl of an electric mixer, using the whisk attachment, beat the remaining 2 cups heavy cream with the orange zest at high speed until soft peaks form. Remove the bowl from the mixer stand. Whisk about ½ cup of the whipped cream into the cooled chocolate. Pour this mixture into the rest of the whipped cream and, using a rubber spatula, gently fold it in. Do not overmix, or the cream will become grainy. Use the filling immediately, or refrigerate for up to 2 hours.

ASSEMBLE THE CAKE

7. Place one of the meringue circles on a cardboard cake round or cake plate. Scoop about 2½ cups of the filling on top and spread it into an even layer, almost to the edges. Arrange a ring of strawberries, cut side down, around the edge of the round, with the pointed ends facing out. Continue making concentric rings of strawberries until the filling is covered. Place the other meringue round on top, smooth side up. Using a small offset metal spatula, spread a thin layer of filling over the meringue, covering it completely.

8. Scrape the remaining filling into a pastry bag fitted with a medium star tip (such as Ateco #6). Pipe 8 large rosettes around the edge of the top and one in the center. Top each rosette with a sliced strawberry. Refrigerate the cake for at least 30 minutes before serving.

STORE *in the refrigerator, uncovered, for up to 8 hours. The meringues can be made ahead and stored in an airtight container in a dry place for up to a month.*

Coconut Meringue Cake

Coconut meringue layers, crisp on the outside, chewy on the inside, and as light as air, make an ideal foil for a rich whipped white chocolate ganache enhanced with coconut and rum. The shiny chocolate glaze gives this celestial cake a sleek finish and a chocolaty endnote.

➤ MAKES ONE 9-INCH CAKE, SERVING 10

COCONUT DACQUOISE

½ cup (2.1 oz/60 g) slivered almonds

1½ cups (6 oz/172 g) confectioners' sugar

2½ cups (7 oz/200 g) unsweetened shredded coconut (available in health food stores)

5 large egg whites, at room temperature

Pinch of salt

¼ teaspoon cream of tartar

½ cup (3.5 oz/100 g) superfine sugar

Whipped White Chocolate Coconut-Rum Ganache (page 319)

⅔ cup Bittersweet Chocolate Glaze (page 306)

GARNISH

⅓ cup (1 oz/28 g) unsweetened shredded coconut

MAKE THE DACQUOISE

1. Position two racks near the center of the oven and preheat the oven to 350°F. Using a cake pan or cardboard cake round as a guide, draw a 9-inch circle on each of two sheets of parchment paper. Turn the sheets over and place each on a baking sheet. Lightly butter each piece of parchment paper.

2. In the bowl of a food processor, combine the almonds and confectioners' sugar and process until the almonds are finely ground. Add the coconut and pulse until blended. Set aside.

3. In the bowl of an electric mixer, using the whisk attachment, beat the egg whites and salt at medium speed until foamy. Add the cream of tartar and beat at medium-high speed until soft peaks begin to form. Gradually add the superfine sugar, about 1 tablespoon at a time, then increase the speed to high and beat the whites until stiff peaks form. Remove the bowl from the mixer stand and, using a large rubber spatula, gently fold in the coconut mixture one-third at a time.

4. Scrape half of the meringue into the center of each of the traced circles. Using a small offset metal spatula, spread it evenly to the edges of each circle. Bake the meringues for 20 to 25 minutes, until they are lightly golden and crisp on top but still soft in the center. Transfer the baking sheets to wire racks and cool completely.

ASSEMBLE THE CAKE

5. Using a pancake turner, carefully transfer one of the dacquoise circles to a cardboard cake round or serving plate. Spread with about 1¼ cups of the whipped ganache. Carefully place the remaining dacquoise round, upside down, on top. Spread the chocolate glaze over the top of the round. Frost the sides of the cake with a thin layer of the remaining whipped ganache. Pat the coconut over the sides, and sprinkle a little on top of the glaze. Refrigerate the cake for at least 1 hour before serving.

STORE *refrigerated for up to 3 days. Bring the cake to room temperature before serving.*

CHOCOLATE DACQUOISE CAKE

Τhe crisp, nutty meringue layers in this cake are lightly flavored with cocoa powder and then sandwiched with a fluffy chocolate buttercream and layers of moist devil's food cake for a delightful contrast in taste and texture. Extra meringue is crumbled up to create the decorative cobbling on the sides of the finished cake.

➤ MAKES ONE 9-INCH CAKE, SERVING 12

COCOA DACQUOISE LAYERS

¾ cup (3.2 oz/90 g) slivered almonds, lightly toasted (see page 37)

¾ cup (3 oz/85 g) confectioners' sugar

2 tablespoons (0.4 oz/10 g) natural (not Dutch-processed) cocoa powder

1½ tablespoons (0.4 oz/11 g) cornstarch

5 large egg whites

⅛ teaspoon salt

½ teaspoon cream of tartar

½ cup (3.5 oz/100 g) superfine sugar

Deeply Dark Devil's Food Cake (page 122)

Chocolate Swiss Meringue Buttercream (page 322)

MAKE THE DACQUOISE

1. Position two racks near the center of the oven and preheat the oven to 200°F. Using a cake pan or cardboard cake round as a guide, draw a 9-inch circle on each of two sheets of parchment paper. Turn the sheets over and place each on a baking sheet.

2. In the bowl of a food processor, combine the almonds, confectioners' sugar, cocoa, and cornstarch and process until the nuts are finely ground. Set aside.

3. In the bowl of an electric mixer, using the whisk attachment, beat the egg whites at medium speed until foamy. Add the salt and cream of tartar and beat at medium-high speed until soft peaks begin to form. Gradually add the sugar, about 1 tablespoon at a time, then increase the speed to high and beat the whites until stiff peaks form.

4. Gently fold the nut mixture into the meringue one-third at a time. Scrape the meringue into a pastry bag fitted with a medium plain tip (such as Ateco #6). Starting at the center of one of the drawn circles, pipe a spiral of meringue out to the edges, filling the circle completely. (Or, if you prefer, scoop some of the meringue into the center of the circle and spread it over the circle with a small metal spatula.) Repeat to form the second circle. Pipe or spoon the remaining meringue mixture in dollops spaced randomly around the circles (these dollops will be crumbled and used for garnish).

5. Bake the meringues for 1 hour. Turn the oven off and leave them in the oven for at least another hour.

6. Remove the meringues from the oven and very carefully peel them off the parchment paper (they break easily).

ASSEMBLE THE CAKE

7. Using a long serrated knife, cut the cake horizontally into 2 layers. Place one of the layers on a cardboard cake round or serving plate. Spread the layer with a generous cup of the buttercream. Top with one of the dacquoise rounds, smooth side up. Spread with another generous cup of buttercream. Repeat the layering with the remaining chocolate cake layer and more buttercream. Top with the remaining dacquoise round, smooth side up. Frost the sides and top of the cake with the remaining buttercream.

8. Crumble the small meringue rounds into chunks in a bowl, then pat the meringue chunks onto the sides of the cake.

9. Refrigerate the cake for at least 1 hour (this will soften the dacquoise layers and make the cake easier to cut). Bring to room temperature before serving.

STORE *in the refrigerator for up to 3 days; bring to room temperature before serving.*

14

FILLINGS AND FROSTINGS

ALMOND FILLING • CREAM CHEESE FILLING • APPLE FILLING • FIG FILLING • WHITE DRIZZLE GLAZE • BITTERSWEET CHOCOLATE GLAZE • SOUR CREAM FILLING AND TOPPING • WHIPPED CREAM CHEESE FILLING • COCONUT-PECAN FILLING AND FROSTING • CREAM CHEESE SPICE FROSTING • CREAM CHEESE MAPLE FROSTING *(variation)* • WHITE CHOCOLATE CREAM CHEESE FROSTING • FLUFFY WHITE FROSTING • CREAMY PEANUT BUTTER FROSTING • FUDGY CHOCOLATE FROSTING • DARK CHOCOLATE SOUR CREAM FROSTING • MILK CHOCOLATE COCONUT GANACHE • MILK CHOCOLATE PEANUT BUTTER GANACHE • WHIPPED WHITE CHOCOLATE GANACHE • WHIPPED WHITE CHOCOLATE LEMON GANACHE *(variation)* • WHIPPED WHITE CHOCOLATE ESPRESSO GANACHE *(variation)* • WHIPPED WHITE CHOCOLATE CINNAMON GANACHE *(variation)* • WHIPPED WHITE CHOCOLATE ORANGE GANACHE *(variation)* • WHIPPED WHITE CHOCOLATE RASPBERRY GANACHE *(variation)* • WHIPPED WHITE CHOCOLATE COCONUT-RUM GANACHE *(variation)* • RICH CHOCOLATE ESPRESSO FROSTING • WHIPPED GANACHE • SWISS MERINGUE BUTTERCREAM • CHOCOLATE SWISS MERINGUE BUTTERCREAM *(variation)* • ORANGE SWISS MERINGUE BUTTERCREAM *(variation)* • FRENCH-STYLE BUTTERCREAM • PISTACHIO BUTTERCREAM *(variation)* • CHOCOLATE BUTTERCREAM *(variation)* • HAZELNUT BUTTERCREAM *(variation)* • RASPBERRY BUTTERCREAM *(variation)* • ALMOND BUTTERCREAM *(variation)* • SILKY CHOCOLATE BUTTERCREAM • CARAMEL ESPRESSO BUTTERCREAM

While some cakes look best plain or with just a simple sprinkling of confectioners' sugar or cocoa powder, most benefit from the addition of a filling, frosting, or glaze (and sometimes all three). Decorating a cake with frosting can be an expression of a baker's creativity and artistry (and it can sometimes cover up a flaw or two). While many of the frostings and fillings in this chapter are meant to be used with particular cakes, feel free to experiment with combinations of various elements on your own. Just keep a few basic guidelines in mind:

➤ Pair richer frostings and buttercreams with lighter cakes, such as chiffon and sponge cakes.

➤ Coat flourless cakes and tortes (which tend to be rich) with a thin layer of glaze instead of a thick layer of frosting.

➤ Whipped cream and light, fluffy frostings can be lavished thickly onto cakes.

➤ When using frostings and fillings that require refrigeration, choose a cake that stays soft when refrigerated (such as chiffon, sponge, or angel food cakes).

➤ Let cakes that have been frosted with buttercream stand at room temperature to soften the buttercream before serving.

➤ If making buttercream ahead of time, bring it to room temperature before using.

➤ Spread ganache fillings and frostings, which are very rich, thinly over cake layers.

➤ Using a pastry bag and a star tip to pipe a few decorations on top of a frosted cake is an easy way to dress up a simple cake for a festive occasion.

ALMOND FILLING

 Use canned almond paste rather than the kind in a tube for the best flavor in this creamy coffee cake filling.

➤ MAKES ABOUT 1 CUP

⅓ cup (3.3 oz/95 g) canned almond paste

⅓ cup (2.3 oz/66 g) granulated sugar

4 tablespoons (2 oz/57 g) unsalted butter, softened

1 large egg

2 tablespoons (0.8 oz/25 g) all-purpose flour

1. In the bowl of a food processor, pulse together the almond paste and sugar until the almond paste is broken up and the mixture is blended. Add the butter and process until smooth. Add the egg and flour and mix until blended. Transfer the mixture to a small bowl, cover, and refrigerate until ready to use.

STORE *in the refrigerator, covered, for up to 3 days.*

Cream Cheese Filling

Lightly scented with orange and vanilla, this sweet cream cheese mixture makes a marvelous filling for Filled Coffee Cake (page 110).

➤ MAKES ABOUT 1⅓ CUPS

8 ounces (227 g) cream cheese, softened

2 tablespoons (1 oz/28 g) unsalted butter, softened

⅓ cup (2.3 oz/66 g) granulated sugar

1 large egg

⅛ teaspoon salt

½ teaspoon finely grated orange zest

½ teaspoon vanilla extract

1. In the bowl of an electric mixer, using the paddle attachment, beat the cream cheese and butter at medium-low speed until well blended and creamy, about 1 minute. Add the sugar and mix until well blended. Add the egg, salt, orange zest, and vanilla extract and mix until blended. Cover the bowl and chill the filling for at least 15 minutes before using.

STORE *in an airtight container in the refrigerator for up to 3 days.*

APPLE FILLING

ull of apple flavor but unfussy, this filling transforms plain coffee cake into something exceptional (see Filled Coffee Cake, page 110).

➤ MAKES ABOUT 2⅔ CUPS

3 cups (15 oz/425 g) diced (¼-inch cubes) peeled Granny Smith apples (about 2½ apples)

1 teaspoon freshly squeezed lemon juice

3 tablespoons (1.5 oz/42 g) unsalted butter, cut into tablespoons

⅔ cup (5 oz/143 g) firmly packed light brown sugar

1 tablespoon (0.3 oz/8 g) all-purpose flour

¾ teaspoon ground cinnamon

½ cup (2.5 oz/72 g) dark raisins

½ cup (2 oz/57 g) coarsely chopped pecans

1. In a medium bowl, toss the apple cubes with the lemon juice to prevent them from browning.

2. In a large skillet, heat the butter over medium-high heat until melted and bubbling. Add the apples and sauté for 2 minutes. Sprinkle over the sugar and cook, stirring frequently, for another 3 minutes, or until the sugar has liquefied and the apples are tender. Add the flour and cook for another minute, stirring constantly. Stir in the cinnamon, raisins, and pecans. Remove the skillet from the heat and cool the filling completely before using.

STORE *in the refrigerator, covered, for up to 3 days.*

FIG FILLING

The warm notes of brandy and cinnamon highlight the sweet fig essence of this jam-like filling for Filled Coffee Cake (page 110).

➤ MAKES ABOUT 1½ CUPS

2 cups (10 oz/283 g) halved dried figs

½ cup (3.5 oz/100 g) granulated sugar

1½ cups (360 ml) water

2 teaspoons finely grated lemon zest

¼ teaspoon salt

1 cinnamon stick

1 tablespoon (15 ml) brandy

½ teaspoon vanilla extract

1. In a medium saucepan, combine the figs, sugar, water, lemon zest, salt, and cinnamon stick and bring to a boil, then reduce the heat until just simmering. Simmer for 25 to 30 minutes, until the figs are tender when pierced with a fork (there should still be some liquid left). Let the mixture cool for 10 minutes.

2. Remove the cinnamon stick and transfer the cooled fig mixture to the bowl of a food processor. Add the brandy and vanilla extract and process until smooth, about 30 seconds. Let cool completely.

STORE *in an airtight container in the refrigerator for up to 2 weeks.*

White Drizzle Glaze

This quick confectioners' sugar glaze is ideal for drizzling onto finished cakes—it's thick enough to hold its shape and won't run off the sides of a Bundt cake. Make the icing right before you're ready to use it.

➤ MAKES A GENEROUS ½ CUP

1 cup (4 oz/115 g) confectioners' sugar

¼ cup (60 ml) heavy cream, plus more if needed

½ teaspoon vanilla extract

1. In a small bowl, combine all the ingredients and stir vigorously with a rubber spatula until it is completely smooth, adding a little more cream if needed.

2. Scrape the glaze into a parchment paper cone (see page 52) or small sealable plastic bag (seal the bag and snip a tiny hole in one of the bottom corners). Drizzle the glaze onto the cake and let set for at least 10 minutes before serving.

STORE: *Use right away, as the glaze will harden upon standing.*

BITTERSWEET CHOCOLATE GLAZE

ere is a glossy dark chocolate glaze that will enhance a variety of cakes. The glaze becomes dull and slightly hard when chilled, so be sure to bring the cake to room temperature (or at least cool room temperature) before serving.

TO DRIZZLE ONTO THE TOP OF A 9- OR 10-INCH CAKE (MAKES ⅔ CUP)

3 ounces (85 g) bittersweet chocolate, coarsely chopped

⅓ cup (80 ml) heavy cream

½ teaspoon vanilla extract

TO GLAZE THE TOP AND SIDES OF A 9-INCH CAKE (MAKES 1⅓ CUPS)

6 ounces (170 g) bittersweet chocolate, coarsely chopped

⅔ cup (160 ml) heavy cream

1 teaspoon vanilla extract

TO GLAZE THE TOP AND SIDES OF A 10-INCH CAKE (MAKES 2 CUPS)

9 ounces (255 g) bittersweet chocolate, coarsely chopped

1 cup (240 ml) heavy cream

1¼ teaspoons vanilla extract

1. Place the chocolate in the bowl of a food processor and process just until finely ground. (Leave the chocolate in the processor.)

2. In a small saucepan, bring the cream to a boil. Remove from the heat and add the chocolate to the pan. Stir until the chocolate is completely melted and the glaze is smooth. Stir in the vanilla extract. Transfer the glaze to a small bowl. Cover the surface of the glaze with a piece of plastic wrap and let cool for about 10 minutes before using.

STORE *in an airtight container in the refrigerator for up to 2 weeks; rewarm gently in a double boiler before using.*

SOUR CREAM FILLING AND TOPPING

With the slight tang of sour cream, this is a wonderful filling, topping, or accompaniment for cakes made with fresh fruit. Try it with Peach Tatin Cake (page 186) or Jasmine and Ginger Plum Upside-Down Cake (page 184).

➤ MAKES A GENEROUS 2 CUPS

1 cup (240 ml) heavy cream

3 tablespoons (1.6 oz/45 g) sour cream

¼ cup (1 oz/29 g) confectioners' sugar

2 tablespoons (0.9 oz/25 g) granulated sugar

1 teaspoon vanilla extract

1. In the bowl of an electric mixer, combine all the ingredients and, using the whisk attachment, beat at medium-high speed until the mixture forms stiff peaks. Use immediately, or transfer to a covered container and refrigerate.

STORE *in the refrigerator, covered, for up to 6 hours.*

WHIPPED CREAM CHEESE FILLING

This whipped cream filling is enhanced by the addition of cream cheese, which stabilizes the cream and gives it a pleasant tang. It is particularly good with devil's food cake, sponge or chiffon cakes, and spice cakes.

➤ MAKES ABOUT 3 CUPS

1 cup (240 ml) heavy cream

6 ounces (170 g) cream cheese, softened

⅓ cup (2.3 oz/66 g) granulated sugar

1 teaspoon vanilla extract

1. In the bowl of an electric mixer, using the whisk attachment, beat the cream at high speed until firm peaks begin to form. Cover and refrigerate.

2. In a clean mixer bowl, using the paddle attachment, beat the cream cheese and sugar at medium speed until creamy and smooth, about 3 minutes, scraping down the sides of the bowl as necessary. Beat in the vanilla extract. Using a rubber spatula, gently fold in one-third of the whipped cream. Fold in the remaining cream. Use immediately or cover and refrigerate.

STORE *in the refrigerator, covered, for up to 4 hours.*

COCONUT-PECAN FILLING AND FROSTING

The classic filling and topping for German Chocolate Cake (page 153), this frosting is oh-so-gooey and sweet.

➤ MAKES ABOUT 3¼ CUPS

1 cup (240 ml) heavy cream or evaporated milk

1¼ cups (8.8 oz/250 g) granulated sugar

4 large egg yolks, lightly beaten

½ cup (1 stick/4 oz/113 g) unsalted butter, cut into tablespoons

1 teaspoon vanilla extract

1½ cups (6 oz/170 g) sweetened flaked coconut

1¼ cups (4.4 oz/125 g) pecans, toasted (see page 37) and chopped

1. In a medium saucepan, combine the cream, sugar, egg yolks, and butter and cook over medium heat, stirring constantly, until the butter has melted and the mixture thickens and bubbles. Reduce the heat to low and cook for 2 minutes longer.

2. Remove the pan from the heat and stir in the vanilla extract, coconut, and pecans. Cool for about 1 hour, or until the mixture is spreadable, before using.

STORE *in an airtight container in the refrigerator for up to 2 weeks; let soften at room temperature before using.*

CREAM CHEESE SPICE FROSTING

This cream cheese frosting, perfect as a topping for gingerbread cake, gets a lift from a trio of spices.

➤ MAKES 1⅓ CUPS

6 ounces (170 g) cream cheese, softened

3 tablespoons (1.5 oz/42 g) unsalted butter, softened

½ teaspoon vanilla extract

⅛ teaspoon ground cinnamon

⅛ teaspoon ground ginger

Pinch of freshly grated nutmeg

Pinch of salt

1 cup (4 oz/115 g) confectioners' sugar, sifted

1. In the bowl of an electric mixer, using the paddle attachment, beat together the cream cheese and butter at medium speed until smooth. Beat in the vanilla extract, spices, and salt. Reduce the speed to low, add the confectioners' sugar, and beat until well blended. Raise the speed to high and beat until light and creamy, about 2 minutes.

STORE *in an airtight container in the refrigerator for up to 1 week; let soften at room temperature before using.*

CREAM CHEESE MAPLE FROSTING: Add ⅛ teaspoon maple flavoring along with the vanilla extract.

WHITE CHOCOLATE CREAM CHEESE FROSTING

White chocolate adds richness and body to this luxurious frosting and tempers the characteristic tang of cream cheese with a mild sweetness. While it's the ideal complement to carrot cake, it's also great lavished over spice, banana, or chocolate cakes.

➤ MAKES 3½ CUPS

3.5 ounces (100 g) high-quality white chocolate, chopped

1 pound (454 g) cream cheese, softened

3 tablespoons (1.5 oz/42 g) unsalted butter, softened

1 tablespoon (15 ml) freshly squeezed lemon juice

1 teaspoon vanilla extract

1⅔ cups (6.7 oz/191 g) confectioners' sugar

1. Melt the white chocolate in the top of a double boiler over barely simmering water, stirring frequently. Remove the chocolate from the heat and set aside to cool slightly.

2. In the bowl of an electric mixer, using the paddle attachment, beat the cream cheese and butter at medium speed until smooth and creamy, about 1 minute. Add the melted white chocolate and mix until blended. Add the lemon juice, vanilla extract, and confectioners' sugar and mix until blended. Increase the speed to high and beat until smooth and creamy, about 1 minute. Use the frosting immediately, as it will begin to harden quickly.

STORE *in an airtight container in the refrigerator for up to 3 days; bring to room temperature before using.*

FLUFFY WHITE FROSTING

This sweet, billowy white frosting, also known as Seven-Minute Frosting, is as light as air and can be piled high on top of cakes and cupcakes. It should be made right before you're going to use it, as it will harden as it stands.

➤ MAKES ABOUT 5 CUPS

3 large egg whites

1½ cups (10.5 oz/300 g) granulated sugar

⅓ cup (80 ml) water

½ teaspoon cream of tartar

Pinch of salt

1 teaspoon vanilla extract

1. Fill a skillet with 1 inch of water and bring to a simmer over medium-high heat. Reduce the heat so that the water is at a bare simmer.

2. In the bowl of an electric mixer, combine the egg whites, sugar, water, cream of tartar, and salt and, using the whisk attachment, beat at medium speed until foamy, about 1 minute.

3. Place the bowl in the skillet of simmering water and stir the mixture with a rubber spatula until it reaches 160°F on an instant-read thermometer. Remove the bowl from the water and place it on the mixer stand. Using the whisk attachment, beat the mixture at high speed until it forms stiff peaks and is cool, 5 to 7 minutes. Add the vanilla extract and mix at medium speed until blended.

STORE: *Use right away, as the frosting hardens upon standing.*

CREAMY PEANUT BUTTER FROSTING

 h, peanut butter. I adore it, whether it's straight from the jar or in a creamy frosting slathered on a chocolate cake. This recipe is designed for a brand-name, commercial peanut butter (my favorite is Jif), not the natural kind found in health food stores.

➤ MAKES 2¾ CUPS

¾ cup (7 oz/200 g) creamy peanut butter (not sugar-free or natural)

4 tablespoons (2 oz/57 g) unsalted butter, softened

1½ teaspoons vanilla extract

3 cups (12 oz/345 g) confectioners' sugar

⅓ cup (80 ml) whole milk

1. In the bowl of an electric mixer, using the paddle attachment, beat the peanut butter and butter at medium speed until well blended. Add the vanilla extract and mix until blended and smooth, scraping down the sides of the bowl as necessary. At low speed, gradually add the confectioners' sugar in three additions, alternating it with the milk in two additions. Beat at low speed until creamy, about 1 minute.

2. Use the frosting immediately, or cover and refrigerate.

STORE *in an airtight container in the refrigerator for up to 4 days; bring to room temperature before using.*

FUDGY CHOCOLATE FROSTING

This rich, chocolaty frosting spreads beautifully and has a luscious sheen. Use it to fill and frost chocolate or vanilla butter cakes.

➤ MAKES 3 CUPS

3 ounces (85 g) unsweetened chocolate, coarsely chopped (I use Scharffen Berger)

3 ounces (85 g) bittersweet chocolate, coarsely chopped

1 cup (2 sticks/8 oz/227 g) unsalted butter, softened

2 cups (8.1 oz/230 g) confectioners' sugar

1 tablespoon vanilla extract

1. Put both chocolates in a medium stainless steel bowl and place the bowl over a pot of barely simmering water. Heat, stirring frequently, until the chocolate is completely melted. Remove the bowl from the pot and set the chocolate aside to cool until tepid.

2. In the bowl of an electric mixer, using the paddle attachment, beat the butter at medium speed until creamy, about 30 seconds. Gradually add the confectioners' sugar and beat at high speed until light and creamy, about 2 minutes. Beat in the vanilla extract. Add the cooled chocolate at low speed, mixing until blended and scraping down the sides of the bowl as necessary. Increase the speed to high and beat until slightly aerated, about 1 minute.

STORE *at room temperature, covered, for up to 3 hours, or refrigerate for up to 5 days. Bring to room temperature before using.*

DARK CHOCOLATE SOUR CREAM FROSTING

Ultra-creamy and rich, this bittersweet frosting has a satiny texture and the subtle tang of sour cream.

➤ MAKES ABOUT 2½ CUPS

6 ounces (170 g) bittersweet chocolate, coarsely chopped

½ cup (1 stick/4 oz/113 g) unsalted butter, softened

½ cup (4.2 oz/121 g) sour cream, at room temperature

2½ cups (10.1 oz/287 g) confectioners' sugar, sifted

1 teaspoon vanilla extract

1. Put the chocolate in a medium stainless steel bowl and place the bowl over a pot of barely simmering water. Heat, stirring frequently, until the chocolate is completely melted. Remove the bowl from the pot and set the chocolate aside to cool until tepid.

2. In the bowl of an electric mixer, using the paddle attachment, beat the butter at medium speed until creamy, about 30 seconds. Add the sour cream and beat at medium speed until blended and smooth, about 1 minute. Gradually add the confectioners' sugar and beat at high speed until light and creamy, about 2 minutes. Beat in the vanilla extract. Add the cooled chocolate at low speed, mixing until blended and scraping down the sides of the bowl as necessary. Increase the speed to high and beat until slightly aerated, about 1 minute.

STORE *in an airtight container at room temperature for up to 3 hours, or refrigerate for up to a week; bring to room temperature before using.*

Milk Chocolate Coconut Ganache

With only two ingredients, this ultra-creamy frosting is dead easy to make, though you'd never guess it from the taste. Use full-fat (not light) coconut milk for the best taste and texture.

➤ Makes 2⅓ cups

12 ounces (340 g) high-quality milk chocolate, finely chopped

1¾ cups (420 ml) coconut milk

1. Put the chocolate in a medium bowl and set aside.

2. In a small saucepan, heat the coconut milk over medium heat, stirring frequently, until bubbles begin to form around the edges of the pan. Pour the hot coconut milk over the chocolate and let it stand for about 1 minute to melt the chocolate, then whisk until the chocolate is melted and the mixture is smooth. Cover the surface of the ganache with plastic wrap and refrigerate until well chilled and firm enough to spread, about 5 hours.

STORE *in an airtight container in the refrigerator for up to a week.*

MILK CHOCOLATE PEANUT BUTTER GANACHE

Something downright magical happens when peanut butter and chocolate get together, as in this indescribably delicious ganache. Use it as a filling or frosting for chocolate or vanilla layer cakes and cupcakes.

➤ MAKES 2½ CUPS

8 ounces (227 g) high-quality milk chocolate, finely chopped

1½ cups (360 ml) heavy cream

½ cup (4.6 oz/133 g) creamy peanut butter (not sugar-free or natural)

Pinch of salt

1. Put the chocolate in a medium bowl and set aside.

2. In a medium saucepan, heat the heavy cream over medium-high heat until bubbles form around the edges of the pan. Add the peanut butter and salt and whisk until completely combined. Pour the hot cream mixture over the chocolate and let stand for about 1 minute to melt the chocolate, then whisk until the chocolate is melted and the mixture is smooth. Cover the surface of the ganache with plastic wrap and refrigerate until firm enough to spread, about 4 hours.

STORE *in an airtight container in the refrigerator for up to a week.*

Whipped White Chocolate Ganache

Used as a filling or frosting for a variety of cakes, this white chocolate ganache is rich, but because it is whipped, it is also quite light. Allow time, as it needs to chill for at least six hours before whipping. And above all, do not overwhip the ganache, or it will become a grainy mess (though it will still taste great!).

➤ Makes about 1¾ cups

6 ounces (170 g) high-quality white chocolate, finely chopped

1 cup (240 ml) heavy cream

1. Place the white chocolate in the bowl of an electric mixer and set aside.

2. In a small saucepan, bring the cream to a gentle boil over medium heat. Pour the hot cream over the chocolate and let it stand for about 1 minute to melt the chocolate, then whisk the mixture until smooth. Cover with plastic wrap and refrigerate for at least 6 hours, or overnight.

3. Using the whisk attachment, beat the ganache at medium-high speed until the whisk begins to leave a trail in it and it is the consistency of softly whipped cream.

STORE *in an airtight container in the refrigerator for up to 3 days.*

Whipped White Chocolate Lemon Ganache: After whisking the ganache until smooth in Step 2, whisk in 1 teaspoon finely grated lemon zest.

Whipped White Chocolate Espresso Ganache: In Step 2, add ⅓ cup espresso beans, coarsely chopped, to the cream and bring to a boil. Remove the pan from the heat and let stand for 15 minutes. Return to a gentle boil, then strain over the white chocolate and proceed as directed.

WHIPPED WHITE CHOCOLATE CINNAMON GANACHE: In Step 2, add 2 cinnamon sticks to the cream and bring to a boil. Remove the pan from the heat and let stand for 15 minutes. Return to a gentle boil, then strain over the white chocolate and proceed as directed.

WHIPPED WHITE CHOCOLATE ORANGE GANACHE: After whisking the ganache until smooth in Step 2, whisk in 1 teaspoon finely grated orange zest.

WHIPPED WHITE CHOCOLATE RASPBERRY GANACHE: After whisking the ganache until smooth in Step 2, whisk in 1 tablespoon raspberry brandy, such as Framboise.

WHIPPED WHITE CHOCOLATE COCONUT-RUM GANACHE: Substitute Lindt White Coconut White Chocolate. After whisking the ganache until smooth in Step 2, whisk in 1 tablespoon dark rum.

RICH CHOCOLATE ESPRESSO FROSTING

This dark chocolate ganache is infused with the flavor of fresh espresso beans. Not as sweet as most frostings, it is ideal sandwiched between dacquoise or meringue rounds, topped with lots of whipped cream.

➤ MAKES ABOUT 2½ CUPS

1¾ cups (420 ml) heavy cream

⅓ cup (0.9 oz/26 g) espresso beans, coarsely chopped

12 ounces (340 g) semisweet chocolate, finely chopped

2 tablespoons (1 oz/28 g) unsalted butter, cut into tablespoons

1. In a medium saucepan, combine the cream and espresso beans and bring to a boil over medium-high heat. Remove the pan from the heat and let the cream infuse for 20 minutes.

2. Place the chocolate in a medium bowl. Set aside.

3. Add the butter to the cream mixture and return it to a boil. Strain the cream through a fine-mesh sieve onto the chocolate (discard the beans). Let stand for 30 seconds to melt the chocolate, then whisk until blended and smooth. Cover the surface of the frosting with plastic wrap and refrigerate, stirring occasionally, until firm enough to spread, about 1½ hours.

STORE *in an airtight container in the refrigerator for up to a week; bring to cool room temperature before using.*

WHIPPED GANACHE

A lthough it is light as a cloud, this silky filling and frosting has a real chocolate kick. This recipe can easily be doubled.

➤ MAKES 3 CUPS

7 ounces (200 g) bittersweet chocolate, finely chopped

2 cups (480 ml) heavy cream

1 teaspoon vanilla extract or 1 tablespoon Cognac, Grand Marnier, Kahlúa, or other liqueur

1. Put the chocolate in the bowl of an electric mixer and set aside.

2. In a medium saucepan, bring the heavy cream to a gentle boil over medium-high heat. Pour the hot cream over the chocolate and let stand for about 1 minute to melt the chocolate, then whisk until the chocolate is melted and the mixture is smooth. Whisk in the vanilla extract or Cognac or liqueur. Cover the surface of the ganache with plastic wrap and refrigerate until firm enough to whip, at least 6 hours.

3. Using the whisk attachment, beat the ganache at medium-high speed until it forms medium peaks and is firm enough to spread, about 1 minute (do not overbeat).

STORE *in an airtight container in the refrigerator for up to a week; bring to room temperature before using.*

SWISS MERINGUE BUTTERCREAM

The great thing about this fluffy egg white buttercream is that it doesn't require you to make a sugar syrup as in the classic French version. Instead, the whites are warmed gently in a skillet of hot water before whipping. The butter should be at cool room temperature (slightly firm, but not soft or squishy) before you add it to the whites.

➤ MAKES A GENEROUS 5 CUPS

1 cup (7 oz/200 g) granulated sugar

5 large egg whites

3 tablespoons (45 ml) water

1 pound (4 sticks/454 g) unsalted butter, slightly softened

1 teaspoon vanilla extract

1. Pour ½ inch of water into a skillet and bring to a simmer. Reduce the heat to medium-low to maintain a simmer.

2. In the bowl of an electric mixer, combine the sugar, egg whites, and water. Place the bowl in the skillet of water and whisk gently until the mixture registers 160°F on an instant-read thermometer.

3. Transfer the bowl to the mixer stand and, using the whisk attachment, beat at medium-high speed until the meringue forms stiff, shiny peaks and is cool, about 5 minutes.

4. Reduce the speed to medium and beat in the butter 1 tablespoon at a time. Beat in the vanilla. Beat at high speed until the buttercream is smooth, about 1 minute.

STORE *in an airtight container at room temperature for up to 6 hours, or refrigerate for up to a week; bring to room temperature before using.*

CHOCOLATE SWISS MERINGUE BUTTERCREAM: In a medium bowl, melt 6 ounces bittersweet chocolate, coarsely chopped, with 3 tablespoons water over a pot of barely simmering water, stirring until smooth. Let cool. Mix the cooled chocolate into the finished buttercream at low speed, then stir the buttercream with a rubber spatula until completely blended.

ORANGE SWISS MERINGUE BUTTERCREAM: Reduce the vanilla extract to ½ teaspoon and add ½ teaspoon orange oil or Fiori di Sicilia (see Sources, page 366) and 1½ tablespoons Grand Marnier or Cointreau.

FRENCH-STYLE BUTTERCREAM

This classic French buttercream is made by pouring a hot sugar syrup into beaten eggs and then adding softened butter. The trick to this finicky frosting is accuracy: The boiling syrup needs to be at 238°F when it is added to the eggs. Too low, and the buttercream will be too thin; too high, and the syrup will clump in the bowl. But get it right, and you'll have a luscious, satiny frosting that will transform even the plainest of cakes into something spectacular.

➤ MAKES 4 CUPS

1½ cups (10.5 oz/300 g) granulated sugar

½ cup (120 ml) water

4 large eggs, at room temperature

1¾ cups (3½ sticks/14 oz/397 g) unsalted butter, slightly softened (but still cool)

1 teaspoon vanilla extract

1. In a small heavy saucepan, combine the sugar and water and bring to a boil over medium heat, stirring to dissolve the sugar. Stop stirring, and increase the heat to high.

2. In the bowl of an electric mixer, using the whisk attachment, beat the eggs at medium speed until the sugar syrup is ready.

3. Cook the sugar syrup until it reaches 238°F on a candy thermometer. Remove the pan from the heat and, with the mixer off, immediately pour about ¼ cup of the hot syrup over the beaten eggs. Beat at high speed until blended, about 10 seconds. Turn the mixer off and add another ¼ cup syrup. Beat at high speed for another 10 seconds. Repeat this process until all of the syrup is used. Using a rubber spatula, scrape down the sides of the bowl, then beat at medium-high speed until the mixture is completely cool, about 5 minutes.

4. Beat in the softened butter 1 tablespoon at a time at medium speed. Add the vanilla extract. Increase the speed to medium-high and beat the buttercream until it is smooth and shiny, about 4 minutes.

STORE *in an airtight container at room temperature for up to 6 hours, or refrigerate for up to a week; bring to room temperature before using.*

PISTACHIO BUTTERCREAM: In Step 4, beat ¼ cup pistachio paste, homemade (page 335) or store-bought (see Sources, page 366), and 2 to 3 drops green food coloring into the finished buttercream.

CHOCOLATE BUTTERCREAM: Omit the vanilla. In Step 4, beat 5 ounces extra bittersweet or bittersweet chocolate, melted and cooled, into the finished buttercream.

HAZELNUT BUTTERCREAM: In Step 4, beat ½ cup praline paste, homemade (page 333) or store-bought (see Sources, page 366), and 2 tablespoons Frangelico (hazelnut liqueur) into the finished buttercream.

RASPBERRY BUTTERCREAM: In Step 4, beat ½ cup seedless raspberry jam, 2 tablespoons Chambord (raspberry liqueur) or kirsch (optional), 1 teaspoon finely grated lemon zest, and 3 to 4 drops red food coloring into the finished buttercream.

ALMOND BUTTERCREAM: Omit the vanilla. In Step 4, beat ½ teaspoon almond extract into the finished buttercream.

SILKY CHOCOLATE BUTTERCREAM

ere's an egg yolk buttercream that has a light, silky texture and an intense chocolate flavor. Use the best chocolate you can for this frosting—it will make all the difference.

➤ MAKES A SCANT 3 CUPS

10 ounces (283 g) high-quality bittersweet chocolate, chopped

⅔ cup (160 ml) water, divided

¾ cup (150 g) granulated sugar

3 large egg yolks

1 cup (2 sticks/8 oz/227 g) unsalted butter, slightly softened

1. Put the chocolate and ⅓ cup of the water in a medium stainless steel bowl and place the bowl over a pot of barely simmering water. Heat, stirring frequently, until the chocolate is completely melted. Remove the bowl from the pot and set the chocolate mixture aside to cool until tepid.

2. In a small heavy saucepan, combine the sugar with the remaining ⅓ cup water and bring to a boil over medium heat, stirring to dissolve the sugar. Stop stirring, and increase the heat to high.

3. Meanwhile, in the bowl of an electric mixer fitted with the whisk attachment, begin beating the egg yolks at medium speed. When the sugar syrup reaches 225°F on a candy thermometer, increase the speed of the mixer to high. Continue to cook the sugar syrup until it reaches 238°F.

4. Remove the pan of syrup from the heat and with the mixer off, immediately pour about ¼ cup of the hot syrup over the beaten eggs. Beat at high speed until blended, about 10 seconds. Turn the mixer off and add another ¼ cup syrup. Beat at high speed for another 10 seconds. Repeat this process until all of the syrup is used. Using a rubber spatula, scrape down the sides of the bowl, and beat at medium-high speed until the egg mixture is completely cool, about 5 minutes.

5. At medium speed, beat in the softened butter 1 tablespoon at a time. Increase the speed to medium-high and beat the buttercream until it is smooth and shiny, about 2 minutes. Reduce the speed to

low and add the cooled chocolate mixture, mixing just until blended. Stir the mixture by hand a few times to make sure it is well blended.

STORE *in an airtight container at room temperature for up to 6 hours or refrigerate for up to a week; bring to room temperature before using.*

CARAMEL ESPRESSO BUTTERCREAM

A classic French-style buttercream, but made with dark brown sugar instead of white sugar, which turns it into caramel. The bold flavor of espresso complements the rich, sweet caramel. Slather it on Sour Cream Chocolate Cake Layers (page 124) or Deeply Dark Devil's Food Cake (page 122).

➤ MAKES 5 CUPS

1¼ cups (10.5 oz/300 g) firmly packed dark brown sugar

1¼ cups (300 ml) heavy cream

½ cup (120 ml) light corn syrup

¼ teaspoon salt

4 large eggs

1 pound (4 sticks/454 g) unsalted butter, slightly softened

2 teaspoons vanilla extract

1 tablespoon (0.1 oz/3 g) espresso powder, dissolved in 1 tablespoon (15 ml) hot water

1. In a medium saucepan, combine the sugar, heavy cream, corn syrup, and salt and cook over medium-high heat, stirring constantly, just until the sugar is dissolved. Stop stirring, and increase the heat to high.

2. Meanwhile, in the bowl of an electric mixer fitted with the whisk attachment, begin beating the eggs at medium speed. When the sugar syrup reaches 225°F on a candy thermometer, increase the speed of the mixer to high. Continue to cook the sugar syrup until it reaches 238°F.

3. Remove the pan from the heat and, with the mixer off, immediately pour about ¼ cup of the hot syrup over the beaten eggs. Beat at high speed until blended, about 10 seconds. Turn the mixer off and add another ¼ cup syrup. Beat at high speed for another 10 seconds. Repeat this process until all of the syrup is used. Using a rubber spatula, scrape down the sides of the bowl, then beat at medium-high speed until the egg mixture is completely cool, about 5 minutes.

4. At medium speed, beat in the softened butter 1 tablespoon at a time. Add the vanilla extract and coffee mixture, increase the speed to medium-high, and beat the buttercream until it is smooth and shiny, about 4 minutes.

STORE *in an airtight container at room temperature for up to 6 hours, or refrigerate for up to a week; bring to room temperature before using.*

15

Basic Recipes
and
Accompaniments

BASIC SOAKING SYRUP • PRALINE PASTE • PRALINE POWDER • PISTACHIO PASTE • CRÈME FRAÎCHE • SUGARED NUTS • ALMOND TOFFEE CRUNCH • CLASSIC WHIPPED CREAM • ESPRESSO CREAM • BROWN SUGAR WHIPPED CREAM • CACAO NIB WHIPPED CREAM • CHOCOLATE WHIPPED CREAM • COCONUT WHIPPED CREAM • MASCARPONE WHIPPED CREAM • WHITE CHOCOLATE WHIPPED CREAM • WHITE CHOCOLATE LEMON WHIPPED CREAM (*variation*) • WHITE CHOCOLATE COCONUT WHIPPED CREAM (*variation*) • CARAMEL CREAM • CARAMEL SAUCE • MINT SYRUP • RED BERRY SAUCE • GINGERED BERRY COMPOTE • WARM CHOCOLATE SAUCE • LEMON CURD • CANDIED ORANGE ZEST • CLASSIC VANILLA CUSTARD SAUCE (CRÈME ANGLAISE) • BANANA ICE CREAM • QUICK BANANA ICE CREAM • COOKIES AND CREAM ICE CREAM • TOASTED ALMOND CRUNCH ICE CREAM • MERINGUE MUSHROOMS • ALMOST FOOLPROOF TEMPERED CHOCOLATE

A few of the recipes in this chapter are for basic cake components (such as Cookies and Cream Ice Cream and Lemon Curd) and some are for cake decorations (e.g., Almond Toffee Crunch and Candied Orange Zest), but most are for delicious things to serve alongside or on top of cakes, such as sauces and flavored whipped creams. Whatever your goal—whether it's to impart flavor and moisture to a cake with a soaking syrup or elevate a slice of pound cake with a zippy fruit compote—you'll find just the right recipe here.

BASIC SOAKING SYRUP

 sed primarily to moisten cake layers, this syrup also adds flavor to cake layers.

TO SOAK 1 OR 2 LAYERS
(MAKES ABOUT 1 CUP)

½ cup (3.5 oz/100 g) granulated sugar

¾ cup (180 ml) water

1½ tablespoons (22 ml) liqueur or
¾ teaspoon vanilla extract

TO SOAK 3 OR 4 LAYERS
(MAKES 1⅓ CUPS)

¾ cup (5.3 oz/150 g) granulated sugar

1 cup (240 ml) water

3 tablespoons (45 ml) liqueur or
1 teaspoon vanilla extract

1. In a small saucepan, combine the sugar and water and bring to a boil over medium heat, stirring to dissolve the sugar. Remove the pan from the heat and let the syrup cool to room temperature.

2. Stir in the liqueur or extract.

STORE *in an airtight container in the refrigerator for up to 6 weeks.*

PRALINE PASTE

Though prepared praline paste is available in gourmet shops and by mail-order (see Sources, page 366), it's easy to make your own. The combination of caramelized almonds, hazelnuts, and fragrant hazelnut oil is a flavorful addition to cakes and buttercreams.

➤ MAKES A GENEROUS 1 CUP

½ cup (2.1 oz/60 g) blanched whole or slivered almonds

½ cup (2.5 oz/71 g) blanched hazelnuts

¾ cup (5.3 oz/150 g) granulated sugar

3 tablespoons (45 ml) water

1 tablespoon (15 ml) hazelnut or vegetable oil

1. Position a rack in the center of the oven and preheat the oven to 350°F.

2. Spread the almonds and hazelnuts on a baking sheet and toast in the oven for 8 to 12 minutes, shaking the pan once or twice, until golden and fragrant. Let the nuts cool completely on the baking sheet.

3. Brush another baking sheet lightly with vegetable oil; set aside. Combine the sugar and water in a medium heavy saucepan and bring to a boil over medium-high heat, stirring to dissolve the sugar and occasionally brushing down the sides of the pan with a wet pastry brush. Continue to cook, without stirring, until the mixture turns a light caramel, 3 to 5 minutes.

4. Remove the pan from the heat and stir in the toasted almonds and hazelnuts. Return the pan to the heat and cook, stirring, until the nuts are completely coated with the caramel and it deepens to an amber color. Immediately pour the caramelized nut mixture onto the oiled baking sheet, spreading it out. Allow the praline to cool for 30 minutes, or until hard.

5. Using a large knife, coarsely chop the praline. Place in a food processor and process for about a minute, until it is the consistency of sand. Add the hazelnut or vegetable oil and process for another 30 seconds, or until it becomes a paste.

STORE *in an airtight container in the refrigerator for up to 1 week.*

PRALINE POWDER

imilar to praline paste but drier, this aromatic powder can be made with a variety of nuts to flavor cakes, frostings, or ice creams—it's also great sprinkled on ice cream.

➤ MAKES ABOUT 1 CUP

½ cup (3.5 oz/100 g) granulated sugar

2 tablespoons (30 ml) water

½ cup (2 oz/57 g) chopped walnuts, blanched almonds, shelled pistachios, or toasted, skinned hazelnuts (see page 37)

1. Brush a baking sheet lightly with vegetable oil; set aside. Combine the sugar and water in a medium heavy saucepan. Bring to a boil over medium-high heat, stirring to dissolve the sugar and occasionally brushing down the sides of the pan with a wet pastry brush. Continue to cook, without stirring, until the mixture turns a light caramel, 2 to 4 minutes.

2. Remove the pan from the heat and stir in the chopped nuts. Return the pan to the heat and cook, stirring, until the nuts are completely coated with the caramel and it deepens to an amber color. Immediately pour the caramelized nut mixture onto the oiled baking sheet. Allow the praline to cool for 30 minutes, or until hard.

3. Using a large knife, coarsely chop the praline. Place in a food processor and process just until it is finely ground.

STORE *in an airtight container in a cool, dry place for up to a month.*

PISTACHIO PASTE

More of a crumbly wet nut mixture than a smooth paste, this pastry-kitchen staple adds just-out-of-the-shell pistachio flavor to buttercreams and other fillings and frostings. Store-bought pistachio paste is available in gourmet and some health food stores or through mail-order (see Sources, page 366), but it's easy to make your own.

➤ MAKES ABOUT 1⅔ CUPS

1¼ cups (6.7 oz/190 g) shelled unsalted pistachio nuts

¾ cup (5.3 oz/150 g) granulated sugar

2 tablespoons (30 ml) water

2 tablespoons (30 ml) pistachio or vegetable oil

1. Position a rack in the center of the oven and preheat the oven to 350°F.

2. Spread the pistachio nuts on a baking sheet and toast in the oven for 5 to 7 minutes, shaking the pan once or twice, until fragrant. Let the nuts cool completely on the baking sheet.

3. Brush another baking sheet lightly with vegetable oil; set aside. Combine the sugar and water in a medium heavy saucepan. Bring to a boil over medium-high heat, stirring to dissolve the sugar and occasionally brushing down the sides of the pan with a wet pastry brush. Continue to cook, without stirring, until the mixture turns to a medium caramel, 3 to 5 minutes.

4. Remove the pan from the heat and stir in the toasted pistachios. Return the pan to the heat and cook, stirring, until the nuts are completely coated with the caramel and it deepens to an amber color. Immediately pour the caramelized nut mixture onto the oiled baking sheet, separating the nuts a bit with a wooden spoon so they are not mounded. Allow the praline to cool for 30 minutes, or until hard.

5. Using a large knife, coarsely chop the praline. Place in a food processor and process for about a minute, until it is the consistency of sand. Add the pistachio or vegetable oil and process for about 30 seconds longer, until blended.

STORE *in an airtight container in the refrigerator for up to 1 week.*

CRÈME FRAÎCHE

These days this rich and tangy cream can be found in the dairy section of many supermarkets, but, in a pinch, it can also be made at home.

➤ MAKES ABOUT 2¼ CUPS

2 cups (480 ml) heavy cream (preferably not ultra-pasteurized)

¼ cup (60 ml) buttermilk

1. Combine the cream and buttermilk in a small saucepan and heat over medium-low just until the mixture registers 110°F on an instant-read thermometer. Pour the mixture into a heatproof glass container.

2. Cover the container loosely, place it in a warm place, such as the top of the refrigerator or the stove, and let stand, without stirring, for 8 to 14 hours (ultra-pasteurized cream may take up to 36 hours), until slightly thickened (it should still be pourable).

3. Transfer the crème fraîche to an airtight container and refrigerate for at least 3 hours before using (it will continue to thicken as it chills).

STORE *in an airtight container in the refrigerator for up to 2 weeks.*

SUGARED NUTS

isarmingly simple to make, these flavorful sugared nuts make a big impact as a cake garnish or topping. They are also superb on their own—serve them in a bowl along with coffee or tea after the dessert course.

➤ MAKES 1½ CUPS

1 large egg white

1½ cups (4.5 oz/128 g) sliced unblanched almonds or pecans, walnuts, or salted peanuts

2 tablespoons (0.8 oz/25 g) granulated sugar

1. Position a rack in the center of the oven and preheat the oven to 325°F. Lightly butter a baking sheet.

2. Place the egg white in a medium bowl, add the nuts, and stir to coat the nuts evenly. Sprinkle over the sugar and toss the nuts to coat evenly with the sugar.

3. Spread the nuts in an even layer on the baking sheet. Bake, tossing the nuts twice, for 20 to 25 minutes, until lightly browned. Cool completely.

4. Store the nuts in an airtight container at room temperature.

STORE *in an airtight container at room temperature for up to a week.*

ALMOND TOFFEE CRUNCH

This delightful toffee crunch is a nice way to break up the vast whiteness of a whipped cream– or buttercream-topped cake or to enjoy as a snack on its own.

➤ MAKES ABOUT ½ CUP

½ cup (2.1 oz/60 g) slivered almonds

4 tablespoons (2 oz/57 g) unsalted butter, cut into tablespoons

½ cup (3.5 oz/100 g) granulated sugar

3 tablespoons (44 ml) water

1 teaspoon freshly squeezed lemon juice

Pinch of salt

½ teaspoon vanilla extract

¼ teaspoon almond extract

1. Position a rack in the center of the oven and preheat the oven to 350°F.

2. Put the almonds on a baking sheet and bake for 8 to 10 minutes, until they are golden and fragrant. Let cool.

3. Lightly butter a jelly-roll pan; set aside. In a medium saucepan, combine the butter, sugar, water, lemon juice, and salt, place over medium heat, and stir with a wooden spoon just until the sugar is dissolved. Stop stirring, raise the heat to medium-high, and boil the mixture until it turns a deep golden brown, about 7 minutes.

4. Remove the pan from the heat and stir in the almonds and extracts. Pour the mixture into the center of the prepared jelly-roll pan, place the pan on a wire rack, and let cool completely.

5. Slide a metal spatula under the toffee and transfer it to a cutting surface. Finely chop the toffee using a chef's knife, or chop it in a food processor. Store in an airtight container at room temperature.

STORE *in an airtight container in a cool, dry place for up to 1 month.*

Classic Whipped Cream

A dollop of freshly whipped cream improves almost any cake, from a simple pound cake to an intensely flavored flourless chocolate cake, and takes minutes to make.

➤ Makes 3 cups

1½ cups (360 ml) heavy cream

3 tablespoons (0.7 oz/21 g) confectioners' sugar, sifted

1½ teaspoons vanilla extract

1. In the chilled bowl of an electric mixer, using the whisk attachment, whip the cream at high speed just until it begins to thicken. Add the sugar and vanilla and beat until soft peaks form. Use immediately, or cover and refrigerate.

Store *in the refrigerator, covered, for up to 2 hours.*

ESPRESSO CREAM

This softly whipped espresso-infused cream is a flavorful alternative to standard whipped cream or crème anglaise. It is really more of a sauce than a whipped cream, meant to be poured rather than dolloped.

➤ MAKES 1¾ CUPS

1¾ cups (420 ml) heavy cream

½ cup espresso beans

2 tablespoons (0.8 oz/25 g) granulated sugar

½ teaspoon vanilla extract

1. In a small saucepan, combine the heavy cream, espresso beans, and sugar and bring to a boil over medium heat, stirring occasionally to dissolve the sugar. Remove the pan from the heat and let stand, covered, for 15 minutes.

2. Pour the cream through a fine-mesh sieve into the bowl of an electric mixer (discard the beans). Cover the bowl and refrigerate for 3 hours, until well chilled.

3. Add the vanilla extract to the cream and, using the whisk attachment, whip the cream until the whisk begins to leave a trail and soft mounds begin to form (the cream should still be pourable). Use immediately, or cover and refrigerate.

4. To serve, spoon a large circle of cream onto each dessert plate and place a slice of cake on top.

STORE *in the refrigerator, covered, for up to 3 hours.*

BROWN SUGAR WHIPPED CREAM

U sing brown sugar in place of granulated sugar adds a subtle caramel flavor and color to whipped cream. This cream goes particularly well with dark chocolate, spice, and fruit cakes.

➤ MAKES ABOUT 2 CUPS

1 cup (240 ml) chilled heavy cream

2 tablespoons (0.9 oz/27 g) firmly packed light brown sugar

¾ teaspoon vanilla extract

1. In the bowl of an electric mixer, using the whisk attachment, whip the cream with the brown sugar and vanilla extract at high speed until soft peaks form. Use immediately, or cover and refrigerate.

STORE *in the refrigerator, covered, for up to 2 hours.*

CACAO NIB WHIPPED CREAM

Cacao nibs are unsweetened shards of roasted cocoa beans that have the taste of chocolate and the texture of nuts. Heavy cream infused with cacao nibs takes on a subtle cocoa flavor that lingers on the palate in a very pleasing way. This softly whipped cream is a luscious complement to any chocolate cake.

➤ MAKES ABOUT 2 CUPS

1 cup (240 ml) heavy cream

¼ cup (1 oz/28 g) cacao nibs, finely chopped (available from www.chocolatesource.com; see Sources, page 367)

2 tablespoons (0.8 oz/25 g) granulated sugar

½ teaspoon vanilla extract

1. In a small saucepan, combine the heavy cream and cacao nibs and bring to a boil over medium heat. Remove the pan from the heat and let stand, covered, for 20 minutes.

2. Pour the cream through a fine-mesh sieve into the bowl of an electric mixer (discard the nibs). Cover the bowl and refrigerate for 3 hours, until well chilled.

3. Add the sugar and vanilla extract to the cream and, using the whisk attachment, whip the cream until it forms soft peaks. Use immediately, or cover and refrigerate.

STORE *in the refrigerator, covered, for up to 2 hours.*

MASCARPONE WHIPPED CREAM

This billowy white cream is sweet but has an unexpected tangy finish.

➤ MAKES ABOUT 1¾ CUPS

½ cup (120 ml) heavy cream

½ cup (4.2 oz/121 g) mascarpone cheese

3 tablespoons (0.7 oz/21 g) confectioners' sugar

1 teaspoon vanilla extract

1. In the bowl of an electric mixer, using the whisk attachment, beat the cream with the mascarpone, sugar, and vanilla extract on high speed until soft peaks form. Use immediately, or cover and refrigerate.

STORE *in an airtight container in the refrigerator for up to 3 hours.*

WHITE CHOCOLATE WHIPPED CREAM

xtra rich and full-bodied, this white chocolate cream is wonderful served alongside simple, light cakes.

➤ MAKES 2¼ CUPS

4 ounces (114 g) high-quality white chocolate, coarsely chopped

1¼ cups (300 ml) heavy cream, divided

1. Place the white chocolate and ¼ cup of the heavy cream in the top of a double boiler and heat over barely simmering water, stirring frequently, until the chocolate is melted and smooth. Remove the chocolate from the heat and let cool to room temperature.

2. In the bowl of an electric mixer, using the whisk attachment, beat the remaining 1 cup heavy cream at high speed until soft peaks begin to form. Remove the bowl from the mixer stand. Whisk about ½ cup of the whipped cream into the chocolate. Pour this mixture into the rest of the whipped cream and, using a rubber spatula, gently fold it in. Do not overmix, or the cream will become grainy. Use immediately, or cover and refrigerate.

STORE *in the refrigerator, covered, for up to 2 hours.*

WHITE CHOCOLATE LEMON WHIPPED CREAM: In Step 2, whisk 1 teaspoon finely grated lemon zest into the chocolate along with the ½ cup of whipped cream.

WHITE CHOCOLATE COCONUT WHIPPED CREAM: Substitute Lindt White Coconut White Chocolate for the white chocolate (this cream will not be completely smooth because of the shredded coconut in the chocolate).

CARAMEL CREAM

Silky smooth with a deep caramel flavor and a subtle tang, this whipped cream is wonderful as an accompaniment to or topping for a cake. Note that the caramel must chill for two hours, so plan ahead.

➤ MAKES ABOUT 3 CUPS

¾ cup (5.3 oz/150 g) granulated sugar

3 tablespoons (45 ml) water

¼ teaspoon freshly squeezed lemon juice

1¼ cups (300 ml) heavy cream, divided

¾ cup (6.4 oz/181 g) mascarpone cheese

1 teaspoon vanilla extract

1. In a small heavy saucepan, combine the sugar, water, and lemon juice and cook over medium heat, stirring constantly, until the sugar dissolves. Increase the heat to high and cook without stirring, occasionally brushing down the sides of the pan with a wet pastry brush, until the syrup caramelizes and turns a golden amber color, about 4 minutes.

2. Remove the pan from the heat and carefully add ½ cup of the heavy cream (the mixture will bubble up), stirring until smooth. Carefully pour the hot caramel into a heatproof glass measure and loosely cover with plastic wrap. Refrigerate the caramel until chilled, about 2 hours.

3. In the bowl of an electric mixer, using the whisk attachment, beat the remaining ¾ cup cream with the mascarpone cheese and vanilla at medium speed until blended. Add the chilled caramel and beat at high speed until the mixture forms soft peaks. Use immediately, or cover and refrigerate.

STORE *in the refrigerator, covered, for up to 8 hours.*

CARAMEL SAUCE

The complex sweetness of rich, creamy caramel sauce works well with many cakes, particularly chocolate ones.

➤ MAKES ABOUT 1 ½ CUPS

1½ cups (10.5 oz/300 g) granulated sugar

½ cup (120 ml) water

1 cup (240 ml) heavy cream

2 tablespoons (1 oz/28 g) unsalted butter

1. In a medium heavy saucepan, combine the sugar and water and cook over medium heat, stirring constantly, until the sugar dissolves. Increase the heat to high and cook without stirring, occasionally brushing down the sides of the pan with a wet pastry brush, until the syrup caramelizes and turns a golden amber color, about 8 minutes.

2. Remove the pan from the heat and very slowly and carefully add the cream (the mixture will bubble up furiously), stirring until smooth (if there are some hardened bits of caramel sticking to the bottom of the pan, place the pan over medium-low heat and stir until they are dissolved). Add the butter and stir until melted.

3. Serve warm, or cool, cover, and refrigerate until ready to use.

STORE *in an airtight container at room temperature for up to 3 days, or refrigerate for up to 3 months. Reheat before using.*

MINT SYRUP

This minty fresh syrup adds a burst of flavor when drizzled onto pound cakes, fresh berries, or ice cream.

➤ MAKES ABOUT ½ CUP

¼ cup (60 ml) loosely packed fresh mint leaves

½ cup (5.8 oz/164 g) light corn syrup

1 teaspoon water

1. Combine all the ingredients in a blender or small food processor and process until the mint is finely chopped. Transfer the syrup to a plastic squeeze bottle or small pitcher and refrigerate until ready to use.

STORE *in an airtight container in the refrigerator for up to 2 weeks.*

IT IS THE DESTINY OF MINT TO BE CRUSHED.
—WAVERLY ROOT

RED BERRY SAUCE

This simple berry sauce comes together in a flash and really dresses up a plain slice of cake. Start by adding the lesser amount of sugar and check the sauce for balance; if needed, add more sugar until it's just right.

➤ MAKES ABOUT 1 ⅓ CUPS

2 cups (8 oz/226 g) fresh raspberries

1 cup (4 oz/113 g) sliced fresh strawberries

⅓ to ½ cup (1.3 oz/38 g to 2 oz/57 g) confectioners' sugar, depending on the sweetness of the berries

2 teaspoons freshly squeezed lemon juice

1. Combine all the ingredients in the bowl of a food processor and process until smooth. Strain the sauce through a fine-mesh sieve. Cover and refrigerate until ready to serve.

STORE *in the refrigerator, covered, for up to 2 weeks.*

GINGERED BERRY COMPOTE

This zingy berry compote is a nice complement to homey cakes like Plainly Perfect Pound Cake (page 91) or Heavenly Angel Food Cake (page 62). A little sweet whipped cream or vanilla ice cream on the side would be a nice accompaniment.

➤ MAKES ABOUT 1 ¼ CUPS

½ cup (120 ml) water

½ cup (3.5 oz/100 g) granulated sugar

A 1-inch piece of fresh ginger, peeled and thinly sliced

1 cup (240 ml) assorted fresh berries, such as raspberries, quartered strawberries, and blueberries

1. In a small saucepan, combine the water and sugar and bring to a boil. Remove the pan from the heat and add the ginger slices. Set aside to infuse for 30 minutes.

2. Place the berries in a medium bowl. Strain the ginger syrup over the berries (discard the ginger). Cover the compote and refrigerate for at least 1 hour, or until ready to serve.

STORE *in the refrigerator, covered, for up to 24 hours.*

WARM CHOCOLATE SAUCE

Like all proper chocolate sauces, this one is rich, shiny, and very chocolaty. Pour it on a slice of cake or serve it in a small pitcher on the side. Use a top-quality bittersweet chocolate, such as the slightly fruity Valrhona Manjari.

➤ MAKES 1½ CUPS

¾ cup (180 ml) heavy cream

⅓ cup (2.3 oz/66 g) granulated sugar

3 ounces (85 g) bittersweet chocolate, finely chopped

¼ cup (2.9 oz/82 g) light corn syrup

2 tablespoons (1 oz/30 g) unsalted butter, cut into tablespoons

1 teaspoon vanilla extract

1. In a medium saucepan, combine the cream and sugar and cook over medium heat, stirring constantly until the sugar is dissolved and the cream begins to boil. Remove from the heat, add the chocolate, and let stand for 30 seconds to melt the chocolate. Whisk until the chocolate is completely melted.

2. Add the corn syrup and butter and cook over medium heat, stirring constantly, until the mixture comes to a simmer. Remove the pan from the heat and whisk in the vanilla extract. Use the sauce immediately, or cover and refrigerate.

STORE *in an airtight container in the refrigerator for up to a week; reheat before using.*

LEMON CURD

ilky smooth and sweet-tart, Lemon Curd makes a lively filling for layer cakes and a delightful spread for pound cake slices.

➤ MAKES 2 CUPS

8 large egg yolks

1¼ cups (8.8 oz/250 g) granulated sugar

2 teaspoons finely grated lemon zest

¾ cup (180 ml) freshly squeezed lemon juice

Pinch of salt

½ cup (1 stick/4 oz/113 g) unsalted butter, cut into tablespoons

1. Set a fine-mesh sieve over a medium bowl and set aside. In a medium heavy nonreactive saucepan, whisk together the egg yolks and sugar until blended. Stir in the lemon zest and juice, salt, and butter and cook over medium heat, whisking constantly, until the mixture thickens, 7 to 10 minutes (do not let the custard boil, or it will curdle). The mixture should leave a path on the back of a wooden spoon when you draw your finger across it. Immediately strain the mixture through the sieve, pressing it through with a rubber spatula.

2. Set the bowl containing the lemon mixture in a large bowl filled about one-third of the way with ice water (be careful that the water doesn't splash into the lemon mixture). Stir the mixture frequently until it is slightly chilled, about 15 minutes. Cover the surface of the curd with plastic wrap and refrigerate until ready to use.

STORE *in an airtight container in the refrigerator for up to 3 weeks.*

CANDIED ORANGE ZEST

Slender glistening strips of candied orange zest are surprisingly easy to prepare and make a pretty garnish for orange-flavored cakes.

➤ MAKES ABOUT 1¼ CUPS

CANDIED ZEST

3 oranges, scrubbed with a vegetable brush

1 cup (7 oz/200 g) granulated sugar

¾ cup (180 ml) water

¼ teaspoon cream of tartar

SUGAR COATING

½ cup (7 oz/200 g) granulated sugar

1. Using a sharp paring knife, remove the peel of each orange in vertical strips, trying not to include any of the bitter white pith. If any of the pith remains, place each strip, pith side up, on a cutting board and use the paring knife, with the blade parallel to the board, to carefully slice it off. Cut the zest into fine julienne strips.

2. Half fill a medium saucepan with water and bring it to a boil. Add the strips of zest, reduce the heat to a simmer, and simmer for about 15 minutes. Drain and rinse the zest.

3. In the same saucepan, combine the sugar, water, and cream of tartar and bring to a boil, stirring constantly to dissolve the sugar. Add the zest, cover the pan, and reduce the heat to low. Let the zest simmer for another 15 minutes. Remove the pan from the heat and cool completely.

4. The zest can be stored in its syrup in an airtight container for up to a month. When you are ready to use it, drain it well and toss it in the granulated sugar, breaking up any lumps of sugar with your hands. Spread the zest out on a baking sheet and let dry at room temperature for at least 2 hours before using.

STORE *in an airtight container in the refrigerator for up to a month.*

Classic Vanilla Custard Sauce (Crème Anglaise)

This is a delicate cooked custard sauce, speckled with vanilla bean seeds and served cold with a variety of desserts. It is particularly good paired with a warm chocolate or upside-down cake. The sauce requires some attention, as it needs to be stirred constantly and will curdle if heated beyond 175°F.

➤ Makes about 2¼ cups

1 cup (240 ml) heavy cream

1 cup (240 ml) whole milk

½ vanilla bean

4 large egg yolks

¼ cup (1.7 oz/50 g) granulated sugar

Pinch of salt

1. In a medium saucepan, combine the cream and milk. Using a paring knife, split the vanilla bean lengthwise in half. Scrape out the tiny seeds from the pod and add them to the pan, along with the pod. Cook the mixture over medium-high heat until bubbles begin to form around the edge of the pan. Remove the pan from the heat, cover, and let steep for 15 minutes.

2. In a medium bowl, whisk together the egg yolks, sugar, and salt until blended. Reheat the cream mixture until bubbles form around the edges of the pan again. Gradually whisk the hot cream mixture into the yolk mixture until blended. Return the mixture to the saucepan and cook over medium-low heat, stirring constantly with a wooden spoon, until the sauce thickens enough so that a path remains when you run your finger across the back of the sauce-coated spoon. The sauce should register 175°F on an instant-read thermometer; don't allow the sauce to boil, or it will curdle.

3. Pour the sauce through a fine-mesh sieve into a medium stainless steel bowl. Set the bowl in a large bowl filled about one-third of the way with ice water (be careful that the water doesn't splash into the sauce). Stir the sauce frequently until it is slightly chilled, about 15 minutes. Cover and refrigerate until ready to serve.

STORE *in the refrigerator, covered, for up to 4 days.*

BANANA ICE CREAM

Here's Melanie Dubberley's recipe for the banana ice cream used in Soused Banana Ice Cream Crunch Cake (page 274). Melanie cleverly heightens the banana flavor in the ice cream with accents of fresh ginger and dark rum. To maximize the banana impact, be sure to use ripe bananas that have a few dark spots on them.

➤ **MAKES ABOUT 5 CUPS**

1½ cups (360 ml) whole milk

1½ cups (360 ml) heavy cream

1 cup (7 oz/200 g) granulated sugar, divided

¼ cup (60 ml) dark rum

⅛ teaspoon salt

1 vanilla bean

2 medium-sized ripe bananas

2 teaspoons finely chopped fresh ginger

6 large egg yolks

---

1. In a medium saucepan, combine the milk, cream, ½ cup of the sugar, the rum, and salt. Using a paring knife, slit the vanilla bean lengthwise. Scrape the tiny vanilla seeds into the cream mixture, add the vanilla pod, and set aside.

2. Peel the bananas and place them in the bowl of a food processor. Process to roughly chop them, then add the ginger and process until smooth and soupy. Add to the cream mixture.

3. Place the pan over medium-high heat and bring to a gentle boil, stirring frequently.

4. Meanwhile, in a medium bowl, whisk the egg yolks with the remaining ½ cup sugar until blended. Remove the cream mixture from the heat and whisk about ¾ cup of it into the yolk mixture. Gradually whisk this mixture into the hot cream mixture in the saucepan. Place the pan over medium heat and cook, stirring constantly with a wooden spoon, until the mixture thickens enough to leave a path on the back of the sauce-coated spoon when you drag your finger across it. The mixture should register 175°F on an instant-read thermometer (do not let boil).

5. Strain the mixture through a fine-mesh sieve into a medium bowl. Set the bowl in a large bowl filled about one-third of the way with ice water (be careful that the water doesn't splash into the banana mixture). Stir the banana mixture frequently until it is chilled, about 25 minutes. Remove the bowl from the ice bath, cover the surface of the banana custard with plastic wrap, and place the bowl in the freezer for about 15 minutes (no longer, or it may freeze), until it is very cold.

6. Pour the ice cream base into an ice cream machine and process according to the manufacturer's instructions. Pack the ice cream into an airtight container and freeze for at least 4 hours, until firm.

STORE *in an airtight container in the freezer for up to 3 months.*

Quick Banana Ice Cream

Store-bought banana ice cream is very difficult to find, and making it from scratch is time-consuming. Here's an excellent alternative, ready in a flash: high-quality vanilla ice cream from the supermarket combined with ripe banana puree and fresh ginger. It's fabulous with chocolate sauce and/or coconut whipped cream.

➤ MAKES 5 CUPS

1 large ripe banana

2 teaspoons finely grated fresh ginger

5 cups (1.2 l) high-quality vanilla ice cream (preferably Häagen-Dazs)

1. Peel the banana and cut it into chunks. Combine the banana chunks and ginger in the bowl of a food processor and process until the banana is pureed and smooth. Scrape the mixture into a small saucepan and place over medium heat. Cook, stirring frequently, until the mixture just begins to bubble, about 1 minute. Let cool, then transfer the mixture to a freezer-safe container and cover it loosely with plastic wrap. Freeze until ready to use.

2. Let the ice cream stand at room temperature for about 15 minutes to soften.

3. Scoop the softened ice cream into the bowl of an electric mixer. Using the paddle attachment, mix the ice cream at low speed until smooth; add the banana mixture and mix just until blended. Scrape the ice cream into an airtight container and freeze for at least 2 hours before using.

STORE *in an airtight container in the freezer for up to a month.*

COOKIES AND CREAM ICE CREAM

I'm not sure whose idea it was, but it was an inspired one—adding crushed Oreos ("America's favorite cookie") to creamy homemade vanilla ice cream. An even better idea? Using it as the basis for a cake (see Chocolate Cookies and Cream Ice Cream Cake, page 276).

➤ MAKES ABOUT 1 QUART

2 cups (480 ml) half-and-half

6 large egg yolks

⅔ cup (4.6 oz/132 g) granulated sugar

1 cup (240 ml) heavy cream

1 teaspoon vanilla extract

10 Oreo cookies, coarsely crushed

1. In a medium saucepan, bring the half-and-half to a gentle boil over medium heat. Remove from the heat.

2. In a medium bowl, lightly beat the egg yolks. Whisk in the sugar until well blended. Whisk about one-third of the hot half-and-half into the yolk mixture. Pour this mixture into the remaining half-and-half in the saucepan. Cook over medium heat, stirring constantly with a wooden spoon, until the mixture thickens enough to leave a path on the back of the sauce-coated spoon when you drag your finger across it. The mixture should register 175°F on an instant-read thermometer (do not let boil).

3. Strain the mixture through a fine-mesh sieve into a medium bowl. Set the bowl in a larger bowl filled about one-third of the way with ice water (be careful that the water doesn't splash into the yolk mixture). Stir the mixture frequently until it is chilled, about 25 minutes.

4. Remove the bowl from the ice bath and stir in the heavy cream and vanilla extract. Pour into an ice cream machine and process according to the manufacturer's instructions. Add the crushed Oreos during the last minute of churning. Pack the ice cream into an airtight container and freeze for at least 4 hours, until firm.

STORE *in an airtight container in the freezer for up to 3 months.*

TOASTED ALMOND CRUNCH ICE CREAM

Freshly toasted almonds impart an exceptional flavor to this creamy ice cream, while chopped Heath Bars add crunch. Great on its own or served alongside chocolate cake, the ice cream is also the star of its own cake—Toasted Almond Chocolate Baked Alaska (page 282).

➤ MAKES ABOUT 1 QUART

2⅓ cups (560 ml) heavy cream

2⅓ cups (560 ml) whole milk

1 cup (7 oz/200 g) granulated sugar, divided

1⅓ cups (5.6 oz/160 g) slivered almonds, toasted (see page 37)

8 large egg yolks

⅔ cup chopped Heath Bars (¼-inch pieces)

1. In a medium saucepan, combine the cream, milk, ¾ cup of the sugar, and the almonds and bring to a gentle boil over medium-high heat. Reduce the heat to low and simmer for 20 minutes. Remove the pan from the heat.

2. In a large bowl, whisk the egg yolks with the remaining ¼ cup sugar until blended. Gradually whisk in the hot cream mixture. Return the mixture to the saucepan and cook over medium heat, stirring constantly with a wooden spoon, until the mixture thickens enough to leave a path on the back of the sauce-coated spoon when you drag your finger across it. The mixture should read 175°F on an instant-read thermometer (do not let boil).

3. Strain the mixture through a fine-mesh sieve into a large bowl (discard the almonds). Set the bowl in a larger bowl filled about one-third of the way with ice water (be careful that the water doesn't splash into the mixture). Stir frequently until the mixture is chilled, about 25 minutes.

4. Pour the ice cream base into an ice cream machine and process according to the manufacturer's instructions. When the ice cream is firm, add the Heath Bar pieces and process just until blended. Pack

the ice cream into an airtight container and freeze for at least 4 hours, until firm.

STORE *in an airtight container in the freezer for up to 3 months.*

MERINGUE MUSHROOMS

ABûche de Noël without meringue mushrooms is like a Christmas tree without ornaments. But these adorable garnishes are not just for show—they add delicious crunch to the Yuletide cake classic as well as to a variety of other cakes and desserts. The best part? They can be made up to eight months (yes, months!) in advance, leaving plenty of time for holiday shopping.

➤ MAKES ABOUT FOURTEEN 1½-INCH DIAMETER (MEASURING THE CAP) MUSHROOMS

2 large egg whites, at room temperature

⅛ teaspoon cream of tartar

Pinch of salt

½ cup (3.5 oz/100 g) superfine sugar

Dutch-processed cocoa powder for sprinkling

1. Position a rack in the center of the oven and preheat the oven to 200°F. Line a baking sheet with parchment paper.

2. In the bowl of an electric mixer, using the whisk attachment, beat the egg whites at medium speed until foamy. Add the cream of tartar and salt and beat at medium-high speed until soft peaks begin to form. Gradually add the granulated sugar, about 1 tablespoon at a time, then increase the speed to high and beat the whites until stiff peaks form.

3. Scrape about ¼ cup of the meringue into a small sealable plastic bag and set aside. Scrape the remaining meringue into a large pastry bag fitted with a medium plain tip (such as Ateco #6). To pipe the mushroom caps, hold the bag perpendicular to the lined baking sheet, with the tip almost touching the sheet. Begin piping the meringue, squeezing the bag with a steady pressure, keeping the tip buried in the meringue, then lifting it as the meringue mounds; pipe a 1½-inch-diameter rounded mound of meringue, then make a quick swirling motion with the tip to cut off the point of the meringue. Repeat to form 14 caps in all. Wet your finger and smooth over any meringue points on top of the caps.

4. To pipe the stems, again hold the bag perpendicular to the baking sheet, with the tip almost touching the sheet. Begin piping the meringue, squeezing the bag with a steady pressure while lifting it slowly up and forming a cone shape that measures about 1½ inches high and about 1 inch in diameter at the base. Repeat to form 14 stems in all.

5. Bake the caps and stems for 45 minutes, or until they are firm to the touch. Remove from the oven. Leave the oven on.

6. Using a pastry tip or a paring knife, make a small hole in the center of the bottom of each cap. Seal the bag containing the reserved meringue and cut a tiny hole in one of the bottom corners of the bag. Pipe a small amount of meringue into the hole in one cap. Push the pointed end of a stem into the hole, and return the mushroom, cap side down, to the baking sheet. Repeat with the remaining caps and stems.

7. Bake the meringue mushrooms for another 30 minutes, or until dry. Cool completely.

8. Lightly sift a little cocoa powder over the mushrooms before using them.

STORE *in an airtight container in a cool, dry place for up to 8 months.*

Almost Foolproof Tempered Chocolate

Tempering is the process that makes chocolate lustrous, brilliant, and professional looking—the way it looks on the confections in the glass cases in a world-famous chocolate shop. The only time you will need to temper chocolate is when the chocolate garnish on your cake needs a glossy shine—such as a band of chocolate that is wrapped around the side of a cake. Tempering will make a huge difference in the look; untempered chocolate will appear dull and may have white streaks on it when it sets. Many competent home bakers quake at the notion of tempering chocolate, but the procedure is actually quite simple.

Tempering involves heating chocolate to between 110°F and 120°F (in order to melt out stable and unstable cocoa butter crystals) and then cooling it to between 80°F and 84°F (at which temperature the stable crystals can reform but unstable ones can't). The chocolate is then heated to between 84°F and 91°F to give it a workable consistency, and it is kept at that temperature while being used. Melt and temper more chocolate than you think you will need; leftover chocolate can be cooled and reused.

➤ SPECIAL EQUIPMENT: HEATING PAD (THE TYPE USED FOR BACKACHES); GOOD-QUALITY DIGITAL OR MERCURY CHOCOLATE THERMOMETER (WITH A GAUGE THAT RUNS FROM 80°F TO 130°F)

1. Wrap the heating pad in plastic wrap to protect it from chocolate stains, and set the control dial to the lowest setting.

2. Set aside a chunk of the chocolate (about 2½ inches square) you are tempering (this chocolate must be in "good temper," shiny and without any white streaks). Chop the remaining chocolate and place it in a medium bowl (or a large bowl, depending on how much chocolate you are working with). Set the bowl over a saucepan of hot but not quite simmering water and heat, stirring occasionally, until the chocolate is melted and reaches a temperature of between 110°F and 120°F. Turn off the heat, and remove the bowl from the saucepan. Add the reserved chocolate chunk to the melted chocolate and let the chocolate cool, stirring frequently, until it reaches 82°F to 84°F for dark chocolate, or 80°F to 82°F for milk and white chocolate. Remove the unmelted portion of the chocolate chunk.

3. Return the bowl to its place over the saucepan (the heat under the pan should still be off) and raise the temperature of the chocolate to between 86°F and 91°F for dark chocolate, or 84°F to 87°F for milk and white chocolate. Be careful not to allow the chocolate to go above the maximum temperatures. Then maintain that temperature range while working with the chocolate by keeping the bowl on the wrapped heating pad.

16

SOURCES

THE A. L. BAZZINI COMPANY
200 Food Center Drive
Hunts Point Market
Bronx, NY 10474
(800) 228-0172;
(718) 842-8644
Roasted nuts, seeds, nuts in the shell, dried fruits, and nut butters. Catalog available.

BERYL'S CAKE DECORATING EQUIPMENT
P.O. Box 1584
North Springfield, VA 22151
(800) 488-2749;
(703) 256-6951
Website: www.Beryls.com
Cake pans, paste and powder food coloring, gum paste tools, fondant, and lots of other cake-decorating supplies. Catalog available.

THE BAKER'S CATALOGUE
P.O. Box 876
Norwich, VT 05055-0876
(800) 827-6836
Website:
www.kingarthurflour.com
Baking ingredients including specialty flours, decorating sugars, Fiori di Sicilia, Grade B maple syrup, candied fruit, cake pans, and utensils. Catalog available.

BRIDGE KITCHENWARE CORP.
711 Third Ave.
New York, NY 10017
(800) 274-3435;
(212) 688-4220

Website:
www.bridgekitchenware.com
General bakeware, candy-maker's tools, and a large selection of cake pans. $3 for catalog, refundable with first purchase.

CHEFSWAREHOUSE.COM
A source for serious amateurs as well as professionals, this website has a good selection of high-end chocolate, vanilla beans, nut pastes, and specialty pastry ingredients.

CHOCOLATESOURCE.COM
A wide range of high-end bar and bulk chocolate, cocoa powder, cacao nibs, and other chocolate products.

A COOK'S WARES
211 37th Street
Beaver Falls, PA 15010
(412) 846-9490
Website: www.cookswares.com
General bakeware, including a large selection of cake pans, chocolate, and extracts.

DAIRY FRESH CHOCOLATE
57 Salem Street
Boston, MA 02113
(800) 336-5536;
(617) 742-2639
Callebaut, Lindt, Peter's, and Valrhona chocolates.

DECHOIX SPECIALTY FOODS
58-25 52nd Avenue
Woodside, NY 11377
(800) 834-6881;
(718) 507-8080
Chocolate, fruit purees and pastes, nuts, and nut products.

EASY LEAF PRODUCTS
6001 Santa Monica Boulevard
Los Angeles, CA 90038
(800) 569-5323;
(213) 469-0856
Website: www.easyleaf.com
All types of gold leaf and related equipment.

GOURMAIL
126A Pleasant Valley #401
Methuen, MA 01844
(800) 366-5900, ext. 96
Website: www.gourmail.com
Valrhona, Callebaut, and Cocoa Barry chocolate; candied violets and chocolate-covered coffee beans for decorating cakes.

INSTAWARES.COM
This restaurant supply site carries cardboard cake rounds in a variety of sizes.

J. B. PRINCE COMPANY
36 E. 31st Street, 11th Floor
New York, NY 10016
(212) 683-3553
Website: www.jbprince.com

Professional-grade bakeware, silicone baking mats, and cake pans.

KITCHENAID HOME
APPLIANCES
P.O. Box 218
St. Joseph, MI 49085
(800) 541-6390
Website: www.kitchenaid.com
Electric mixers and food processors. Catalog available.

LA CUISINE
323 Cameron Street
Alexandria, VA 22314-3219
(800) 521-1176;
(703) 836-4435
Website: www.lacuisineus.com
General bakeware, nut pastes, meringue powder, coarse sugar, dragees, and other cake-making and decorating supplies. Catalog available.

NEW YORK CAKE AND
BAKING DISTRIBUTORS
56 West 22nd Street
New York, NY 10010
(800) 94-CAKE-9;
(212) 675-CAKE
Website: www.nycake.com
General bakeware, including specialty cake pans, cake-decorating supplies, acetate transfer sheets, and chocolate.

PENZEY'S SPICES
P.O. Box 933
Muskego, WI 53150
(800) 741-7787
Website: www.penzeys.com
Spices, herbs, and extracts. Catalog available.

ROYAL PACIFIC FOODS
(THE GINGER PEOPLE)
2700 Garden Road, Suite G
Monterey, CA 93940
(800) 551-5284
Website:
www.gingerpeople.com
Ginger, in all its glorious forms, including crystallized, candied, and ground.

SUR LA TABLE
Pike Place Farmers Market
84 Pine Street
Seattle, WA 98101
(800) 243-0852
Website: www.surlatable.com
General bakeware, including decorative cake pans. Catalog available.

SWEET CELEBRATIONS
(FORMERLY MAID OF
SCANDINAVIA)
7009 Washington Avenue S.
Edina, MN 55439
(800) 328-6722
Website: www.sweetc.com
Baking equipment and ingredients, including cake pans, pastry tips, cake separators, chocolate, and decorating sugars. Catalog available.

TROPICAL NUT & FRUIT
P.O. Box 7507
1100 Continental Boulevard
Charlotte, NC 28273
(800) 438-4470;
704-588-0400
Website:
www.tropicalnutandfruit.com
Chocolate, dried fruits, and nuts.

WILLIAMS-SONOMA
100 North Point Street
San Francisco, CA 94133
(800) 541-2233
Website:
www.williams-sonoma.com
General bakeware and specialty cake pans, as well as extracts and flavoring oils. Catalog available.

WILTON INDUSTRIES
2240 West 75 Street
Woodridge, IL 60517-0750
(800) 994-5866
Website: www.wilton.com
Pastry bags and tips, specialty cake pans, meringue powder, flower nails, and a wide selection of other cake-making and decorating ingredients and equipment.

INDEX

A

All-purpose flour, 7–8
Almond(s)
    about, 16
    Biscuit, 82–83
    Buttercream, 325
    Chocolate-Coconut Cake, 206–207
    Chocolate Torte, 200–201
    Cream Cheese Pound Cake, Cherry-,
        98–99
    Filling, 301
    Génoise, 76–77
    Praline Paste, 333
    Praline Powder, 334
    to toast, 37
    Toasted, Baked Alaska, Chocolate,
        282–283
    Toasted, Crunch Ice Cream, 360–361
    Toasted, Pound Cake, 92–93
    Toffee Crunch, 338
    White Chocolate Raspberry Cake,
        192–193
Almost Foolproof Tempered Chocolate,
    364–365
Angel Food Cake(s)
    about, 59
    Chocolate, Double, Michael's, 64–65
    Heavenly, 62–63
    pan preparation, 33
Apple
    Cake with Maple Frosting, 175
    Charlotte, Classic, 177–179
    Cheesecake Brûlée, 230–232
    Filling, 177, 303

B

Baked Alaska, Toasted Almond Chocolate,
    282–283
Baking powder, 13
Baking soda, 13
Banana
    Cake with Caramel Espresso Frosting,
        156–157
    Chiffon Cake, Walnut, 67
    Chocolate Quick Cake, 125
    Ice Cream, 356–357
    Ice Cream Cake, Crunch, Soused,
        274–275
    Ice Cream, Quick, 358
    Walnut Cake, 176

Basic Golden Cake Layers, 120
Basic Soaking Syrup, 332
Basic White Cake Layers, 119
Basket weave decoration, 48–49
Bellas, Michael, 64
Bench scraper, 23
Berry(ies). *See also* specific berries
    Compote, Gingered, 351
    Sauce, Red, 350
    Topping, 288, 291
Biscotti Crust, 240
Biscuit, Almond, 82–83
Bittersweet Chocolate
    about, 15
    Ganache, 276
    Glaze, 306
    Mousse Cake, 246–247
Black Forest Cake, 194–195
Blackout Cake 2003, Brooklyn, 158–160
Blueberry
    Crumb Cake, Sour Cream–, 106–107
    Topping, Lemon Soufflé Cheesecake
        with, 226–227
Boston Cream Pie, 78–79
Bourbon, Date, Fig, and Golden Raisin Cake
    with, 180–182
Bread flour, 8
Brioche Cake with Caramel Custard Cream,
    112–114
Brooklyn Blackout Cake 2003, 158–160
Brownie Latte Cheesecake, 242–243
Brown Sugar
    about, 10
    Date Cake, 136–137
    –Ginger Plum Topping, 184
    Whipped Cream, 341
Brûlée, Apple Cheesecake, 230–232
Bûche de Noël, Chocolate Hazelnut, 85–87
Bundt Cake(s)
    Fig and Marsala Wine, 182–183
    Pound, Buttermilk, Cinnamon Swirl,
        98–99
    Pound, Cream Cheese, Cherry-Almond,
        98–99
    Pound, Ginger, Lemon-Soaked, 96–97
    Pound, Luxe, 94–95
    Pound, Rich Marble, with Chocolate
        Glaze, 102–103
    Pound, Sour Cream, Deep Chocolate,
        104–105
    Sticky Toffee Pudding Cake, 136–137
Butter
    about, 9
    to cream sugar and, 35
    softening, 34
Butter Cake(s). *See also* Pound Cake(s); Coffee
    Cake(s)

about, 117–118
    Banana, with Caramel Espresso
        Frosting, 156–157
    Blackout 2003, Brooklyn, 158–160
    Chocolate Banana Quick, 125
    Chocolate Buttermilk, Individual
        Glazed, 142–143
    Chocolate Cake Layers, Sour Cream,
        124
    Chocolate Coconut Cupcakes, 144–145
    Chocolate, German, 153–155
    Chocolate Guinness, 130–131
    Chocolate Pudding, Saucy, 133
    Coconut Cake Layers, 119
    Cornmeal, Lemon, 129
    Devil's Food, Deeply Dark, 122–123

    Fudge, Sour Cream, with Peanut Butter
        Frosting, 140–141
    Gingerbread, 128
    Ginger Spice, Fresh, 126–127
    Golden Cake Layers, Basic, 120
    Lemon Lust, 164–166
    Orange Grove, 167–169
    Poppy Seed, Sour Cream, with
        Whipped White Chocolate
        Lemon Ganache, 138–139
    "Seven Layer," 148–149
    Toffee Pudding, Sticky, 136–137
    Torte, Chocolate Walnut, with Cognac
        Cream, 161–163
    Torte, Sacher, 150–152
    Tres Leches, 134–135
    White Cake Layers, Basic, 119
Buttercream
    Almond, 325
    Caramel Espresso, 328
    Chocolate, 83–84, 86–87, 325
    Chocolate, Silky, 326–327
    Coconut, 171
    Espresso, 83–84
    food coloring in, 46
    French-Style, 324
    Hazelnut, 86–87, 325
    Lemon, 165
    Meringue, Swiss, 322
    Meringue, Swiss Chocolate, 322
    Meringue, Swiss Orange, 323
    Orange, 168
    piped decorations, 45
    Pistachio, 325
    Raspberry, 325
Buttermilk
    Apple Cake with Maple Frosting, 175
    Blackout Cake 2003, Brooklyn,
        158–160

Buttermilk (*continued*)
  Chocolate Cakes, Individual Glazed, 142–143
  Coffee Cake, Peach, 108–109
  Pound Cake, Cinnamon Swirl, 98–99

C

Cacao Nib Whipped Cream, 342
Cake divider, 23
Cake flour, 7, 8
Cake Layers. *See also* Layer Cake(s); Mousse Cake(s)
  Banana, 156
  Chocolate, Sour Cream, 124
  Coconut, 119
  to fill and frost, 43–44
  Génoise, Almond, 76–77
  Génoise, Classic, 74–75
  Golden, Basic, 120
  Lemon, 164
  Orange, 167
  stacked, 44
  to trim and divide, 43
  White, Basic, 119
Cake leveler, 23
Cake making. *See also* Decorations; Ingredients
  equipment, 23–29
  high-altitude baking, 38–39
  mail order sources, 367–368
  techniques, 33–37
  troubleshooting guide, 39
Cake pans
  about, 23–24
  to prepare, 33–34
  sizes, 29
Cake rounds, cardboard, 24
Cake tester, 24
Cake turntable, 24
Candied Orange Zest, 354
Candy thermometer, 27–28
Caramel
  Cream, 347
  Custard Cream, Brioche Cake with, 112–114
  Espresso Buttercream, 328
  Peach Topping, 186
  Sauce, 348
  Whipped Cream, Brown Sugar, 341
Carrot Cake, Solid Gold, 146–147
Cashews, about, 16
Charlotte, Apple, Classic, 177–179
Cheesecake, Brownie Latte, 242–243
Cheesecake(s)
  about, 215–216
  Apple Brûlée, 230–232

Cherry-Topped Cups, 222–223
Chocolate, Rich, 220–221
freezing, 37
Goat Cheese, with Fig Topping, 236–237
Hazelnut Vanilla, 228–229
Lemon, Raspberry-Topped, 238–239
Lemon Soufflé, with Blueberry Topping, 226–227
Marbled Mascarpone, 240–241
New York, Classic, 218–219
Pumpkin, Creamy, with Ginger-Pecan Crust, 224–225
Ricotta Torte, 217
White Chocolate Peach, 233–235
Cherry(ies)
  -Almond Pound Cake, Cream Cheese, 98–99
  Black Forest Cake, 194–195
  Cheesecake Cups, -Topped, 222–223
  Soaking Syrup, 194
  Topping, Tart, 223
  Whipped Cream, 194
Chiffon Cake(s)
  about, 60
  Banana Walnut, 67
  Banana Walnut, with Maple Mousse, 252–253
  Chocolate Sheet, 85–86
  Classic, 66–67
  Lemon, 264
  Lemon Sheet, 80–81
  Lime, 67
  Lime, with Ginger Mousse, 272–273
  Orange, 70–71
  pan preparation, 33
  Spiced, 67
  Vanilla-Flecked, 68–69
Chocolate. *See also* Chocolate decorations
  Buttercream, 83–84, 86–87, 325
  Buttercream, Silky, 326–327
  Buttercream, Swiss Meringue, 322
  Crust, Cookie, 246
  Crust, Crumb, 220
  Crust, Wafer, 262
  Drizzle, White, 209, 210, 212
  Frosting, 153–154. *See also* Ganache
  Frosting, Dark, Sour Cream, 315
  Frosting, Espresso, Rich, 320
  Frosting, Fudgy, 159, 314
  Frosting, White Chocolate Cream Cheese, 311
  Glaze, Bittersweet, 306
  to melt, 36
  morsels, about, 16
  Pudding Filling, 159
  Sauce, Warm, 352

storage of, 15
Tempered, Almost Foolproof, 364–365
types of, 14–16
Whipped Cream, 343
Whipped Cream, White Chocolate, 346
Chocolate Cake(s). *See also* Chocolate Mousse Cake(s); Chocolate Torte(s); Flourless Cake(s); White Chocolate Cake(s)
  Angel Food, Double, Michael's, 64–65
  Banana Quick, 125
  Black Forest, 194–195
  Blackout 2003, Brooklyn, 158–160
  Bûche de Noël, Hazelnut, 85–87
  Buttermilk, Individual Glazed, 142–143
  Cheesecake, Brownie Latte, 242–243
  Cheesecake, Marbled Mascarpone, 240–241
  Cheesecake, Rich, 220–221
  Cheesecake, White Chocolate Peach, 233–235
  Chiffon Sheet, 85–86
  Cupcakes, Coconut, 144–145
  Dacquoise, 296–297
  Devilishly Moist, 121
  Devil's Food, Deeply Dark, 122–123
  German, 153–155
  Guinness, 130–131
  Ice Cream, Cookies and Cream, 276–277
  Layers, Sour Cream, 124
  Meringue, White Chocolate Strawberry, 292–293
  Pound, Rich Marble, with Chocolate Glaze, 102–103
  Pound, Sour Cream, Deep, 104–105
  Pudding, Saucy, 133
  Sour Cream, 256–257
  Sour Cream, Fudge, with Peanut Butter Frosting, 140–141
Chocolate decorations
  bands, 53
  curls, 55
  grated chocolate, 55
  leaves, 54–55
  ruffles, 54
Chocolate Mousse Cake(s)
  Bittersweet, 246–247
  Coconut, 254–255
  Layer, 256–258
  Milk Chocolate–Espresso, 270–271
  Peanut Butter, 262–263
  White Chocolate Eggnog, 280–281
  White Chocolate Espresso Icebox, 248–249
Chocolate Torte(s)
  Almond, 200–201

Sacher, 150–152
Sunken, 204–205
Walnut, with Cognac Cream, 161–163
Cinnamon
Graham Cracker Crust, 230
Swirl Buttermilk Pound Cake, 100–101
White Chocolate Ganache, Whipped, 319
Classic Apple Charlotte, 177–179
Classic Chiffon Cake, 66–67
Classic Génoise, 74–75
Classic New York Cheesecake, 218–219
Classic Vanilla Custard Sauce (Crème Anglaise), 355
Classic Whipped Cream, 339
Cocoa powder, 16
Coconut
Buttercream, 171
Cake Layers, 119
-Chocolate Almond Cake, 206–207
Chocolate Cupcakes, 144–145
Cream, 170, 171
Creamy Cake, 170–171
Custard, 170
Meringue Cake, 294–295
Milk Chocolate Ganache, 316
Mousse Cake, Chocolate, 254–255
-Pecan Filling and Frosting, 309
-Rum White Chocolate Ganache, Whipped, 319
Whipped Cream, 344
Whipped Cream, White Chocolate, 346
Coffee. See also Espresso
Syrup, 252
Coffee Cake(s)
about, 89
Brioche, with Caramel Custard Cream, 112–114
Buttermilk Peach, 108–109
Filled, 110–111
Sour Cream–Blueberry Crumb, 106–107
Cognac Cream, Chocolate Walnut Torte with, 161–163
Cognac Syrup, 162
Compote, Gingered Berry, 351
Confectioners' comb, 23, 44–45
Confectioners' sugar, 10
Cookies and Cream Ice Cream, 359
Cookies and Cream Ice Cream Cake, Chocolate, 276–277
Cornelli lace decoration, 52
Cornmeal Cake, Lemon, 129
Cornstarch, 13
Corn syrup, 10
Cream. See also Sour Cream; Whipped Cream

Caramel Custard, Brioche Cake with, 112–114
in Chocolate Valentine Cake, 211–213
Coconut, 170, 171
Crème Fraîche, 336
Lime, Individual Meringue Cups with Fresh Berries and, 290–291
Mascarpone, 250
Cream Cheese. See also Cheesecake(s)
Filling, 302
Filling, Lemon, 164, 165
Filling, Whipped, 308
Frosting, Maple, 310
Frosting, Spice, 310
Frosting, White Chocolate, 311
Pound Cake, Cherry-Almond, 98–99
Creaming butter and sugar, 35
Cream of tartar, 13
Creamy Peanut Butter Frosting, 313
Creamy Pumpkin Cheesecake with Ginger-Pecan Crust, 224–225
Crème Anglaise, 355
Crème Fraîche, 336
Crumb Topping
Buttermilk Peach Coffee Cake, 108–109
Ricotta Torte, 217
Sour Cream–Blueberry Cake, 106–107
Crunch(ies)
Almond, Toasted, Ice Cream, 360–361
Almond Toffee, 338
Sesame, 274
Crust(s)
Biscotti, 240
Chocolate Cookie, 246
Chocolate Crumb, 220
Chocolate Wafer, 262
Ginger-Pecan, 224
Graham Cracker, 218, 222, 226
Graham Cracker, Cinnamon, 230
Graham Cracker, Honey, 236, 238
Hazelnut, 228
Pastry, 233
Crystallized sugar, 10
C scroll decoration, 48
Cupcakes
Cheesecake Cups, Cherry-Topped, 222–223
Chocolate Coconut, 144–145
Curd, Lemon, 353
Custard
Caramel Cream, Brioche Cake with, 112–114
Coconut, 170
Filling, Vanilla, 78
Sauce, Classic Vanilla (Crème Anglaise), 355

D

Dacquoise
about, 285
Chocolate Cake, 296–297
Coconut, 294
Dark Chocolate Sour Cream Frosting, 315
Date(s)
Brown Sugar Cake, 136–137
Fig, and Golden Raisin Cake with Bourbon, 180–182
Fruitcake, Rum-Sopped, 188–189
Decorating comb, 23, 44–45
Decorations, 43–57. See also Chocolate decorations; Frosting
to fill and frost layers, 43–44
gold leaf, 56
marzipan, 56–57
Meringue Mushrooms, 362–363
piped, 45–52
piped writing, 52
to prepare cake layers, 43
stenciled, 53
textured patterns, 44–45
Deeply Dark Devil's Food Cake, 122–123
Devilishly Moist Chocolate Cake, 121
Devil's Food Cake, Deeply Dark, 122–123
DiFrancesco, David, 206
Dot decoration, 46
Double boiler, 25
Dredger, 24
Dried Fruit. See Fruit, Dried
Drop flower decoration, 49
Dubberley, Melanie, 274, 356

E

Earl Grey Syrup, 259
Eggnog White Chocolate Mousse Cake, 280–281
Eggs
about, 14
to beat, 35
to separate, 35
Equipment
mail order sources, 367–368
types of, 23–29
Espresso
Buttercream, 83–84
Buttercream, Caramel, 328
Chocolate Frosting, Rich, 320
Cream, 340
Latte Cheesecake, Brownie, 242–243
Meringue Rounds, 286–287

Espresso *(continued)*
    —Milk Chocolate Mousse Cake,
        270–271
    Syrup, 82, 83, 250
    White Chocolate Ganache, Whipped,
        318
    White Chocolate Icebox Cake, 248–249

F

Fats
    about, 9
    in pan preparation, 33
Fig(s)
    Date, and Golden Raisin Cake with
        Bourbon, 180–182
    Filling, 304
    Fruitcake, Rum-Sopped, 188–189
    and Marsala Wine Cake, 182–183
    Topping, Goat Cheese Cheesecake with,
        236–237
Filled Coffee Cake, 110–111
Filling(s). *See also* Buttercream; Ganache
    about, 300
    Almond, 301
    Apple, 177, 303
    Chocolate Pudding, 159
    Coconut Cream, 170, 171
    Coconut-Pecan, 309
    Cream Cheese, 302
    Cream Cheese, Whipped, 308
    Crumb, 108
    Custard, Vanilla, 78
    Fig, 304
    Lemon Cream Cheese, 164, 165
    Lemon Curd, 353
    Lemon Silk, 80
    Orange, 167, 168
    to prepare cake layers for, 43–44
    Raspberry, 151, 192
    Sour Cream, 307
    Strawberry, 190
    Whipped Cream, 190–191, 288
    Whipped Cream, Raspberry, 208, 209
Flavor accents, 18–19
Fleur-de-lis decoration, 47
Flour
    to measure, 8, 34
    types of, 7–8
Flourless Cake(s)
    about, 197
    Chocolate Almond-Coconut, 206–207
    Chocolate, Individual Warm, 198–199
    Chocolate Intensity (Death by
        Chocolate), 202–203
    Chocolate Raspberry Roll, 208–210

Chocolate Valentine, 211–213
Flourless Torte(s)
    about, 197
    Chocolate Almond, 200–201
    Chocolate, Sunken, 204–205
Flower decorations, piped, 49–52
Flower nail, 25
Fluffy White Frosting, 312
Folding technique, 35–36
Food coloring, 46
Food processor, 25
Freezing tips, 37–38
French-Style Buttercream, 324
Fresh Ginger Spice Cake, 126–127
Frosting. *See also* Buttercream; Topping(s)
    about, 300
    of cake layers, 44
    Chocolate, 153–154. *See also* Ganache
    Chocolate, Dark, Sour Cream, 315
    Chocolate, Espresso, Rich, 320
    Chocolate, Fudgy, 159, 314
    Chocolate, White, Cream Cheese, 311
    Coconut-Pecan, 309
    Cream Cheese Maple, 310
    Cream Cheese, Spice, 310
    Cream Cheese, White Chocolate, 311
    food coloring in, 46
    Meringue, 135
    Peanut Butter, Creamy, 313
    piped decoration with, 45
    Sour Cream Dark Chocolate, 315
    Whipped Cream, 190–191, 277
    White, Fluffy (Seven Minute), 312
Fruit-Based Cake(s). *See also* Fruit, Dried
    about, 173
    Apple Charlotte, Classic, 177–179
    Apple, with Maple Frosting, 175
    Banana Walnut, 176
    Black Forest, 194–195
    Lemon Soufflé, 174
    Peach Tatin, 186–187
    Plum Upside-Down, Jasmine and
        Ginger, 184–185
    Raspberry White Chocolate Almond,
        192–193
    Strawberry Shortcake, 190–191
Fruit, Dried
    about, 18
    Date, Fig, and Golden Raisin Cake with
        Bourbon, 180–182
    Fig and Marsala Wine Cake, 182–183
    Fruitcake, Rum-Sopped, 188–189
Fruit decorations, marzipan, 57
Fruit Topping, 288, 291
Fudge Sour Cream Cake with Peanut Butter
    Frosting, 140–141
Fudgy Chocolate Frosting, 159, 314

G

Ganache
    Bittersweet, 276
    Milk Chocolate Coconut, 316
    Milk Chocolate Peanut Butter, 317
    piped decorations, 45
    Whipped, 321
    Whipped, White Chocolate, 318–319
Génoise
    Almond, 76–77
    Classic, 74–75
    Orange, 267–268
German Chocolate Cake, 153–155
Ginger(ed)
    in Banana Crunch Ice Cream Cake,
        Soused, 274–275
    Berry Compote, 351
    in Fruitcake, Rum-Sopped, 188–189
    and Jasmine Plum Upside-Down Cake,
        184–185
    Mousse, Lime Chiffon Cake with,
        272–273
    -Pecan Crust, 224
    Pound Cake, Lemon-Soaked, 96–97
    Spice Cake, Fresh, 126–127
    Syrup, 264, 265
Gingerbread, 128
Glaze(s)
    Bittersweet Chocolate, 306
    Marsala, 182, 183
    White Drizzle, 305
Goat Cheese Cheesecake with Fig Topping,
    236–237
Golden Cake Layers, Basic, 120
Gold leaf, decorating with, 56
Graham Cracker Crust, 218, 222, 226
    Cinnamon, 230
    Honey, 236, 238
Granulated sugar, 10

H

Harlam, Carole, 177
Hazelnut(s)
    about, 17
    Bûche de Noël, Chocolate, 85–87
    Buttercream, 86–87, 325
    Crust, 228
    Praline Paste, 333
    Praline Powder, 334
    Syrup, 86
    to toast, 37
    Vanilla Cheesecake, 228–229
Heavenly Angel Food Cake, 62–63

High-altitude baking, 38–39
Honey(ed)
about, 12
Raspberries, Yogurt Mousse Cake with
Mint Syrup and, 259–261
Honey Graham Cracker Crust, 236, 238
Hot Milk Sponge Cake, 72–73

I

Icebox Cake, White Chocolate Espresso,
248–249
Ice Cream
Banana, 356–357
Banana, Quick, 358
Cookies and Cream, 359
Toasted Almond Crunch, 360–361
Ice Cream Cake(s)
about, 245
Baked Alaska, Toasted Almond
Chocolate, 282–283
Banana Crunch, Soused, 274–275
Cookies and Cream, Chocolate,
276–277
Icing. *See also* Frosting
White Drizzle Glaze, 305
Individual Glazed Chocolate Buttermilk Cakes,
142–143
Individual Meringue Cups with Lime Cream
and Fresh Berries, 290–291
Individual Warm Chocolate Cakes, 198–199
Ingredients, 7–19
chocolate, 14–16
dried fruits, 18
eggs, 14
fats, 9
flavor accents, 18–19
flours, 7–8
leaveners, 13–14
mail order sources, 367–368
measurement of, 8, 34
nuts, 16–18
stabilizers, 13
sugar and sweeteners, 10–13
Italian Meringue, 282–283

J

Jasmine and Ginger Plum Upside-Down Cake,
184–185

K

Kahlúa Cream, 204, 205, 270
Knives, 25

L

Lace decoration, 52
Latte Cheesecake, Brownie, 242–243
Layer Cake(s). *See also* Cake Layers
Banana, with Caramel Espresso
Frosting, 156–157
Black Forest, 194–195
Blackout 2003, Brooklyn, 158–160
Coconut, Creamy, 170–171
Devil's Food, Deeply Dark, 122–123
German Chocolate, 153–155
Lemon Lust, 164–166
Orange Grove, 167–169
"Seven Layer," 148–149
Leaveners, 13–14
Leaves
chocolate, 54–55
piped, 51
Lemon
Buttercream, 165
Cake, Lemon Lust, 164–166
Cheesecake, Raspberry-Topped,
238–239
Chiffon Cake, 264
Chiffon Sheet Cake, 80–81
Cornmeal Cake, 129
Curd, 353
Filling, Cream Cheese, 164, 165
Filling, Silk, 80
Ganache, White Chocolate, Whipped,
318
Ginger Pound Cake, -Soaked, 96–97
Mousse Cake with Fresh Raspberries,
264–266
Poppy Seed Pound Cake, 91
Roll, 80–81
Soaking Syrup, 165
Soufflé Cake, 174
Soufflé Cheesecake with Blueberry
Topping, 226–227
Syrup, 96–97
Whipped Cream, White Chocolate, 346
Lime
Chiffon Cake, 67
Chiffon Cake with Ginger Mousse,
272–273
Cream, Individual Meringue Cups with
Fresh Berries and, 290–291

Poppy Seed Pound Cake, 91
Syrup, 272
Loaf Cake(s)
Chocolate Banana Quick, 125
Fruitcake, Rum-Sopped, 188–189
Pound, Lemon Poppy Seed, 91
Pound, Lime Poppy Seed, 91
Pound, Plainly Perfect, 90
Pound, Toasted Almond, 92–93
Luxe Pound Cake, 94–95
Lyle's golden syrup, 12

M

Macadamias, about, 17
Mail order sources, 367–368
Maple Frosting, Cream Cheese, 310
Maple Mousse, Banana Walnut Chiffon Cake
with, 252–253
Marbled Mascarpone Cheesecake, 240–241
Marble Pound Cake, Rich, with Chocolate
Glaze, 102–103
Marsala Glaze, 182, 183
Marsala Wine and Fig Cake, 182–183
Marzipan decorations, 56–57
Mascarpone
Cheesecake, Marbled, 240–241
Tiramisu Cake, 250–251
Whipped Cream, 345
Measuring equipment, 26
Measuring ingredients, 8, 34
Meringue
Buttercream, Swiss, 322
Buttercream, Swiss Chocolate, 322
Buttercream, Swiss Orange, 323
Cups, 290
Italian, 282–283
Layers, 292
Mushrooms, 362–363
Shell, 288
Topping, 135, 282–283
Meringue Cake(s)
about, 285
Chocolate Dacquoise, 296–297
Coconut, 294–295
Espresso Rounds, 286–287
Individual Cups with Lime Cream and
Fresh Berries, 290–291
Mousse, Milk Chocolate–Espresso,
270–271
Pavlova, Perfect, 288–289
White Chocolate Strawberry, 292–293
Michael's Double Chocolate Angel Food Cake,
64–65
Milk
Sponge Cake, Hot Milk, 72–73

Milk *(continued)*
    Tres Leches Cake, 134–135
Milk Chocolate
    about, 15
    Ganache, Coconut, 316
    Mousse Cake, –Espresso, 270–271
    Peanut Butter Ganache, 317
Mint Syrup, 349
Mixers, electric, 25
Mixing bowls, 26
Molasses, 13
Mousse Cake(s)
    about, 245
    Banana Walnut Chiffon Cake with
        Maple Mousse, 252–253
    Bittersweet Chocolate, 246–247
    Chocolate Coconut, 254–255
    Chocolate Layer, 256–258
    Chocolate Peanut Butter, 262–263
    Ginger Mousse, Lime Chiffon Cake
        with, 272–273
    Lemon, with Fresh Raspberries,
        264–266
    Milk Chocolate–Espresso, 270–271
    Oranges and Cream, 267–269
    Raspberry, 278–279
    Tiramisu, 250–251
    White Chocolate Eggnog, 280–281
    White Chocolate Espresso Icebox,
        248–249
    Yogurt, with Honeyed Raspberries and
        Mint Syrup, 259–261
Muscovado sugar, 12

N

New York Cheesecake, Classic, 218–219
Nut(s). *See also* specific nuts
    about, 16–18
    to blanch, 36–37
    Praline Powder, 334
    Sugared, 337
    to toast, 37
Nut Paste
    about, 18
    Pistachio, 335
    Praline, 333

O

Oil, about, 9
Oil-Based Cake(s)
    about, 118
    Banana, with Caramel Espresso
        Frosting, 156–157

Carrot, Solid Gold, 146–147
Chocolate, Devilishly Moist, 121
Pumpkin Walnut, 132
Opera Cake, 82–84
Orange(s)
    Buttercream, 168
    Cake, Orange Grove, 167–169
    Chiffon Cake, 70–71
    and Cream Cake, 267–269
    Filling, 167, 168
    Génoise, 267–268
    Layer Cake, 167–168
    Mousse, 268
    Soaking Syrup, 168
    Syrup, 267, 268, 278–279
    White Chocolate Ganache, Whipped,
        319
    Zest, Candied, 354
Oven temperature, 26
Oven thermometer, 26, 27

P

Pans. *See* Cake pans
Parchment paper, 26
Pastry bag, 26–27, 45
Pastry brush, 27
Pastry Crust, 233
Pastry tips, 27
Pavlova, Perfect, 288–289
Peach
    Coffee Cake, Buttermilk, 108–109
    Tatin Cake, 186–187
    White Chocolate Cheesecake, 233–235
Peanut(s), about, 17
Peanut Butter
    Chocolate Mousse Cake, 262–263
    Frosting, Creamy, 313
    Milk Chocolate Ganache, 317
Pecan(s)
    about, 17
    -Coconut Filling and Frosting, 309
    -Ginger Crust, 224
    to toast, 37
Perfect Pavlova, 288–289
Piped decorations, 45–52
Pistachio(s)
    about, 17
    Buttercream, 325
    Paste, 335
    Praline Powder, 334
Plainly Perfect Pound Cake, 90
Plum Upside-Down Cake, Jasmine and Ginger,
    184–185
Poppy Seed
    Pound Cake, Lemon, 91

Pound Cake, Lime, 91
Sour Cream Cake with Whipped White
    Chocolate Lemon Ganache,
    138–139
Pound Cake(s)
    about, 89
    Almond, Toasted, 92–93
    Buttermilk, Cinnamon Swirl, 98–99
    Cream Cheese, Cherry-Almond, 98–99
    Ginger, Lemon-Soaked, 96–97
    Lemon Poppy Seed, 91
    Lime Poppy Seed, 91
    Luxe, 94–95
    Marble, Rich, with Chocolate Glaze,
        102–103
    Plainly Perfect, 90
    Sour Cream, Deep Chocolate, 104–105
Praline Paste, 333
Praline Powder, 334
Pudding Cake(s)
    Chocolate, Saucy, 133
    Toffee, Sticky, 136–137
Pumpkin
    Cheesecake, Creamy, with Ginger-Pecan
        Crust, 224–225
    Walnut Cake, 132
Pumpkin Seeds, Sugared, 335

Q

Quick Banana Ice Cream, 358

R

Raisin(s)
    about, 18
    Fruitcake, Rum-Sopped, 188–189
    Golden, Date, and Fig Cake with
        Bourbon, 180–182
Ranhofer, Charles, 282
Raspberry(ies)
    Berry Sauce, Red, 350
    Buttercream, 325
    Chocolate Roll, 208–210
    Chocolate Valentine Cake, 211–213
    Filling, 151, 192
    Fresh, Lemon Mousse Cake with,
        264–266
    Honeyed, Yogurt Mousse Cake with
        Mint Syrup and, 259–261
    Lemon Cheesecake, -Topped, 238–239
    Mousse Cake(s), 278–279
    Topping, 239
    Whipped Cream Filling, 209, 210

White Chocolate Almond Cake, 192–193

White Chocolate Ganache, Whipped, 319

Red Berry Sauce, 350

Rich Chocolate Cheesecake, 220–221

Rich Chocolate Espresso Frosting, 320

Rich Marble Pound Cake with Chocolate Glaze, 102–103

Ricotta Torte, 217

Roll

    Bûche de Noël, Chocolate Hazelnut, 85–87

    Chocolate Raspberry, 208–210

    Lemon, The Ultimate, 80–81

Rope decoration, 47–48

Rosebud decoration, 50

    half rose, 50

Rose decoration, 50–51

Rosette decoration, 46

Ruffles, chocolate, 54

Rum

    Banana Crunch Ice Cream Cake, Soused, 274–275

    -Coconut White Chocolate Ganache, Whipped, 319

    Fruitcake, -Sopped, 188–189

    Soaking Syrup, 170, 171

    Syrup, 150, 151, 280

S

Sacher Torte, 150–152

Salt, 19

Sanding sugar, 12

Sauce(s)

    Caramel, 348

    Chocolate, Warm, 352

    Custard, Classic Vanilla (Crème Anglaise), 355

    Red Berry, 350

    Toffee, Sticky, 136

Saucy Chocolate Pudding Cake, 133

Self-rising cake flour, 8

Semisweet chocolate, 15

Sesame Crunchies, 274

"Seven Layer" Cake, 148–149

Seven-Minute Frosting, 312

Sheet Cake(s)

    Buttery, 148–149

    Chocolate Chiffon, 85–86

    Lemon Chiffon, 80–81

Shell decoration, 47

    reverse, 47

Shortcake, Strawberry, 190–191

Shortening, 9

Sieve, 27

Sifter, 27

Silicone baking mats, 27

Silky Chocolate, Buttercream, 326–327

Soaking Syrup

    Basic, 332

    Cherry, 194

    Lemon, 165

    Orange, 168

    Rum, 170, 171

Solid Gold Carrot Cake, 146–147

Soufflé Cake, Lemon, 174

Soufflé Cheesecake, Lemon, with Blueberry Topping, 226–227

Sour Cream

    Chocolate Cake, 256–257

    Chocolate Cake Layers, 124

    in Cornmeal Cake, Lemon, 129

    Crumb Cake, –Blueberry, 106–107

    Filling and Topping, 307

    Frosting, Dark Chocolate, 315

    Fudge Cake with Peanut Butter Frosting, 140–141

    in German Chocolate Cake, 153–155

    in Lemon Soufflé, Lemon, 174

    in Peach Tatin Cake, 186–187

    Poppy Seed Cake with Whipped White Chocolate Lemon Ganache, 138–139

    Pound Cake, Deep Chocolate, 104–105

Soused Banana Crunch Ice Cream Cake, 274–275

Spatulas, 27

Spice(d)

    Cake, 180–181

    Chiffon Cake, 67

    Cream Cheese Frosting, 310

    Ginger Cake, Fresh, 126–127

Sponge Cake(s)

    about, 59

    Almond Génoise, 76–77

    Boston Cream Pie, 78–79

    Flourless Chocolate, 208–209

    Hot Milk, 72–73

S scroll decoration, 48

Stabilizers, 13

Stacked cakes, 44

Star decoration, 46

Stenciled decoration, 53

Sticky Toffee Pudding Cake, 136–137

Storage tips, 37

Strawberry(ies)

    Berry Sauce, Red, 350

    Filling, 190

    Shortcake, 190–191

    Syrup, 190

Streusel. See also Crumb Topping

Cinnamon Swirl Buttermilk Pound Cake, 98–99

Sugar. See also Brown Sugar

    boiled syrup, stages of, 11

    Brûlée Topping, 231

    to cream butter and, 35

    types of, 10, 12–13

    White Drizzle Glaze, 305

Sugared Nuts, 337

Sugared Pumpkin Seeds, 335

Sunken Chocolate Torte, 204–205

Superfine (castor) sugar, 12

Sweet pea decoration, 49

Swiss Meringue Buttercream, 322

    Chocolate, 322

    Orange, 323

Syrup. See also Soaking Syrup

    boiled sugar stages, 11

    Coffee, 252

    Cognac, 162

    Earl Grey, 259

    Espresso, 82, 83, 250

    Ginger, 264, 265

    Hazelnut, 86

    Lemon, 96–97

    Lime, 272

    Lyle's Golden, 12

    Mint, 349

    Orange, 267, 268, 278–279

    Rum, 150, 151, 280

    Strawberry, 190

T

Tea

    Earl Grey Syrup, 259

    Jasmine and Ginger Plum Upside-Down Cake, 184–185

Tempered Chocolate, Almost Foolproof, 364–365

Thermometers, 26, 27–28

Timer, 28

Tip saver, 28

Tiramisu Cake, 250–251

Toasted Almond Chocolate Baked Alaska, 282–283

Toasted Almond Crunch Ice Cream, 360–361

Toasted Almond Pound Cake, 92–93

Toffee Crunch, Almond, 338

Toffee Pudding Cake, Sticky, 136–137

Topping(s). See also Crumb Topping

    Blueberry, 227

    Brown Sugar-Ginger Plum, 184

    Brûlée, 231

    Caramel Peach, 186

    Cherry, Tart, 223

Toppings *(continued)*
    Fig, Goat Cheese Cheesecake with, 236–237
    Fruit, 288, 291
    Peach, 234
    Raspberry, 239
    Sour Cream, 307
    Whipped Cream, 275
    Whipped Cream, Kahlúa, 204, 205, 270
Torte(s)
    Chocolate Almond, 200–201
    Chocolate, Sunken, 204–205
    Chocolate Walnut, with Cognac Cream, 161–163
    flourless, about, 197
    Ricotta, 217
    Sacher, 150–152
Tres Leches Cake, 134–135
Truffle Cake, 202–203
Turbinado sugar, 12

U

Ultimate Lemon Roll, The, 80–81
Unsweetened chocolate, 15
Upside-Down Cake, Jasmine and Ginger Plum, 184–185

V

Vacherin, 285
Valentine Cake, Chocolate, 211–213
Vanilla
    about, 19
    Chiffon Cake, -Flecked, 68–69
    Custard Filling, 78
    Custard Sauce, Classic (Crème Anglaise), 355
    Hazelnut Cheesecake, 228–229
Vanilla sugar, 12
Vegetable oil, 9
Vegetable shortening, 9

W

Walnut(s)
    about, 17
    Banana Cake, 176
    Banana Chiffon Cake, 67
    Banana Chiffon Cake with Maple Mousse, 252–253
    Chocolate Torte with Cognac Cream, 161–163

Praline Powder, 334
Pumpkin Cake, 132
to toast, 37
Warm Chocolate Sauce, 352
Whipped Cream
    Brown Sugar, 341
    Cacao Nib, 342
    Caramel, 347
    Cherry, 194
    Chocolate, 343
    Classic, 339
    Coconut, 344
    Cognac, Chocolate Walnut Torte with, 161–163
    Espresso, 340
    Filling, 190–191, 288
    Filling, Raspberry, 209, 210
    Frosting, 190–191, 277
    Kahlúa, 204, 205, 270
    Mascarpone, 345
    piped decorations, 45
    Topping, 281
    White Chocolate, 346
    White Chocolate Coconut, 346
    White Chocolate Lemon, 346
Whipped Cream Cheese, Filling, 308
Whipped Ganache, 321
    White Chocolate, 318–319
Whisks, 28
White Cake, 134
White Cake Layers, Basic, 119
White Chocolate
    about, 15
    Cream Cheese Frosting, 311
    Drizzle, 209, 210, 211, 212
    Ganache, Whipped, 318–319
    Whipped Cream, 346
    Whipped Cream, Coconut, 346
    Whipped Cream, Lemon, 346
White Chocolate Cake(s)
    Cheesecake, Peach, 233–235
    Espresso Icebox, 248–249
    Meringue, Strawberry, 292–293
    Mousse, Eggnog, 280–281
    Raspberry Almond, 192–193
White Drizzle Glaze, 305
White Frosting, Fluffy (Seven Minute), 312
Whole wheat flour, 8
Wire racks, 28
Wooden spoons, 28

Y

Yeast
    about, 14

Brioche Cake with Caramel Custard Cream, 112–114
Coffee Cake, Filled, 110–111
Yockelson, Lisa, 94, 180
Yogurt Mousse Cake with Honeyed Raspberries and Mint Syrup, 259–261

Z

Zest, Candied Orange, 354
Zester, 29